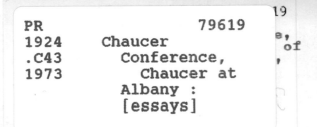

DATE			
fac			

© THE BAKER & TAYLOR CO.

Middle English Texts & Contexts 2
Rossell Hope Robbins
General Editor

Chaucer
at Albany

haucer

at

lbany

Edited by

ROSSELL HOPE ROBBINS

Burt Franklin & Co., Inc.

Designed by Harold Franklin
Printed in the United States of America

Library of Congress Cataloging in Publication Data

Chaucer Conference, State University of New York,
Albany, 1973.
Chaucer at Albany.

1. Chaucer, Geoffrey, d. 1400—Criticism and
interpretation—Congresses. I. Robbins, Rossell Hope,
1912- II. Title.
PR1924.C43 1973 821'.1 75-24816
ISBN 0-89102-065-9

This book has been printed on
Warren 66 Antique Offset,
chosen for its high
degree of permanency, good quality,
and acid-free characteristics.

Contents

Preface

ROSSELL HOPE ROBBINS

These ten essays were first pre-
sented at the Chaucer Conference at the State University of
New York at Albany in November, 1973. Since then, the
contributors have prepared their original papers for a reading rather than a listening public, in much the same way (I
imagine) Chaucer did. All are here printed for the first time.

Viewed as a unit, these ten essays present a wide range of
literary approaches, from the scholarly traditional to the in-
novative and exploratory. Following the pattern of the sessions, I have arranged the ten essays into three major
groupings: those dealing with the minor poems, those with
the *Canterbury Tales,* and those with literary criticism.

In the first set, James Wimsatt shows Chaucer's indebtedness in the *Book of the Duchess* to Machaut's *Lay de Confort,* a rarely read *dit amoureux.* The *House of Fame* is the
subject of two divergent interpretations: Donald K. Fry
considers it as expressing Chaucer's opposition to *auctoritee,* while Beryl Rowland sees it as reflecting the theory
of artificial memory. Pursuing the implications of the *Legend of Good Women,* Robert W. Frank, Jr., warns that in
the *Canterbury Tales,* "pilgrims are there to make the stories possible; the stories are not there to make the pilgrims
possible."

The central block of essays continues with the *Canterbury
Tales.* Robert M. Jordan examines the concept of genre,
and concludes that our critical interests should be directed
to narrative structure rather than to genre. "St. Nicholas
and Saintly Allusion" shows Ann Haskell meticulously reading the text to reveal a new dimension of ironic association.
Having written so extensively on the developing concept of

7

the *Canterbury Tales,* Charles A. Owen, Jr., now gives his final, definitive position.

Finally, three essays discuss the positive and negative aspects of the exegetical approach to Middle English literature. Robert O. Payne considers it "aesthetic suicide to commit ourselves to the aesthetic charade we have been offered recently as 'historical criticism.'" Perhaps the most pungent essay in the collection is that by Martin Stevens, who urges us to examine "the craft of poetry" as the first and foremost concern of Chaucerians. Modifying the positions taken in these two papers attacking the exegetes, is a reasoned study by Carol Kaske on the limitation of perspective.

Though he will find many areas of disagreement, the reader of these essays will, I believe, see a common critical approach: A concern to examine the lines as Chaucer wrote them—or as nearly as we can ascertain; to look for meanings hitherto hidden to us, though not necessarily to Chaucer's audience; and to eschew forcing *parti pris* interpretations into lines that cannot sustain them.

STATE UNIVERSITY OF NEW YORK AT ALBANY

Chaucer
at Albany

1

Machaut's Lay de Confort and Chaucer's Book of the Duchess

JAMES WIMSATT

By count of word and line borrowings, the poetry of Guillaume de Machaut provides by far the most important source for the *Book of the Duchess*. The writers whose work ranks next in such calculations, the authors of the *Roman de la Rose*, Froissart, and Ovid, even taken together do not begin to rival Machaut's contribution. What this indicates is certainly debatable. Critics properly have reservations about using such statistics to assess literary influence. But there is always the danger that in ignoring statistical evidence one is simply rationalizing his own predilections and distorted perceptions. Thus modern tastes have appreciated strong narrative lines and dense semantic texture. Not finding these in Machaut's work, the critics have usually underrated his effect on Chaucer's art. Scholarly correctives are not lacking. Wolfgang Clemen's *Junge Chaucer*[1] and my more specialized *Chaucer and the French Love Poets*[2] have shown that the neglect of Machaut by Chaucer scholars is not justified—that the artistic influence is real. Even these studies, however, have paid negligible attention to Machaut's lyrics.

This paper will explore further Machaut's effect on Chaucer by scrutinizing the important relationships between one of the lyrics, the *Lay de Confort*,[3] and the *Book of the Duchess*.[4] At the same time it will indicate that Machaut's lyrics were worthy of Chaucer's use. Through most of the fourteenth and fifteenth centuries Machaut was the most admired and imitated poet and musical composer of France. The close imitations of his forms and narratives by Froissart, Deschamps, Christine de Pisan, Alain Chartier, and Charles d'Orléans, together with Chaucer's use of his poetry, witness particularly to the height and duration of Machaut's prestige as poet.

There are two good reasons for choosing this particular work. In the first place the *Lay de Confort* is a definite if minor source for the wording in the *Duchess,* and it can be shown to have an important place in the tradition from which the work developed. Secondly, it is a good representative of Machaut's lays, using well the lyric form that allowed him best to exploit the fine nuances of sentiment and rhetoric which provide the essence of his poetry.

The most obvious connection between the *Lay de Confort (LC)* and the *Book of the Duchess (BD)*, that which establishes Chaucer's dependence on the poem, is found in the Black Knight's explanation of his tearful condition:

> For there nys planete in firmament,
> Ne in ayr ne in erthe noon element,
> That they ne yive me a yifte echone
> Of wepynge when I am allone. (*BD* 693–96)

This derives from the *Lay* (10–15), where the identical image is likewise used in a complaint against Fortune. Perhaps also indebted to this Machaut poem are the Black Knight's words against Fortune which describe her as a hyprocrite and traitor (*LC* 90; cf. *BD* 620, 813); moreover, it has been suggested that the Knight's claim about Fair White, "hit were beter to serve hir for noght Than with another to be wel" (*BD* 844–45), is modeled on the claim in the *Lay* that just knowing Hope is better than having power over another lady (*LC* 166–69).

A typical analysis of this small inventory of line borrowings might indicate that even though Chaucer as a young man had access to no better contemporary court poetry than such a dull lay of Machaut, nevertheless his unerring poetic instinct picked out a few worthwhile phrases and images, and later he recalled and made use of these, leaving the rest of the French poem to molder on the rubbish heaps beside Parnassus. It is hardly prudent, however, to draw such a conclusion before looking further into the relationships between the poems.

When we do look further we find that the *Duchess* had indeed other ties with the *Lay de Confort.* The *Lay* is the second in a small group of related works, to which the *Duchess* belongs, in which the governing rhetorical structure involves a statement of complaint toward the beginning, answered by proffered comfort in the later part. The *Lay* is, furthermore, the first in a sub-group of these works, of which Chaucer's poem is again a member, which is clearly addressed to the poet's highly-placed patron in an identifiable time of trouble. By his borrowings Chaucer makes clear that he knows all four of Machaut's poems of the complaint-and-comfort type.

The first of these is the *Remede de Fortune,*[5] probably written around 1340, a major source of the *Book of the Duchess,* particularly for the Black Knight's complaints. The narrator in this long poem is a lover who begins by complaining against Fortune and Amour, and is eventually comforted and assisted by a godlike Esperance. If there is a real-life situation behind this poem it probably involves a literary affair of gallantry with a court lady.

Machaut did not return to the complaint-and-comfort pattern for about sixteen years, until he composed the *Lay de Confort,* a much shorter poem than the *Remede.* In the *Lay* the lady who narrates throughout complains first against Fortune for both herself and her "ami," and then in the later stanzas finds comfort in Hope and exhorts the lover to do likewise. Her mention of his "prison" (262), along with a later reference to this poem in the related *Confort d'Ami,*[6] indicates that the work was written by Machaut on behalf of an unknown—or even imaginary—lady to the young king Charles of Navarre, whom King John of France put in prison in 1356. Machaut composed the *Confort d'Ami* the next year for the same king, still in prison. This longer work does not have the typical complaint-and-comfort progression, since the comfort is offered from the beginning to the end in a series of exempla, supplemented with pious moralizing, and the only complaint is one imagined in the middle of the work (2057–2102). From the sanctimonious advice that Machaut offers in the poem, utilizing no fictional persona to soften the impact, one might suppose that he was ready to part with Charles, who was proving intransigent in his quarrel with the French. This seems to have been the actual case, since Charles—often called "le Mauvais"—never appears again in Machaut's works, not even in an autobiographical summary.

Machaut did not innately lack a sense of diplomacy. As a bourgeois who enjoyed the patronage of the highest-placed nobility of France for over forty years, he obviously had need of and utilized considerable tact. When in 1361 he came to comfort another young royal patron on his imprisonment, the very structure of the narrative shows his sensitivity and his understanding of how one genuinely consoles. In the *Dit de la Fonteinne amoureuse,*[7] written for the Duke of Berry when he went as hostage to England under the terms of the Treaty of Brétigny, the narrator-poet puts himself in an unobtrusive ancillary position. At the opening of the poem he overhears a princely lover complaining in well-formed stanzas about an impending trip overseas which will separate him from his beloved, and in the latter stages of the story the lover is comforted by his lady in a dream which the narrator shares with him and thus is able to report.

The *Fonteinne amoureuse* is probably the most significant source for the *Book of the Duchess.* But there is still another complaint-and-comfort poem that Chaucer uses, written subsequent to the *Fonteinne,* the *Paradys d'Amours,*[8] composed by Froissart some time between 1362 and 1368 when he was in England as Queen Philippa's secretary. This work reflects major aspects of the *Remede de Fortune;* just as in Machaut, the narrator is a lover who complains against Fortune and Amour; the ensuing comfort is offered by Esperance; and the work seems to commemorate a personal affair of the poet.

In using the complaint-and-comfort mode to console John of Gaunt on the death of Blanche of Lancaster, Chaucer put the type to a new use. The dramatic situation in the *Book of the Duchess* also displays a new variation. As in the *Fonteinne amoureuse,* the narrator overhears the lover's complaint, but instead of the lady's consoling him in a dream, it is the narrator himself who does the comforting. To Chaucer's fellow poets this solution to the dramatic problem proved especially attractive. Comparable situations were handled similarly by the poet of the *Songe vert,*[9] by Oton de Granson,[10] and by Froissart when he utilized the complaint-and-comfort type once more on the occasion of a patron's imprisonment in the *Dit dou Bleu Chevalier,*[11] written for Duke Wenceslas of Brabant after he was captured at the Battle of Bastweiler by the Duke of Juliers in 1371.

The *Book of the Duchess* thus grew out of a French literary development and became an integral part of that development. Chaucer's poem of 1369 or 1370 is the only English member[12] of this series of closely-related works composed between 1340 and 1375. As the *Chaucer's Life Records* shows, there is a gap in the Chaucer documents in the poet's formative years between 1360 and 1367: nothing to prove where he was and what he was doing.[13] Nevertheless, these literary filiations of the *Duchess* indicate strongly that he was a serious and devoted student of contemporary French poetry in this period. In the early 1360's he must have taken advantage of his proximity to the sources of this poetry. He surely spent much time with Froissart at Westminster where the poets could read and discuss Machaut together. In all probability in these discussions there joined at times the very subject of the *Fonteinne amoureuse*, one of the great art patrons of history, the Duke of Berry, who while captive in England resided at the Savoy, John of Gaunt's palace. In addition at the Savoy Chaucer no doubt met the Duke's father, John II of France, who had put Machaut's young friend, Charles of Navarre, in prison just the year before he was himself taken in captivity to England. The works with which Chaucer associated his elegy for Blanche were part of London court life and part of history, and perhaps it would not have occurred to the poet at the time to separate the spheres.

The poetic tradition I have reviewed, with whose development Chaucer was clearly familiar, suggests that Chaucer would have seen the *Lay de Confort* as an integral member in the restricted series of works from which the *Book of the Duchess* developed. Consequently, one may reasonably assert that all aspects of the *Lay* have a bearing on Chaucer's poem. While a similar claim may be made for many of Machaut's lyrics, it is particularly valid for this work. Wherein the *Lay de Confort* is like Chaucer's work, wherein it is unlike, and wherein it is either valuable or not valuable as literature—all are significant to the Chaucer scholar.

Though I suggested earlier that Machaut's lyrics are aesthetically worthwhile, few modern critics have agreed with such a judgment.[14] The fault most often alleged is excessive attention to form. Whether or not one agrees to the stricture, it must be admitted that complex versification is the most obvious distinguishing feature of fourteenth- and fifteenth-century French lyrics, and that Machaut's example and authority prescribed the so-called *formes fixes* of the period—balade, rondel, virelay, chanson royale, and lay.

Among these demanding forms, the lay had a reputation as the most difficult to compose. Froissart claims that writing a lay takes six months. One must allow for some exaggeration, since it is doubtful that Machaut spent over twelve years writing his twenty-five lays; nonetheless, the task was not easy. Each lay is supposed to have twelve pairs of stanzas, with stanza length varying from six to twenty lines. In each pair the stanzas have identical form and there are but two rhyme endings. Among the pairs, the form, the rhyme endings, and the accompanying music are not to be repeated, except for the first and last pairs which are to be identical. Though there is no set rule for line length, two- and three-stress lines tend to predominate. Rhymes are often *riche* or *leonine* or otherwise complicated.

For modern sensibilities such complex demands of form point to either madness or foolishness. When inspection of the content of these poems reveals everywhere conventional figures, conventional diction, and a very restricted range of subject matter, then the judgment seems confirmed. It appears that the poetaster is attempting to cover his defective invention and understanding with virtuoso performances in versifying. Yet there may be an alternative explanation: the poet for good reason chose to bind his matter in a tight form and to express it in a narrow range of diction and imagery.

Form and convention are characteristic of literature of all time. Their basic function is to civilize, to bring under control the apparent wildness and formlessness of life and the seeming chaos that underlies it. This function was particularly useful to the fourteenth-century court poet. His noble patron had a double faith: in the order with which God informs creation, and in the order mirroring God's plan by which a court society can tame the crude and undisciplined occasions of life. An insistence on refined living, a demanding code of courtesy, a rigid exclusion of the villainous— such were the means by which one maintained serenity in the face of the War, Plague, Separation, and Death which characterized the period. Similarly in court poetry the forces of disorder and dissolution could be kept under control within the tight constraints of form and convention. The *Lay de Confort* illustrates well how this can work.

The twelve sections of the *Lay* feature two conventional personifications: Fortune and Hope. In the first five sections the mischief of Fortune is attacked; in the last seven the value of Hope is asserted. The narrator is a lady who muses aloud, speaks directly to her lover, and at one point addresses Hope. She says almost nothing which allows inferences about the specific circumstances of the poem: who she and the lover are, what they look like, where and how they live, or what Fortune has done to them. His being in prison is mentioned only at the end of the poem, and this circumstance could comprehend many real or metaphoric situations. It is only by external evidence of manuscript dating, the poet's associations, historical events, and the reference to the *Lay* in the *Confort d'Ami,* that we can identify the prisoner and the occasion of his imprisonment.

The discussion of Fortune which dominates the first half of the poem is carried on exclusively in terms that derive from venerable authorities like Boethius and the *Roman de la Rose.* In the first pair of stanzas the subject and treatment recall strongly the *Consolation of Philosophy.* The *Consolation* like the *Lay* opens with a discussion of composing sad songs; and like Boethius the lady's complaint is against Fate and Fortune:

S'onques dolereusement	[If ever I could make,
Sceus faire ne tristement	sadly and sorrowfully,
Lay ou chanson	a lay or chanson
Ou chant à dolereus son	or a song with an unhappy sound
Qui sentement	which has the sentiment
Ait de plour et de tourment,	of tears and torment,
Temps et saison	I have time and season
Ay dou faire et occoison	and occasion for doing it
Presentement.	right now.
Qu'en terre n'a element	For in the world there is no
Ne planette en firmament	element, nor planet in the
Qui de pleur don	firmament which does not make me
Ne me face et, sans raison,	a gift of tears, and without cause
Mon cuer dolent;	makes my heart unhappy.
Et Fortune m'a dou vent	And Fortune
D'un tourbillon	with a whirlwind
Tumé jus de sa maison	has tumbled me down from her home
En fondement. (1–18)	into the dungeon.]

The expression and figures are thoroughly conventional; at the same time in the image of the whirlwind poet finds a striking way of evoking the violent revolution of Fortune's wheel.

The complaint continues in conventional terms for the next four sets of stanzas. Within such limits as convention sets, the individual verse form and music of each stanza pair mark distinctive subject matter and approach. In the second pair the lady states what Fortune has done to her; with a half-look Fortune has wounded her and now mistreats her as if she were a baby in a crib, and her grief increases when she sees many *paillart, coquart,* and *couart* carried high on Fortune's seat. With this statement of personal experience and observation as a basis, in the next section the lady generalizes about Fortune's habitually capricious behavior. In mostly two-stress lines a great spate of "ist" rhymes is broken only occasionally by the closely related "it."

Ainsi Fortune se chevist	[Fortune so manages
Que l'un norrist,	that she feeds one
L'autre amaigrist,	and starves the other,
L'un enrichist,	makes one rich,
L'autre apovrist.	the other poor.
Se l'un en pleure, l'autre rist.	If one cries because of her,
En tels fais se delite.	the other laughs. In such things
Se l'un fait grant, l'autre amenrist	she delights. If she makes one
Par droit despist.	great, she diminishes the other
Son fait honnist;	with true spite. Her deed shames;
Autre apetist,	she has not other taste
N'autre delist	nor delight.
N'a: je ne prise son profit	I do not value her profit
Une troée mite.	A clipped sou.

Elle se boute en maint abist;	She breaks many boundaries;
Se l'un garist,	if she heals one,
L'autre mourdrist,	she murders another.
Quanqu'elle dist	Whatever she says,
Tantost desdist.	immediately she denies it.
Adès est contraire à son dist.	She is always contrary to her word.
La fausse, l'ypocrite	The false, the hypocrite
M'a si blecié en l'esperist	has so wounded my spirit
Que ja descrist	that it could never be described
N'iert par escrist.	in writing.
Einsi languist	My heart thus languishes
Mes cuers et vist	and lives
En grief qui n'est pas plus petist	in a grief which is no smaller
Des .x. plaise d'Egypte. (47–73)	than the ten plagues of Egypt.]

The brief lines, hissing sibilants, and abrupt dentals provide fine support to this standard statement about the suddenness and spite of the fickle goddess.

The fourth section of the *Lay* returns to the earlier image of Fortune's wounding half-look. Had Fortune looked at her full, muses the lady, the perverse traitor would have killed her; she wishes she had died, her suffering is now so great. In the following transitional section the lady summarizes what she has said, for the first time addressing the lover directly:

Einsi en grant desconfort	[Thus in great discomfort, sweet
Dous amis, se desconforte	friend, my heart is depressed
Mes cuers qui t'aimme si fort	which loves you so much
Qu'amours ne fu mais si forte,	that love was never so strong,
Dont joie n'a ne deport	whence it has neither joy nor pleasure
Pour les griés qui li tiens porte.	because of the grief that yours bears.
S'en ay en moy tel remort	From this I have such sadness
Que bien vorroie estre morte.	That I wish indeed to be dead.
Car Fortune nous fait tort	Now Fortune misuses us
Par diverse voie et torte;	in different manners and wrongs;
Mais en Esperence au fort	but in Hope finally
Un tres petit me conforte;	I comfort myself a very little;
Et en cest espoir ay sort:	and in this hope I place my fate:
Que Raison soit de ta sorte	that Reason may govern your acts
Et qu'encor venras au port	and that you will yet come to the haven
D'Onneur par la droite porte.	of Honor by the right entrance.]
(95–110)	

The second stanza here provides a double transition. It applies the complaint against Fortune to the lover as well as the lady, and it changes the focus from the misdeeds of Fortune to the consolations of Hope.

In the second half, the lady now states that when she is sad, Espoirs comes and tells her to remember her love and put aside her sadness; then Espoirs acts as a very sweet physician against Fortune and her tricks. The personification Hope thus is presented as a comforting Lady Philosophy. In the section that follows, the lady exhorts her lover to find his comfort in Hope:

Pren confort en ta souffrence	[Take comfort in your suffering
D'Esperance	from Hope
Main et soir.	morning and evening.
Se tu le fais sans doubtance	If you do so without doubt
D'Esperence,	of Hope,
Nul pooir	there is no power
N'a de toy faire grevence.	that can give you grief.
C'iert vaillence,	This will be valor,
C'iert savoir,	this will be wisdom,
C'iert joie, pais, aligence;	this will be joy, peace, relief;
C'iert plaisence—	this will be pleasure—
De l'avoir.	to have her.

Et s'Yre ou Despit te lance	And if Anger or Spite wound you
De sa lance,	with their lance,
Recevoir	you should receive it
Dois en bonne pacience;	in good patience;
Ne t'avence	nor would it advance you
De mouvoir,	to move away,
Car au goust de souffissance	since for the enjoyment
To pesence	of sufficiency
Dois avoir.	you must endure sadness.
Miex vaut assez s'acointence	Just knowing her (Hope) is much better
Que puissence	than having power
D'autre avoir. (143–66)	over another.]

In this advice to the lover that he accept all with patience, the lady sounds rather like the poet in the *Confort d'Ami* superciliously advising Charles, or perhaps like Criseyde in the last book of *Troilus and Criseyde* solemnly chiding Troilus for his impatience.

The theme of warring abstractions, initiated with the attacks of Spite and Anger on the lover in the stanzas just quoted, is continued in the eighth section where the battle is an interior one. Echoing the God of Love's advice in the *Roman de la Rose,* the lady tells her lover to oppose Hope and Sweet Thought to the torments of Desire. In the ninth section she rather abruptly expresses some doubts about the lover's faithfulness to her; at the same time she declares her own faithfulness. Then in the tenth stanza-pair she addresses Hope, describing the emotional consequences of her misgivings about the lover; while Hope shines, she has joy, but when Hope leaves, she falls in a well of sorrow.

The final two sections are devoted respectively to the lady's concluding remarks about herself and to her advice to the lover. For herself she recalls that when he is with her all her lamenting is quenched, and she resolves to rejoice and stop complaining. Her counsel to him is to make Hope his lady and to pray to God:

Pour ce, amis, pren de ta gent	[Therefore, friend, take from your
Espoir, le tres biau corps	gentle Hope the very lovely body
Et le dous nom	and the sweet name
Qui tout veint de bon renom;	which surpasses all in good fame;
Et vraiement,	and truly,
S'en toy d'eus has fermement	if you have firmly in yourself
L'impression,	their image,
Tu vivras en ta prison	you will live in your prison
Joieusement.	happily.
Se tu le fais autrement,	If you act otherwise,
En dolour, dolentement,	in sadness, sorrowfully,
Confusion,	you still often have
Pleur et lamentation	confusion,
Aras souvent.	tears and lamentation.
Loe Dieu devotement	Praise God devoutly
Et a bas ton:	in a low voice;
N'i voy milleur ne si bon	I see no better nor so good
Esbatement. (255–72)	entertainment.]

A nice ambiguity involving the lady and Hope is found here and other places in the latter part of the poem. Hope and the lady both take the part of the Boethian adviser; and both of them are depicted as the beloved. In this tendency to equate the two there is a certain idealization of the lady and humanization of Hope.

The final lines of the *Lay* in which the lover is advised to pray to God appear to take the poem out of the realm of Fortune and Hope and into the sphere of true enjoyment, Heaven. To say this, however, would be to distort a formula. The ending provides no Boethian solution to the complaint, but instead is a simple reminder to the lover to say his prayers, an injunction which has little more significance than the *Dieu* in *Adieu*. I think we must recognize that in this poem, as in Machaut's earlier Boethian *Remede de Fortune* and in the *Book of the Duchess,* the stronger remedies of Lady Philosophy do not figure; God and Providence are not effectively asserted. This does not mean that Machaut and Chaucer were ignorant of the final books of the

Consolation. Rather in these poems they were interested in providing consolation on a worldly level, and the consolation they offer derives from art rather than philosophy.

In the course of her haphazard dealings with men, Fortune has separated the lovers of *Lay de Confort.* This goddess is a vicious hypocrite who feeds only to starve, cures only to murder. The victim in prison apparently can do little against this force, except to adopt the remote hope that he will one day be free.

Nevertheless, he can control what Fortune represents by adhering to a courtly code of behavior, by maintaining courtesy, dignity, and equanimity. The poem likewise can control this monster of disorder and evil; it can fence her in within the complex order of the verse, hobble her with a standard set of images, and bridle her with the conventions of the love narrative. Thus tamed, Fortune can be put through her paces. The poem further can promote Hope— the force intent on restoring equilibrium to the lovers—into a worthy opposite of Fortune, who is after all a product of rhetoric.

The situation of Chaucer's Black Knight is, of course, more desperate than that of Machaut's prisoner. There is no reversing the final stroke of Fortune, Death. The dreamer in the *Duchess* never mentions Hope; it is irrelevant to the poem. The best he can suggest is the example of Socrates, a model of fortitude, but that remote and austere virtue has little to recommend it to a bereft young lover. Yet there remains the consolation provided by the controlling power of the poetic conventions. If it is true that the Black Knight is consoled by the very process of telling his story, much of his consolation and that of the audience must arise from the act of constraining those bogeys of Fortune and Death itself, with a series of standard epithets within a conventional narrative. If these ugly figures cannot be kept out of court life, they can at least be controlled and curbed with courtly behavior, and the poets of the court can hold them in tight literary bounds.

In evaluating the *Book of the Duchess,* the modern critic almost reflexively points to features that show Chaucer breaking out of the mold of French court poetry. There are such features, of course. But this approach puts a premium on disregarding the basic elements of the poem. Its central situation, its narrative, and its rhetoric are products of the contemporary French court tradition. Like Machaut, but more resourcefully than Machaut, Chaucer in this poem finds happy variations within the narrow confines of the conventional: in the story of love, the description of the lady, the complaint against Fortune. Chaucer's chess game, like Machaut's whirlwind, involves original variation, but it is within the tradition. In such adherence to tradition lies the primary consoling power of Chaucer's poem.

The *Lay de Confort,* then, is of the family of the *Book of the Duchess.* There is a true kinship, manifested particularly in the use and function of poetic convention in the work. Furthermore, while the *Lay* does not rank as high in the Court of Praise as Chaucer's elegy, it is no relative to be ashamed of.

THE UNIVERSITY OF NORTH CAROLINA AT GREENSBORO

FOOTNOTES

1. Wolfgang Clemen, *Der Junge Chaucer* (Bochum-Langendreer: Poppinghaus, 1938). See also his *Chaucers frühe Dichtung* (Göttingen: Vandenhoeck & Ruprecht, 1963); trans. C. A. M. Sym, *Chaucer's Early Poetry* (New York: Barnes & Noble, 1964).

2. James Wimsatt, *Chaucer and the French Love Poets* (Chapel Hill: Univ. of North Carolina Press, 1968).

3. V. Chichmaref, ed., *Poésies lyriques* (Paris: Champion, [1909]).

4. All Chaucer quotations are from *The Works of Geoffrey Chaucer,* ed. F. N. Robinson, 2nd ed. (Boston: Houghton-Mifflin, 1957).

5. *Oeuvres de Guillaume de Machaut,* ed. Ernest Hoepffner, SATF, 57 (Paris: Firmin-Didot, 1908, 1911, 1921), 2. 1–157.

6. Op. cit., 3. 1–142.

7. Op. cit., 3. 143–244.

8. *Oeuvres de Froissart:* Poésies, ed. August Scheler, 3 vols. (Bruxelles: V. Devaux et Cie, 1870–1872), I, 1–52.

9. Leopold Constans, "Le Songe vert," *Romania,* 33 (1904), 490–539.

10. Arthur Piaget, *Oton de Grandson Sa Vie et ses Poésies* (Lausanne: Librairie Payot, 1941), e.g., "Complainte de Saint Valentine," pp. 183–93.

11. Scheler, op. cit., 1 (1870), 348–62. References to the battle in Auguste Longnon, *Méliador par Jean Froissart,* SATF, 36 (Paris: Firmin-Didot, 1895), 1. lxvi–ii.

12. Evidence for composition of *BD* in 1368 has been presented by John N. Palmer, "The Historical Context of the *Book of the Duchess*: A Revision," *Chaucer Review,* 8 (1974), 253–61.

13. Martin M. Crow and Clair C. Olson, *Chaucer Life-Records* (Austin: Univ. of Texas Press, 1966). Chapter 3 ends with 1360 and Chapter 4 starts with 1366.

14. Cf. Hoepffner, I. viii.

2

The Ending
of the House of Fame

DONALD K. FRY

The House of Fame begins with a survey of
dream theories. Then Geoffrey falls asleep on the night of
December 10 and dreams of a temple of glass, on whose
walls he sees painted a distorted version of Virgil's *Aeneid*.
He steps outside into a desert, where he feels disoriented.
Jove's eagle carries Geoffrey off, delivering interminable
lectures on the mechanics of sound and the cosmos before
depositing him in the sky at the Palace of Fame. Inside,
Geoffrey sees the goddess Fama and her assistant Eolus,
god of the winds, whimsically distorting pleas for reputations, deserved and undeserved. A bystander asks Geoffrey
if he came there for fame, and he replies, "No, I trust only
my own art." The eagle gives Geoffrey a lift into the whirl-
ing wicker house next door, where he finds millions of people playing gossip. Suddenly, a man of great authority appears, and the poem breaks off in midsentence. So much
for plot; but the meaning of all this remains muddy.

Some recent interpretations include Koonce's Robertsonian reading, Bennett's notion of a vindication of poetry,
satire on French love poems, attack on the trivium, legal
wranglings, a frame for a series of tales, and stage for an an-
nouncement concerning Richard or John of Gaunt or
somebody.[1] I find none of these readings compelling, and
offer in this paper a new interpretation: the *House of Fame*

27

demonstrates metaphorically the unreliability of transmitted secular knowledge by satirizing the "man of great authority" and authorities in general, breaking off as a deliberate fragment.

Fifty-one lines after the opening of the poem, the theories of the causes of dreams are all rejected:

> But why the cause is, noght wot I.
> Wel worthe, of this thyng, grete clerkys,
> That trete of this and other werkes;
> For I of noon opinion
> Nyl as now make mensyon.[2] (52–56)

This skeptical refusal to take sides precedes an invocation to God to bring joy to those who hear his own dream and "take hit wel and skorne hyt noght" (91), coupled with a violent curse on any who

> . . . hyt mysdemen in her thoght
> Thorgh malicious entencion.
> And whoso thorgh presumpcion,
> Or hate, or skorn, or thorgh envye,
> Dispit, or jape, or vilanye,
> Mysdeme hyt. (92–97)

In this proem and invocation Chaucer typically sounds indirectly the first notes of his subject: a distrust of old theories and their interpreters, extended to a dislike of misinterpreters of his poetry.

The narrator tells us he dreamed he entered a temple of glass, finding there a retelling of the *Aeneid* on a brass tablet. Although lines 143–48 accurately translate the beginning of Virgil's epic, Chaucer changes the plot and details considerably. As many scholars have noted, he draws on various sources, especially Ovid, to emphasize the pathetic love story of Dido.[3] But he also removes two key elements from the *Aeneid* version, the substitution of Cupid for Ascanius and the cave scene, and lets Dido be captivated by

Aeneas through the efforts of Venus.[4] Chaucer emphasizes his plot manipulation to his own audience by immediately refusing to embroider:

> What shulde I speke more queynte,
> Or peyne me my wordes peynte
> To speke of love? Hyt wol not be;
> I kan not of that faculte.
> And eke to telle the manere
> How they aqueynteden in fere,
> Hyt were a long process to telle,
> And over-long for yow to dwelle. (245–52)

The inability and brevity topoi show us an author distorting his source, albeit for legitimate reasons. He then introduces Dido's lament, unparallelled in the *Aeneid,* with an assertion of his own authority:

> In suche wordes gan to pleyne
> Dydo of her grete peyne,
> As me mette redely;
> Non other auctour alegge I. (311–14)

Dido concludes:

> "O, wel-awey that I was born!
> For thorgh yow is my name lorn,
> And alle myn actes red and songe
> Over al thys lond, on every tonge.
> O wikke Fame! for ther nys
> Nothing so swift, lo, as she is!
> O, soth ys, every thing ys wyst,
> Though hit be kevered with the myst.
> Eke, though I myghte duren ever,
> That I have don, rekever I never,
> That I ne shal be seyd, allas,
> Yshamed be thourgh Eneas,
> And that I shal thus juged be,—

'Loo, ryght as she hath don, now she
Wol doo eft-sones, hardely;'
Thus seyth the peple prively." (345–60)

The narrator cynically observes that "al hir compleynt ne al
hir moone, Certeyn, avayleth hir not a stre" (362–63). She
kills herself, and Geoffrey sends us off to read Virgil and
Ovid if we want more details, excusing himself again with
the brevity topos. He then introduces a list of masculine be-
trayals with this observation:

But wel-away! the harm, the routhe,
That hath betyd for such untrouthe,
As men may ofte in bokes rede,
And al day sen hyt yet in dede,
That for to thynken hyt, a tene is. (383–87)

We can interpret "such untrouthe as men may ofte in bokes
rede" ambiguously, in the two senses of men's infidelity
and the lies told by the books. This Dido episode shows us
a narrator deliberately distorting a well-known source for
his own purposes, while highlighting the distortion process. Dido emerges as more of a victim, who suffers from
love, suicide, and finally a wicked reputation. Chaucer
shows us, by doing it before our very eyes, how authors
contribute to the faulty transmission of knowledge from the
past; and the Dido theme leads us to expect further examples of coupled love and fame—exactly the "tidings" the
eagle promises in Book II.

Once in the air, the eagle explains to Geoffrey the mechanics of transmission of human speech in terms of its ultimate destination. He says:

"[Fame's] paleys stant, as I shal seye,
Ryght even in myddes of the weye
Betwixen hevene, erthe, and see;
That what so ever in al these three
Is spoken, either privy or apert,

The way therto ys so overt,
And stant eke in so juste a place,
That *every soun* mot to hyt pace,
Or what so cometh from any tonge,
Be hyt rouned, red, or songe,
Or spoke in suerte or in drede,
Certeyn, hyt moste thider nede."
            (713–24, my emphasis)

The notion of a house in the sky reached by all human speech originates in Ovid's *Metamorphoses,* Book XII, in a context of tales of the Trojan War, and would have been familiar to medieval audiences; but, just to be sure no one misses the point, the tiresome eagle repeats it three more times:

"Now hennesforth y wol the teche
How *every speche,* or noyse, or soun,
Thurgh hys multiplicacioun,
Though hyt were piped of a mous,
Mot nede come to Fames Hous." (782–86)

"That *every speche* of every man,
As y the telle first began,
Moveth up on high to pace
Kyndely to Fames place." (849–52)

"That *every word* that spoken ys
Cometh into Fames Hous, ywys."[5]
            (881–82; my emphases)

The repeated emphasis on "every soun," "every speche," "every word" means, I think, just what it says: every human utterance flies to Fame's House. The matter of all this human speech includes not only everyday talk, everything spoken aloud, but "what so cometh from any tonge, be hyt rouned, *red,* or songe" would also include private reading, since medieval readers seem generally to have read to

themselves aloud. Chaucer here uses sound as synech-
doche for all transmitted human knowledge; his source
was probably Dante's *De Vulgari Eloquentia,* I, 3. Dante
theorizes that angels know one another's minds by celestial
extra-sensory perception, or through the mirror of God's
intelligence, while

> the human spirit is held back by the grossness and
> opacity of its mortal body. It was therefore neces-
> sary that the human race should have some sign, at
> once rational and sensible, for the intercom-
> munication of its thoughts, because the sign, hav-
> ing to receive something from the reason of one
> and to convey it to the reason of another, had to
> be rational; and since nothing can be conveyed
> from one reason to another except through a me-
> dium of sense, it had to be sensible; for, were it
> only rational, it could not pass [from the reason of
> one to that of another]; and were it only sensible it
> would neither have been able to take from the rea-
> son of one nor to deposit in that of another. Now
> this sign is that noble subject itself of which we are
> speaking; for in so far as it is sound, it is sensible,
> but in so far as it appears to carry some meaning
> according to the pleasure [of the speaker], it is
> rational.[6]

The windy eagle immediately undercuts the seriousness of
this metaphor in his explanation of the physics of sound:

> "Soun ys noght but eyr ybroken,
> And every speche that ys spoken,
> Lowd or pryvee, foul or fair,
> In his substance ys but air;
> For as flaumbe ys but lyghted smoke,
> Ryght soo soun ys air ybroke." (765–70)

John Leyerle has recently shown the relation of this imagery of broken wind to flatulence.[7]

Geoffrey's journey through the air parallels the flight of sound from earth to Fame's house. The flight proves dangerous, subject to distortions, but without seriousness. Geoffrey's initial fright in the eagle's grasp serves as a symbol of the hazardous flight, and the very length of Book II, 481 lines, gives us a sense of the great distances and times involved.[8] The eagle himself at once poses an intellectual hazard and provides comedy. For example, his speech on the mechanics of sound as broken air occupies 98 lines, says the same thing four times, prides itself on its lack of rhetoric (in a rhetorical catalogue), and ends:

> "Pardee, hit oughte the to lyke!
> For hard langage and hard matere
> Ys encombrous for to here
> Attones; wost thou not wel this?"
> And y answered and seyde, "Yis." (860–64)

Scholars generally interpret Geoffrey's monosyllabic "yis" as tongue-tied fright, but perhaps Chaucer the oral reader delivered it with a yawn of boredom: YIS. . . .[9]

Indeed, hazards fill this void of air. Geoffrey looks down at the pinpoint earth, and we get a sense of frightening height, whereupon the eagle tells Geoffrey that he has just set a new altitude record for dreams:

> ". . . for half so high as this
> Nas Alixandre Macedo;
> Ne the kyng Daun Scipio,
> That saw in drem, at poynt devys,
> Helle and erthe and paradys;
> Ne eke the wrechche Dedalus,
> Ne his child, nyce Ykarus,
> That fleigh so highe that the hete

> Hys wynges malt, and he fel wete
> In myd the see, and ther he dreynte,
> For whom was maked moch compleynte." (914–24)

Icarus reminds Geoffrey (and us) of the potential disasters in the air; just then the eagle admonishes Geoffrey to look up "and behold this large space, this eyr" (926–27) and not fear "the eyryssh bestes" (932). Before Geoffrey identifies the airish beasts and decides whether he should really fear them or not, the eagle tells him the story of Phaeton, who burned up both air and earth when frightened by the Scorpion constellation, finally to fall dead through the air to earth far below.

Then, in a most puzzling passage, the eagle offers Geoffrey a guided tour of the stars: "Lat be . . . thy fantasye! Wilt thou lere of sterres aught?" (992–93). Geoffrey refuses with four lame excuses:

1. For y am now to old. (995)

2. No fors. (999)

3. No fors . . . hyt is no nede.
   I leve as wel, so God me spede,
   Hem that write of this matere,
   As though I knew her places here;

4. And eke they shynen here so bryghte,
   Hyt shulde shenden al my syghte,
   To loke on hem. (1011–17)

Most commentators assume that Geoffrey rejects direct apprehension of experience here, bookishly preferring his authors, but McCollum sensibly describes the refusal as "a rejection of the eagle's propensity for lengthy elucidation. When the dreamer had a question, . . . he did not hesitate to ask for information."[10] In addition, Chaucer underlines his distrust of commentators. Geoffrey says:

> For more clere entendement
> Nas me never yit ysent.
> And than thoughts y on Marcian,
> And eke on Anteclaudian,
> That sooth was her descripsion
> Of alle the hevenes region,
> As fer as that y sey the preve;
> Therfore y kan hem now beleve. (983–90)

Geoffrey says that his celestial experience confirms the accuracy of Martianus Capella's *De Nuptis inter Philologiam et Mercurium* and Alanus de Insulis' *Anticlaudianus*. He does not reject direct experience; rather, he rejects the eagle's commentary on his experience. The eagle reads Geoffrey's mind, perceives there that Geoffrey "sey the preve," and still persists in offering a tour and commentary three times; again Chaucer satirizes the compulsive pedant.

Geoffrey then hears a great roaring sound, which the eagle identifies as speech in Fame's house, but which reminds Geoffrey of the

> ". . . betynge of the see,
> . . . ayen the roches holowe,
> Whan tempest doth the shippes swalowe;
> And lat a man stonde, out of doute,
> A myle thens, and here hyt route;
> Or elles lyk the last humblynge
> After the clappe of a thundringe,
> Whan Joves hath the air ybete.
> But yt doth me for fere swete!" (1034–42)

Again, thunder and tempest and shipwreck demonstrate the dangers of the air.[11]

All of Book II shows the path of sound to Fame's House, with Geoffrey's responses in his parallel flight reminding us of the hazards and distortions in space. At the beginning of Book III, Geoffrey tours the palace, while sound would continue its flight directly to the wicker house. Geoffrey emerges 827 lines later, the eagle picks him up, and Geoffrey resumes his flight parallel to the rising sounds.

The wicker house, sixty miles in diameter, weakly constructed of twigs, spins insanely in the air. Millions of exits pierce it, and the thousand gates have no porters to bar entrance. A roar like a ballista stone emerges, the wicker reverberates with "gygges" and "chirkynges" (1942–43), and the house

> Ys ful of rounynges and of jangles
> Of werres, of pes, of mariages,
> Of reste, of labour, of viages,
> Of abood, of deeth, of lyf,
> Of love, of hate, acord, of stryf,
> Of loos, of lore, and of wynnynges,
> Of hele, of seknesse, of bildynges,
> Of faire wyndes, and of tempestes,
> Of qwalm of folk, and eke of bestes;
> Of dyvers transmutacions,
> Of estats, and eke of regions;
> Of trust, of drede, of jelousye,
> Of wit, of wynnynge, of folye;
> Of plente, and of gret famyne,
> Of chepe, of derthe, and of ruyne;
> Of good or mys governement,
> Of fyr, and of dyvers accident. (1960–76)

The members of the crowd inside, as the eagle told Geoffrey earlier (1074–82), represent in human form the sounds which flew up through the air from earth. But, despite the eagle's assurance four times that every sound reaches this house, this seemingly comprehensive list excludes religious matters altogether. Chaucer has sharpened his focus to include only secular transmitted knowledge.[12] This crowd occupies every foot of space in the wicker house, everyone speaking directly into another's ear, playing the children's game of gossip, which inevitably magnifies every tiding, true or false. In this chaos of noise and distortion, off in a corner, Geoffrey finds the man of great authority, and the poem breaks off.

As readers we see this man of great authority at the end of the journey, while in fact he stands at the middle of it. For whatever he says, whatever anyone says in this house of Daedalus, father of Icarus, who fell from the air, must return eventually to earth. It will grow as it passes from tongue to tongue in the gossip game, until it flies up to a hole in the wicker, joined with its opposite:

> And somtyme saugh I thoo at ones
> A lesyng and a sad soth sawe,
> That gonne of aventure drawe
> Out at a wyndowe for to pace;
> And, when they metten in that place,
> They were achekked bothe two,
> And neyther of hem moste out goo
> For other, so they gonne crowde,
> Til ech of hem gan crien lowde,
> "Lat me go first!" "Nay, but let me!
> And here I wol ensuren the
> Wyth the nones that thou wolt do so,
> That I shal never fro the go,
> But be thyn owne sworen brother!
> We wil medle us ech with other,
> That no man, be they never so wrothe,
> Shal han on [of us] two, but bothe
> At ones, al besyde his leve,
> Come we amorwe or on eve,
> Be we cried or stille yrouned."
> Thus saugh I fals and soth compouned
> Togeder fle for oo tydynge.
> Thus out at holes gunne wringe
> Every tydynge streght to Fame,
> And she gan yeven ech hys name,
> Aftir hir disposicioun,
> And yaf hem eke duracioun,

> Somme to wexe and wane sone,
> As doth the faire white mone,
> And let hem goon. Ther myghte y seen
> Wynged wondres faste fleen,
> Twenty thousand in a route,
> As Eolus hem blew aboute. (2088–120)

A pair of these coupled sounds would fly all the way through Fame's palace, retracing in reverse Geoffrey's steps in Book III, past the goddess herself, whimsically distorting the sounds, personified as petitioners of varying merit, through the imagery of farting surrounding Eolus's black trumpet, passing the caryatid statues of the great poets who support famous heroes' reputations, squabbling among themselves over Homer's alleged lies, noting how Fame and her hall grow larger as one pays attention to them (emblematic of her seductiveness) or how her beryl walls magnify, past the rows of statues of famous minstrels degenerating into mere pipers and magicians, and past the names carved in ice shaded by Fame's temple, and on down to earth through the perilous air. Indeed, the coupled lie and truth face more distortion on their way back to earth than they did on the hazardous journey up through the air.

The man of authority stands in the middle of this whole insane process, personifying something said on earth. Whatever tidings he represents would have been badly distorted on the way up. In short, nothing he says can have any validity, and any validity it might possibly have had will disintegrate in its return through Fame's palace to earth.[13] The figure is ironic; there is no authority, much less great authority, possible in secular human affairs. When a bystander asks Geoffrey if he came for fame, he replies:

> "Nay, for sothe, frend . . .
> I cam noght hyder, graunt mercy,
> For no such cause, by my hed!
> Sufficeth me, as I were ded,
> That no wight have my name in honde.

> I wot myself best how y stonde;
> For what I drye, or what I thynke,
> I wil myselven al hyt drynke,
> Certeyn, for the more part,
> As fer forth as I kan myn art" (1873–82).

Among medieval authors, Geoffrey Chaucer paid the most ostensible homage to *auctoritees*, but he also distorted those sources, combined them, mistranslated them, and even invented "Lollius," whom he mentions 400 lines earlier in this very poem (1468).[14] The skeptical Geoffrey Chaucer mistrusted his *auctoritees*, mistrusted the distortions of transmitted knowledge, trusted only his own art.

Chaucer makes his point by undercutting his own creation, the *man of gret auctorite*. Since nothing this character says can have any validity, he abruptly cuts him off.[15] I picture the first reading of this poem to the court ending something like this. Chaucer reads the closing lines: "Atte laste y saugh a man, Which that y [nevene] nat ne kan; But he semed for to be A man of gret auctorite," closes his manuscript volume, and sits down smiling, to a rising crescendo of shocked surprise, laughter, understanding, and finally applause.

STATE UNIVERSITY OF NEW YORK AT STONY BROOK

FOOTNOTES

1. A full bibliography of recent interpretations appears in A. C. Watts, "Chaucerian Selves—Especially Two Serious Ones," *Chaucer Review*, 4 (1970), 235, fn. 11.

2. All Chaucer quotations are from *The Works of Geoffrey Chaucer*, ed. F. N. Robinson, 2nd ed. (Boston: Houghton-Mifflin, 1957).

3. Robinson, pp. 780–81, fn. 240 ff; A. C. Friend, "Chaucer's Version of the *Aeneid*," *Speculum*, 28 (1953), 317–23; and L. B. Hall, "Chaucer and the Dido-and-Aeneas Story," *Mediaeval Studies*, 25 (1963), 148–59.

4. Hall, loc. cit., 156; but then Chaucer does set the brass plate in Venus' temple, so we might expect a magnified role for her.

5. The eagle's notion of multiplied sound (787–821) parallels Dante's *Convivio,* I, iii; P. H. Wicksteed, trans., *The Convivio of Dante Alighieri,* 2nd ed. (London: Dent, 1908), pp. 16–17.

6. Trans. by Thomas Bergin in his *Dante* (New York: American Heritage Press, 1968), p. 66.

7. John Leyerle, "Chaucer's Windy Eagle," *UTQ,* 40 (1971), 255.

8. J. I. McCollum, Jr., "The House of Fame Revisited," in N. G. Lawrence and J. A. Reynolds, eds., *A Chaucerian Puzzle and other Medieval Essays* (Coral Gables: Univ. of Miami Press, 1961), p. 78.

9. Magdalene College, Cambridge, Pepys MS. 2006, followed by Caxton, omits lines 827–64; Robinson, p. 900.

10. McCollum, loc. cit., 79; J. A. W. Bennett, *Chaucer's Book of Fame* (Oxford: Clarendon Press, 1968), pp. 93–95 obscurely ascribes it to "no more . . . than a certain shortsightedness," compares a similar refusal by Jonece in Froissart's *Le Joli buisson de Jonece,* and postulates a satire on Alanus' rhetoric.

11. Cf. *Hous of Fame,* 198–221 and 435–38; Dunbar's "Harry, harry, hobbillschowe," lines 65–68 [James Kinsley, ed., (Oxford: Clarendon Press, 1958), #46]; Ovid's *Metamorphoses,* II, 178 ff. and *Heroides,* VII, 41 ff.

12. The list of inhabitants in 2121–30 does include pardoners, but there they represent the lies of travelers, not necessarily religious knowledge. Also see Bennett, pp. 175 ff.

13. McCollum, loc. cit., 81; P. F. Baum, "Chaucer's 'The House of Fame,'" *ELH,* 8 (1941), 255.

14. For other views on Lollius, see Robinson, p. 786.

15. Dante's *Convivio* and *De Vulgari Eloquentia* are both fragments, perhaps deliberate.

3

Bishop Bradwardine, the Artificial Memory, and the House of Fame

BERYL ROWLAND

An explanation for the capacity and re-
tentive power of the medieval memory may be found in the
writings on rhetoric in the section which treats of memory.
As Frances Yates has shown in her remarkable studies,[1]
medieval writers modified and used an ancient mnemonic
system for which the principal source was the anonymous
treatise *Ad Herennium*,[2] addressed to students of rhetoric
circa 86 to 82 B.C. The essential features of the system are
astonishingly similar to those used by modern psycholo-
gists to describe mental structures. The frame of reference
frequently used by both is that of a house or large building
in which images are stored. Jung's memory house has many
rooms;[3] the medieval storehouse is a gothic creation with
niches, columns, and corners, on which to place visual images—a palace of memory, St. Augustine calls it, an expan-
sive court or chamber, innumerably full of innumerable
kinds of things.[4]

How the system worked is not entirely clear. Although
mnemonic images are set in their places by way of illustration, their use is never explained in detail. The method ap-

pears to rely for its success on an ability, now lost, to make visual impressions of extraordinary intensity and complexity. The recommendations in Caxton's *Mirrour,* though differing in some respects from those in *Ad Herennium,* emphasize the essential features:

> ¶ Memory Artyfycyall is that which men call Ars memoratiua / The crafte of memory / by which craft thou mayste wryte a thynge in thy mynde / & set it in thy mynde as euydenty as thou mayst rede and se the wordes whych thou wrytest with ynke vpon parchement or paper / Therfore in this arte of memory thou muste haue places which shal be to the lyke as it were perchement or paper to wryte vpon / Also instede of thy lettres thou must ymagyn Images to set in the same places / Therfore fyrst thou shalt chose thy places fyrste As in some greate hous that thou knowest well / and begyn at a certayn place of that hous / & marke som poste / corner / or wall / beynge. there as they stande arow / and within .x. or .xii. fote and not past .xx. fote asonder marke som other poste or wall // and so alway procedyng forthe one way tyll thou haue marked or notyd .C. or .CC. places / or as many as thou canste haue /
> ¶ Also in this crafte as I sayde before thou must haue euer ymages of corporall thynges that thou muste se with thyn eye whiche thou muste ymagyn in thy mynde that thou seest them sette in the places
> ¶ And so of euery corporall thynge thou muste ymagyn that thou seest the same comporall thyng in the place /
> ¶ As whan thou wylte remembre a man / a horse / a byrde / a fysshe / or suche other to Imagyn that thou seest the same man / hors / byrde / or fisshe / in thy place and so of euery corporall thyng / But yf thou canst not haue a cor-

porall ymage of the same thynge / as yf thou
woldest remembre a thynge whyche is of it selfe
no bodely nor corporall thyng but incorporall /
That thou muste yet take an ymage therfore that is
a corporall thynge / As yf thou woldest remember
thys word / to rede / than thou maist ymagyn
one lokynge on a boke / or for this word. walk /
to ymagin a payre of legges / or for this worde
wysedome an olde man wyth a whyt hed so that
euery ymage must be a bodely & a corporal thyng.[5]

Here the application is secular and the intent is faithful to
that of Ciceronian teaching. Caxton concludes with observations on pronunciation and delivery. Albertus Magnus
and Thomas Aquinas, however, justified the cultivated
memory as a means of visualizing spiritual intentions:
archetypal images were to be imprinted on the mind, with
the cosmic order itself as the framework. Just as the Scrip-
tures, under the guise of corporeal things, instructed in
spiritual matters, so did the images in the mind.[6]

Of Chaucer's contemporaries, Petrarch, according to
Romberch, the Dominican,[7] was an authority on the artificial memory, but no trace of his writings on the subject remains. Chaucer would, however, have most probably read
the instructions in *Ad Herennium* and Cicero's recommendations in *De Oratore*. Another possible source of knowledge is the treatise by Bishop Bradwardine. This treatise exists in two manuscripts: British Museum, Sloane 3744, ff.
7v–9r, and FitzWilliam Museum, Cambridge McClean 169,
ff. 254–56. I have examined the second manuscript, which
begins with the rubric "concerning the Artificial Memory"
and concludes "here ends the treatise of Master Thomas
Bradwardine of acquiring the artificial memory. Thanks be
to God, says R. Emylton." Like other treatises, it repeats in
general the techniques described in *Ad Herennium*—rules
for places, images, things, and words. The opening sentence is one which is almost standard in the treatises, but I
have not found his subsequent illustrations elsewhere. Two

things are necessary for the artificial memory, places *(loci)* and images *(ymagines).* He continues, "the places, however, are fixed like tablets on which we write, the images like letters written on them. The places, however, are perpetual and fixed; the images, indeed, are like letters, at one time represented pictorially, at another erased." As in *Ad Herennium,* the places should "neither be obscure nor conspicuous, and should contrast with each other. The first locus may be like an empty and vacant land *(inanis et vacua),* the second like a pleasure garden, the third as having hay lying about or crops as in a time of harvest, the fourth as having stubble after the crops have been collected, the fifth like black ground, the stubble completely burned." Again, as in *Ad Herennium,* Bradwardine avoids using places which will occur frequently in the memory, and emphasizes the importance of the novel or the marvellous. With regard to images themselves, he advises establishing an obvious connection between one image and another, using *ymagines agentes.* Three, five, or seven images (and not many more) may be grouped together, and they should be deliberately coordinated in a striking way. To illustrate his method of remembering images he takes the signs of the zodiac:

> Let him picture to himself next to the beginning of the first place a very white ram, standing upright on its hind feet, with gilded horns, if he wishes. Also, let him put a very red bull on the right of the ram, kicking the ram with the hind feet. The ram, indeed, standing erect, is to strike with the right foot the huge and immoderately inflated testicles of the bull so as to draw blood copiously (and by the testicles one is reminded that it is a bull, not a castrated ox or a cow). Likewise to the bull is to be opposed a woman, as though laboring in childbirth. . . .

Metrodorus of Scepsis was reputed to have recorded on the images of the zodiac all that he wished to remember.

Bradwardine may be alluding to a similar system when he says that if one wants to be reminded of more things, he should put "images in the places following in the same way." He adds, "when this is done, he who is recalling can recite those things in the order which he wishes, that is to say directly or backward."[8]

As distinct from remembering things, Bradwardine then considers the method for remembering words in sentences. The subject is puzzling, because the things to be remembered, so that the sentence can be recalled, seem more difficult to remember than the sentence itself. The technique advocated in *Ad Herennium* required elaborate visual representations, which might involve play on the sound of words. Bradwardine begins with a scheme for memorizing first the vowels, and then composite syllables:

> For five vowels picture to yourself five images in this manner, for A picture to yourself gold *(aurum)*, azimuth or Adam, covering his bare shameful parts with leaves. . . . For E put Eve, naked, hiding her shameful parts with green leaves or other such things . . . for the syllable "ab" picture to yourself one wellknown thing, an abbot, with due appendages; for ba a crossbowman *(balistarius)* with a girdle and the other things which he wears, and for other such syllables, do the same. If however you wish to work more speedily, let there be designated for you an abbot standing upright "ab", upside down "ba"; the *balistarius* standing upright "ba", upside down "ab." And so you may place only one image for both syllables according to the varying situations. Concerning syllables of three letters with two consonants on the outside and the vowel in the middle, the same pattern is used for all. For the syllable "bar" you are to picture Bartholomew skinned alive; for "rab", indeed Rahab the notable prostitute, or for both syllables you are to put merely this one or that one according to one likeness or another as is said.

He next considers words, and then devices for remembering whole sentences, using, as in *Ad Herennium,* visual images which involve action and some play on words. Finally, he provides a method for remembering numbers:

> For one you may picture a unicorn, for two Moses, with two horns namely or two tablets, for three a tripod or trinity, as it is accustomed to be depicted in churches, for four one of the animals of Ezekiel having four faces, for five Christ tormented with five wounds, for six an angel with six wings, for seven a lamb having seven horns or seven eyes, for eight an eight-handed emperor, for nine an angel clothed with a snowy white garment having nine very red stripes across it, three at the top, three below, and three in the middle, which may signify to you the nine orders of angels, or perhaps a man, having cut his thumb, bandaging his wound with the other hand then indeed only nine fingers remain. For ten a cipher may be established or a written mark, etc., to work according to the skill of the augrim.

Bradwardine is not explicit concerning the specific application of the artificial memory,[9] but the original purpose seems never to have been forgotten. Albertus Magnus and Thomas Aquinas did not write their *ars memorativa* as part of treatises on rhetoric. Nevertheless, as has already been observed, Caxton dealt with the artificial memory in conjunction with the techniques of oratory. The orator, while speaking, passed in imagination along the rows of memorized places, plucking from them the images which were to enable him to speak at length with unfailing accuracy. Caxton's contemporary, Stephen Hawes, actually represented Dame Rhetoric applying this ancient memory system to the needs of the poet, reciting his poems aloud to an audience. The poet was to envisage his leathern wallet as a useful system of places, and he was to go through it mentally to remind himself of the images associated with the respective tales stored in the compartments inside:

> Yf to the crature many a sundry tale
> One after other treatably be tolde
> Than sundry ymages in his closed male
> Eache for a mater he doth than well holde
> Lyke to the tale he doth than so beholde
> And inwarde a recapytulacyon
> Of eche ymage the moralyzacyon
> Whiche be the tales he grounded pryuely
> Vpon these ymages sygnyfycacyon
> And whan tyme is for hym to specyfy
> All his tales by demonstracyon
> In due ordre maner and reason
> Than eche ymage inwarde dyrectly
> The oratoure doth take full properly
> So is enprynted in his propre mynde
> Euery tale with hole resemblaunce
> By this ymage he dooth his mater fynde
> Eche after other withouten varyaunce
> Who to this arte wyll gyue attendaunce
> As therof to knowe the perfytenes
> In the poetes scole he must haue intres.[10]

The metaphor of the *male* reminds us of the same word used figuratively twice in the *Canterbury Tales*—in the *Prologue to the Miller's Tale:* ". . . Unbokeled is the male. / Lat se now who shall telle another tale" (I, 3115–16), and in the *Prologue to the Parson's Tale:* "For every man, save thou, hath toold his tale. / Unbokele, and shewe us what is in thy male" (X, 25–26).[11]

I am not the first to consider the artificial memory in relation to Chaucer's works. Donald Howard has observed that Chaucer's account is based on a fiction of a remembered past experience, and appears to be structured on the principles of the cultivated memory. For mnemonic purposes the characters are arranged in associations which are easy to remember, those of class, alliance, and dependency. The arbitrary shape or placement in the *General Prologue* resembles the artificial order imposed on words and images as an aid to memory. The *Prologue* is, therefore, not the introduction, but the heart or backbone of the whole work.[12]

In my view, the *House of Fame* may be seen as an externalization of this memory process. In the framework of a dream, the narration in itself purports to consist of things remembered. It is also an *avisio,* involving prophetic meaning. The images, like memory images, are not dismissed from the mind; they continue to exist in order that inferences can be made. The poet moves through a series of spaces or buildings sharply differentiated from one another. He reveals the *loci* for various images and explains the significance which the images retain in the memory. The Temple of Glass is an ideal memory house:

> In which ther were moo ymages
> Of gold, stondynge in sondry stages,
> And moo ryche tabernacles,
> And with perre moo pynacles,
> And moo curiouse portreytures,
> And queynte maner of figures
> Of olde werk, then I saugh ever. (*HF* 121–27)

With Venus "naked fletynge in a see" as the *ymago agens,* the temple introduces the story of Troy. Although Geoffrey purports to "read" what he narrates, his version is subjective. The brass tablet is the touchstone, and after a close rendering of the first few lines of the *Aeneid,* Chaucer demonstrates by his own treatment of the narrative the way in which poets or historians are responsible for the reputation of their subjects—a theme to which he is to return in his recollection of the seven pillars in the hall of Fame. Whether Chaucer's images for words are here corporeal is not clear. He may be visualizing words in the memory places, as Quintilian advocated, or some kind of shorthand *notae,* a practice traditionally ascribed to the Greeks.[13] His reitera-

tion of "I saw" more than a dozen times in the first book indicates that he has dramatically recreated Virgil's epic by
means of visual memory, and his conclusion directly alludes to images and the memory house, two essential re-
quirements of artificial memory:

> "A, Lord! . . . that madest us
> Yet sawgh I never such noblesse
> Of ymages, ne such richesse
> As I saugh graven in this chirche." (*HF* 470–73)

The poet then chooses a sharply contrasting location,
and since memory was part of rhetoric, the eagle, traditionally the symbol of eloquent speech,[14] is the appropriate vehicle to transport the dreamer to another world. Here, it
seems to me, the eagle demonstrates all the Ciceronian
embellishments of the art, while Geoffrey enumerates the
memory images which form the substance of it. If Dante's
Inferno can be regarded as a kind of memory system for recalling hell and its punishments, as Frances Yates suggests,
the upper world is an admirable location for *ficta loca* of
those who have served the Muses. In the second book the
eagle repeatedly instructs the narrator to look, and every
glance conjures up clusters of vivid images. In the third
book the dreamer is an indefatigable observer on his own
account, and he uses more than twenty references to sight
before reaching the castle. The interior of Fame's Palace is a
typical memory hall, and because the memory figures exemplify the arbitrary nature of Fame, the poet, while assert-
ing that he could name many more names, identifies only
the most outstanding (1430–1512). He sees seven pillars. On
them are writers of Jewish, Greek, and Roman matter, an
arrangement which medieval scholars would regard as
approximately chronological. Recorders of mighty civiliza-
tions that flourished under the Old Law, they are tied
together by various mnemonic devices, in which the focal
aid to memory is the pillar. The lead metal in Josephus' pillar associates him with Saturn, and points to his great age,

to the title of his work, and to its subject, cruelty and destruction; the iron in the pillar is associated with Mars, as the poet states:

> Therfor was, loo, thys piler
> Of which that I yow telle her,
> Of led and yren bothe, ywys,
> For yren Martes metal ys,
> Which that god is of bataylle;
> And the led, withouten faille,
> Ys, loo, the metal of Saturne,
> That hath a ful large whel to turne. (*HF* 1443–50)

The concluding reference to the two metals and to the turning of Saturn's planet makes use of alliteration to mark the transition. Chaucer moves to a pillar with tiger's blood and from thence to the Tholosan, the author of the *Thebaid*. This second pillar is in itself a mnemonic device for recalling Statius' work:

> Thoo stoden forth, on every rowe,
> Of hem which that I koude knowe,
> Though I hem noght be ordre telle,
> To make yow to longe to duelle,
> These of whiche I gynne rede.
> There saugh I stonden, out of drede,
> Upon an yren piler strong
> That peynted was, al endelong,
> With tigres blode in every place,
> The Tholosan that highte Stace,
> That bar of Thebes up the fame
> Upon his shuldres, and the name
> Also of cruel Achilles. (*HF* 1451–63)

Iron is again associated with Mars and the tigers with Dionysus and with an incident in the third book of the *Thebaid,* which caused the renewal of the war. The reference to Achilles in the last line provides the transitional link to the iron pillar of Homer, and the group of detractors surrounding him, and from consideration of the attitudes of writers towards the Trojan war an easy transition is effected to the "tynned yren" pillar of Virgil:

> Tho saugh I stonde on a piler,
> That was of tynned yren cler,
> That Latyn poete, Virgile,
> That bore hath up a longe while
> The fame of Pius Eneas. (*HF* 1481–85)

This pillar provides associations with Jupiter, Mars, and Venus, and uses word play to make further associations. "Tinyren," a carpenter's repairing tool,[15] appropriately conveys Virgil's bearing up of Aeneas' fame. From Virgil's pillar we move to one of copper; from the allusion to Venus' son to Venus' clerk, with ironic reference reinforcing memory and a possible pun on Aeneas and *aeneus*. Ovid, even in his lifetime, was censured for his treatment of love, and in his *Achilleid* Aeneas is a philanderer. Bad fame to Caesar, Aeneas' descendant, is the next connecting idea, expressed with some irony through the image of Lucan on his pillar of iron.

> Thoo saugh I on a piler by,
> Of yren wroght ful sternely,
> The grete poete, daun Lucan,
> And on hys shuldres bar up than,
> As high as that y myghte see,
> The fame of Julius and Pompe. (*HF* 1497–1502)

The last pillar again takes up the idea of bad fame. Sulphurous, evil smelling, the pillar supports Claudian who tells of hell, implicitly the ultimate location of all these pagan writers and their heroes:

> And next him on a piler stood
> Of soulfre, lyk as he were wood,

> Daun Claudian, the sothe to telle,
> That bar up al the fame of helle,
> Of Pluto, and of Proserpyne,
> That quene ys of the derke pyne. (*HF* 1507–12)

But if these writers have names, they are also corporeal
similitudes used to express the teachings of Boethius. Lady
Philosophy treated fame as if influenced by the historians,
and showed how it was to be viewed from a lofty cosmic
perspective, against the background of eternity.[16] Chaucer
names writers who, despite their claims to be accurate,
gave divergent accounts, and who themselves experienced
the vicissitudes of fame: Josephus suffered from political
factions, as he reveals in his biography; Statius failed to win
the coveted chapelet of oak leaves; the poets dealing with
the matter of Troy had their veracity frequently assailed, as
Chaucer indicates; Ovid was banished by Augustus; Lucan
lost the favor of Nero after defeating him in a poetry contest; Claudian, while acknowledged as a panegyric poet of
highest quality, was denounced as alienated from the
faith.[17] Appropriately, they are dismissed in an *occupatio,*
and the suggestion of contempt is reinforced by the comparison to rooks' nests on trees, a colloquial phrase which,
despite its facetiousness, recalls death itself and Virgil's
tree in hell where dreamland phantoms rest their wings.[18]
Traditionally associated with death, rooks are the only crea-
tures to benefit from a man's demise; his good reputation
does not necessarily live on.

Finally, as the ideal house of fictions, Chaucer presents
the House of Rumor. No one has found satisfactory parallels for its location in a valley immediately below the hill of
Fame, nor for the style and material of the building. Bradwardine advised that *loci* should be on different levels with
strongly contrasting features, and among these *loci* he specifically cites a roof of straw for a house, and a foundation
strewn with grass and straw. This house is made of rushes
and twigs. It has innumerable vents, entrances, angles, and
windows in the interstices of the wicker work, in which to

place the images. It is a suitable place for the tidings which are the raw materials on which the poet works. Whereas Lady Fame sits in the middle of the hall and dominates, we find Rumor in a corner, and it is in an angle of the building that Chaucer visualizes his most important image before ending the poem. This final scene is of crowding and confusion, with men running hither and thither around a commanding figure. The protagonist seems to be a man of great authority. He does in fact reflect the terrible power of the dissemination of rumor itself. Chaucer explicitly states that he did not know the man personally. He was not an acquaintance to be placed in a memory niche in order to recall him and his circumstances, as the treatises advised. He is an *ymago agens* invented to embody an abstract idea. Surrounded by an excited mass of people, treading on each other's heels, he is no other than a corporeal similitude of the tidings which the poet had come to find. If this imposing cynosure of all eyes is the iconographic figure of love tidings, then the poem has reached its conclusion. The final line assures us that the Dreamer is confronted in his mind with the object of his search. There is no more to tell. The demonstration of the memory process is over. "But natheles," as the poet has said earlier, "al the substance / I have yit in my remembrance" (1181–82).

YORK UNIVERSITY
TORONTO

FOOTNOTES

1. Frances Yates, *Giordano Bruno and the Hermetic Tradition* (London: Routledge & Kegan Paul, 1964); Frances Yates, *The Art of Memory* (London: Routledge & Kegan Paul, 1966). Raymond D. Di Lorenzo, "The Collection Form and the Art of Memory in *Libellus super ludo Schachorum* of Jacobus de Cessolis," *Mediaeval Studies*, 35 (1973), 205–21, has demonstrated that Jacobus de Cessolis used the artificial memory with reference to chessmen in order to recall moral teachings.

2. Trans. Harry Caplan, Loeb Library (London: Heineman, 1964); Aristotle's *De Memoria et Reminiscentia* refers to the places (*topoi*) of artificial memory (452a 8–16), and his observations were conflated by Albertus Magnus and Thomas Aquinas with those contained in *Ad Herennium*. See Yates, *The Art of Memory*, p. 32. Johannes de Mirfeld also claimed familiarity with Aristotle's techniques—see the *Proemium* to his *Breviarum Bartholomei* in *Johannes de Mirfeld of St Bartholomew's Smithfield*, ed. Sir Percival Horton-Smith and Harold Richard Aldridge (Cambridge: University Press, 1936), p. 50.

3. C.G. Jung, *Contributions to Analytical Psychology*, trans. H.G. and Cary F. Baynes (New York: Harcourt Brace, 1928), pp. 118–19; see also Gaston Bachelard, *The Poetics of Space*, trans. Maria Jolas (1958; rpt. Boston: Beacon Press, 1970), pp. 14–15.

4. *S. Augvstini Confessionvm*, ed. P. Knoll (Leipzig: Teubner, 1919), x, viii, xvii.

5. *The myrrour: & dyscrypscyon of the worlde with many meruaylles* ([London, 1527?]), sig. D3r–D3v. The first two editions of the *Mirrour*, which were from Caxton's press at Westminster, ca. 1481, 1490, do not contain this section. The third edition from the press of Laurence Andrewe is the first to discuss *ars memoratiua*. See W.S. Howell, *Logic and Rhetoric in England,* 1500–1700 (Princeton: Princeton Univ. Press, 1956), p. 87.

6. Albertus Magnus, *Opera Omnia,* ed. H. Kühle, C. Feckes, B. Geyer, W. Kübel, *Monasterii Westfalorum, in Aedibus Aschendorff,* 28 (1951), 246–52; Thomas Aquinas, *In Aristotelis Stagiritae,* (Parma: Fiaccadori, 1866), III, 197–204. *Summa Theologiae, Opera Omnia* ed. S.E. Fretté and P. Maré (Paris: Vivés 1871–80), 6822, II, II, *quaestio,* xlix. art. 1.

7. *Congestorium Artificiose Memorie* (Venice, 1533), pp. 27v–28.

8. See Appendix following for complete text.

9. Bradwardine concludes: "Qui autem sciverit artem notoriam, huius artis summa perfeccionem attinget." According to Yates, *The Art of Memory*, p. 43, *ars notoria* was a magical art of memory attributed to Apollonius or to Solomon. The practitioner of the art gazed at "figures or diagrams curiously marked and called 'notae' whilst reciting magical prayers. . . It was regarded as a particularly black kind of magic and was severely condemned by Thomas Aquinas." In the *Summa Theologiae*, Aquinas stated that the *ars notoria* was "illicita . . . et inefficax" (*Opera Omnia*, II, II, *quaestio,* xcvi, art. 1). The following entries are from M.R. James, *The Ancient Libraries of Canterbury and Dover* (Cambridge: University Press, 1903); p. 93, no. 959: "ars notoria item ars notoria que appellatur noua ars" (Christchurch); p. 276, no.

767: "Barth[i] de Rippa Romea Oraciones extracte de arte notoria"; p. 374, no. 1538: "ars notoria cum figuris de anulis Salamonis"; p. 386, no. 1603: "Item ars notaria (sic) salominis Item lib de anulo salomonis" (St. Augustine's Abbey).

10. *The Pastime of Pleasure,* ed. William Edward Mead, EETS, 173 (London, 1927), p. 52, lines 1247–67.

11. *The Works of Geoffrey Chaucer,* ed. F.N. Robinson, 2nd ed. (Boston: Houghton Mifflin, 1957). All citations are to this edition.

12. Donald R. Howard, "The Canterbury Tales: Memory and Form," *ELH,* 38 (1971), 319–28.

13. See Yates, *Art of Memory,* p. 25. Quintilian stated that a long journey was most suitable for *loci*—see *Institutio Oratoria,* tr. H. E. Butler, Loeb Library (London: Heinemann. 1953), IV, lib. xi, ii, 20–22.

14. See William S. Wilson, "The Eagle's Speech in Chaucer's *House of Fame.*" *QJS,* 50 (1964), 158; Du Cange, *Glossarium Mediae Infimae Latinitatis,* s.v. *aquila.*

15. James Raine, ed., *The Fabric Rolls of York Minster,* Surtees Soc., 35 (Durham: Andrews, 1859), pp. 17–18, 358.

16. *Boece,* 2: pr. 7; m. 7.

17. F.J.E. Raby, *A History of Secular Latin Poetry in the Middle Ages* (Oxford: Clarendon Press, 1957), p. 97.

18. Today, most writers sometimes claim to be writing from "the crow's nest," i.e., from a vantage point. Chaucer may, however, be simply referring to the large number.

APPENDIX

FitzWilliam Museum, Cambridge, MS. 169

(f. 254r)   De Memoria Artificiali

Ad artificialem memoriam duo necessaria requiruntur,
scilicest loca certa, ymagines quoque rerum; loca autem
sunt quasi tabule quibus inscribimus, ymagines quasi
littere eis inscripte; loca autem sunt perpetua atque
5 fixa, ymagines vero nunc pinguntur ut littere, nunc
delentur; loca autem ymaginibus sunt priora, ideo de
eis primitus est dicendum. Circa loca igitur sexta
notantur, scilicet quantitas, figura, qualitas, numerus,
ordo, et distancia intercepta. Sit autem quantitas
10 mediocris, quantum scilicet visionis [MS visiam] virtus distincte

uno intuitu comprehendit, ut parvum herbarium vel area
camerule. Memoria vero maxime causatur a sensu, maxime
quoque a visu, quarum in memoria accidit sicut in visu
accidere consuevit. Figura vero sit sicut quadranguli
15 oblongi. Circa qualitatem quattuor sunt scienda, scilicet quod loca non ponantur nimis obscura quia tunc non
faciliter nec prompte a memoria capientur, nec multum
splendida, quia tunc impedirent apprehensionem ymaginum
inscriptarum. Secundo sciendum est quod loca non debent
20 poni in loco frequentato, ut est ecclesia, forum, et cetera,
quia ymagines rerum frequentancium illa loca que memorie
frequenter occurrent, alias rerum ymagines impedirent.
Sed ponantur in regione derelicta ab hominibus et deserta.
Tercio sciendum est quod magis expedit quod loca sint vera
25 quam tantum ymaginata vel ficta, tunc vero potest illa
frequenter inspicere, et sic habitum illorum per frequen-
ciam intendere et firmare. Per loca tamen ex ficcione
propria fabricanda potest quis operari si velit. Quarto
est utile, quod ponantur dissimilia, quod et cum numero
30 locorum possit simile ostendi. Sit vero locus primus
quasi terra inanis et vacua; secundus quasi viridarium;
tercius quasi habens fenum dispersum vel fruges velud in
tempore messis; quartus quasi habens stipulam post fruges
collectas; quintus quasi terra nigra, stipula totaliter
35 combusta. Deinde pone tibi alia quinque loca elevaciora
si velis, ut lectum magnum et altum, deinde archam, tunc
mensam, tunc sepulcrum, tunc altare. Deinde si velis
magis ascendere per alia quinque loca, pone primo tectum
domus de ligno, secundo de stramine, tercio de lapidibus,
40 quarto de tegula rubea, et quinto [sic] Deinde si velis
quasi alios quinque fundos solarii: primum quasi terreum,
secundum quasi viridi lapide pavatum, tercium tegulis
pavatum, quartum stratum herbis vel stramine, et quintum
paratum tapetis vel pannis. Hec autem quatenus quinque
45 loco omnium memoratorum sufficiunt. Ymmo decem istorum
vel forsan pauciora, nisi hoc voluerit facere mirabilia
inaudita. Ordinem vero valet quod habeant continuum et
directum, ut memoria possit de facili omnes locis in-
scriptas ymagines, directe vel retrograde faciliter in–
50 venire. Circa locorum distancium duo sunt notanda,
scilicet quantitas et qualitas. Sit autem quantitas
mediocris que loca competenter distinguat; qualitas autem
distancie sit nulla, sed vacuum et inane. Ex parte autem memor-
atoris, quantum loca concernit, tria utiliter requiruntur,
55 scilicet clarus habitus et infixus in memoria de hiis

locis, qui fit per frequentem illorum inspeccionem, vel
saltem cogitet de illis; secundo quod sciat prompte sine
calculacione quotus quilibet sit locorum; tercio quando
debet per aliquem locorum aliud operari fingat se positum
60 in distancia optima et sic insipiciat illum locum. Hec
sufficiant nobis de locis; nunc ad ymagines transeamus ubi
quattuor consideranda occurrunt, scilicet quantitas, qualitas,
ordo, et numerus. Sit autem quantitas mediocris, ut est
dictum superius de (f. 254v) locis. Qualitas vero sit
65 mirabilis et intensa, quia talia in memoria imprimuntur
profundius et melius retinentur, talia autem ut plurimum non
sunt media sed extrema, ut summe pulchrum vel turpe, delecta-
bile vel triste, venerandum vel aliquod ridiculum deridendum,
res multum digna vel vilis, aut vulneratum in vulnere multum
70 patente notabili rivo sanguinis defluente, vel aliter detur-
patum, vestis extranea et omnis mirabilis apparatus, color
quoque multum lucidus et intensus, ut intense rubeus et
sintillans, et omnis color visum vehementer immutans. Habeat
quoque omnis ymago aliquam aliam qualitatem vel mocionem,
75 ut sic melius quam per quietem vel ocium, memorie commen-
dantur. Pro ordine ymaginum est taliter operandum. Primo
rei de qua memorari volueris: constitue tibi ymaginem
tantem et talem ut dictum est quas ponas in principio primi
loci, constitue quod si possis ymagini dexteram et sinistram,
80 ymaginem que secundam teneat, trahat, percuciat, vel circa
ipsam aliquid huiusmodi operetur; vel secunda econtra se
habeat ad primam, ita quod operacio sit quasi quedam col-
ligacio ordinis inter illas, et hic inter omnes ymagines
in eodem consequenter additas observetur, pones que si
85 possis terciam quasi equitantem circa secundam vel circa
ipsam aliquid aliud facientem tercie que quartam adiunge
si potes, et sinistre parti ymaginis trade quartem [MS quintam] et quinte
sextam si possis. Si vero velis tot ymagines in uno loco
congere, pone primam ymaginem ut est dictum, secundam vero
90 ad eius dexteram, et terciam ad sinistram, et transiens ad
secundum locum, in ipso et in quocumque sequer cium quot
libuit [liberuit], ymagines collocabis. Hoc autem diligerter advertas
quod corpus cuiuscumque ymaginis est prius in ordine qual bet
sui parte; manus vero vel pes propinquior loci principio
95 cum suis annexis prior est parte remociori et rebus illius.
Pro numero ymaginum est notandum quod in uno loco possunt
congrue statui tres ymagines, quinque vel septem, sed non
multo plures, ne illarum superflua multitudo suam distincti-
onem perturbetur. Memoratori autem circa ymagines duo valent.
100 Primum ne nimis curiose fabricet sibi ymagines, sed per

aliquantulum temporis quamlibet sui partem imprimat profunde
et stabiliter cogitando. Secundum est quod non solum ipsam
ymaginem, sed et eius ordinem ad precedentem proximam et
sequentem similiter diligenter memorie recommendet, ut quo
105 voluerit eundo vel redeundo possit de singulis faciliter
memorari. Sed contingit dupliciter memorari: uno modo
facili scilicet de ipsis rebus tantum; alio modo difficili,
scilicet de nominibus earundem; oportet habere artem dup-
licem memorandi, et primo memoria rerum tractabitur. Res
110 inquam memorande sunt duplices: quedam sensibiles et
quedam insensibiles. Sensibilium quedam visibiles et
quedam non; visibilium quedam sunt nimis magne, quedam nimis
parve, et alie mediocres. Primo ergo de mediocribus est
dicendum. Ponatur enim quod aliquis duodecim signa celestia
115 debeat memorari, scilicet arietem, taurum, et cetera. Con-
stituat ergo sibi iuxta principium primi loci arietem candi-
dissumum stantem et erectum super posteriores eius pedes,
cum cornubus si voluerit deauratis, taurum quoque rubissimum
ponat ad dexteram arietis cum pedibus posterioribus per-
120 cucientem arietem; aries vero stans erectus dextero pede
percuciat taurum super testiculos eius magnos et ultra
modum (f. 255r) inflatos ad effusionem sanguinis copiosam,
et per testiculos memorabitur quod sit taurus, non bos
castratus nec vacca. Similiter taurem anteponatur mulier
125 quasi laborans in partu, et in utero eius quasi rupto a
pectore fingantur duo gemelli pulcherimi exeuntes et cum
cancro horribili et intense rubro ludentes, qui unus par-
vulorum captam manum detineat, et sic ipsum ad fletum et
ad signa talia compellat, reliquo parvulo admirante, et
130 nihilominus cancrum pueriliter contrectante; vel ponantur
ibi duo gemelli non de muliere sed de tauro mirabili modo
nasci, ut rerum paucitas observetur. Ex parte sinistra
arietis ponatur leo horribilis, qui aperto ore erectis que
pedibus virginem pulchre ornatam vestes eius lacerando in-
135 vadat. Aries sinistro pede leoni in capite vulnus infligat.
Virgo vero in dextera manu libram teneat cui canonicum
argenteum appendiculo de serico rubeo appensa vero aurea
fabricetur; in sinistra vero eius ponatur scorpio mirabiliter pungens eam ita ut totum brachium infletur, quem
140 nitatur quasi in libra predicta librare. In secundi vero
loci principio ponatur sagittarius in congruo apparatu
tenens archum extensum mirabilem, in quo mirabilior sit
sagitta, nitatur que sagittarius capram stantem interius
prope in eodem loco erectum hirsutum mirabiliter et villosum,
145 mirabile cornu habentem et barbam auream et prolixam, teneat

que in dextero pede vas aquarium et notabile, in sinistro
vero pisses mirabiles, quibus superfundat aquam clarissimam
de aquario supradicto, et si de pluribus debeat memorari,
ymagines illorum in locis sequentibus simili modo ponat.
150 Quo facto potest memorator ordine quo voluerit res illas
directe scilicet vel retrograde recitare. Si ergo de rebus
extreme magnitudinis volueris memorari in magno vel in parvo,
cuiusmodi sunt mundus, exercitus, civitas, milium, iotha,
aut vermiculus minimus, fingat illarum ymagines medias vel
155 tales quales a pictoribus depinguntur, vel per aliquam rem
eis contrarium similem vel aliqualiter attinentem memoriam
talium comparabit. Si autem de rebus sensibilibus invisi-
bilibus memorari volueris ut de dulci, pone aliquem cibantem
se aliqua re dulci ut zucario, melle, lacte, vel aliquid
160 huiusmodi hilariter degustantem. Pro amaro vero pone aliquem cibantem se aliqua re amara et statim turpiter ipsam
evomentem. Pro fetido pone aliquem fetentem in conspectu
alicuius, qui una manu nares quasi pro fetore concludat,
altera vero istam rem contemptibiliter ostendat. Pro re
165 vero omnino insensibili cuiusmodi sunt deus, angelus,
vacuum infinitum, et talia, pone ymaginem ut faciunt de-
pingentes, vel per aliam rem ei contrariam similem vel
aliter pertinentem eius memoriam procurabis.

Dicto de rerum memoria, iam memoria verborum exigit
170 tempus suum, pro qua ista conclusio declaratur de memoria
sillabarum propositarum, sillabam memorie artificialiter
commendare. Pro qualibet sillaba habeat memorator ymaginem
sibi promptam semper in habitu remanentem, qua cum voluerit
libere potest uti, et hoc faciat isto modo consideret et
175 scribat sibi totum istum numerum possibilem sillabarum,
consideret que tot res bene visibiles sibi notas quarum
nomina in latino vel vulgari propio aut in alia ydiomate
(f. 255v) facilius sibi noto illis sillabis inchoetur vel
contineatur omnino quod est utilius, et quia apud diversas
180 linguas ymmo apud diversos in eadem lingua, diversarum rerum
diversa sunt nomina crebrius usitata, que memorie occurrunt
facilius, non possibile bene dare particularem doctrinam
omnibus hominibus generalem, sed istam doctrinam quilibet
secundum memorie sue modum sibi studeat comparare et com-
185 paratam prudencius, inviolabiliter conservare. Cum ergo
de sillaba aliqua memorari volueris rem aliquam cuius nomen
per illam sillabam incipiat, vel totaliter contineatur. in
certo loco reponat ut superius docebatur, per quam statim
apprehendet nomen illius, cuius primam sillabam sibi sumat,

190 et similiter de qualibet sillaba operetur. Qui ergo istum
laborem abbreviare voluerit, faciat hoc tantum in uno ydiomate
sibi not cuius prompta memoria sibi videbitur plus valere,
nam in uno ydiomate qualicumque in quo pauciores sunt sillabe,
quam omnes que universaliter possunt esse. Sed certe istius
195 negocii longe contractior et utilior est doctrina. Ecce
omnis sillaba est vocalis vel ex vocali et consonante resul-
tans. Pro quinque vocalibus constitue tibi quinque ymagines
isto modo: pro A constitue tibi aurum, azinum, vel adam nuda
verenda sua foliis tegentem, vel aliquam rem talem cuius
200 nomen per A inchoat vel taliter comprehendas in ydiomate
tibi facilius occurrente. Pro E pone evam nudam pudenda
cum viridibus folis abscondentem, vel aliquid huismodi
ut prius dictum est. Et pro reliquis vocalibus reliquas tibi
ymagines similiter fabricabis. Pro sillabis ergo compositis
205 minimis, scilicet ex una vocali et consonante unica con-
stitutis, consimiliter operare. Nam pro 'ab' sillaba, constitue tibi unum notum abbatem cum debito apparatu, pro
'ba' unum balistarium cum zona et ceteris que incumbunt, et
de ceteris sillabis talibus idem age. Si autem brevius
210 volueris operari signetur tibi abbas erectus 'ab,' eversus
'ba' balistarius vero erectus, 'ba' eversus vero 'ab'.
Ideoque tantum unam ymaginem pro amabus sillabis secundum
varium situm ponas, de sillabis autem trium litterarum,
consonantibus duabus extremis, vocali autem mediante, simile
215 est per omnia documentum. Nam pro 'bar' sillaba bartholo-
meum excoriatum constituas, pro 'rab' vero illam raab
egregiam meretricem, vel pro amabus sillabis ponas tantum-
modo hanc vel illa, secundum unam similitudinem vel aliam
ut dictum est. Si autem adhuc facilius illud habere volu-
220 eris, constitue tibi ymagines omnium sillabarum vel saltem
illarum que ut plurimum solent anteponi vel postponi sillabis
duarum litterarum, cuiusmodi sunt 'l' et 'r' cum consimilibus
exceptis paucis, pro 'l' igitur consonante si sis anglicus
potes constituere tibi ulnam, que dicte consonanti in no-
225 mine et figura concordat. Si autem de 'bal' volueris memorari, ymaginem 'ba' sillabe tibi loces eversum abbatem, vel
erectum balistarium si habere velis teneat que ulnam in ore
per medium ex transverso vel alio modo ad balistarii ex-
tremum superius applicetur ad signandum quod 'ba' sillabe
230 debeat 'l' postponi, sillaba vero 'lab' per eandem ymaginem
habentem situacionem contrariam signari debuit. Sed pro
'bla' sillaba memoraliter retinenda, loca balistarium
habentem in medio sui ulnam in manu, scilicet sub zona qui
tibi significet 'l' debere 'ba' sillabam mediare, et sic ti-

235 bi 'bla' sillabam figurabit. Alie vero sunt sillabe plurium
litterarum et ad illas potest prudens satis extendere artem
istam; hec igitur sufficiant pro memoria sillabarum.

A modo tractemus de memoria diccionum de qua talis conclusio premittatur de memoria dicciones prolate artifici-
240 aliter (f. 256r) recordari. Hec conclusio sequitur ex
priori, quelibet enim diccio habet sillabas teriatas et
ideo habita memoria sillabarum, habetur et memoria diccionum. Aliter autem brevius et utilius licet incertius
Hoc probatur miscendo realem memoriam cum verbali. Si
245 enim de aliqua diccione debeas memorari que rem ymagina-
bilem tibi significet, rei illius ymaginem tibi loca pro
talia memoria diccionis. Si autem ymago rei note tibi
possit occurrere que deserviat proposite diccioni, capi-
atur nomen rei, cuius nomen in duabus sillabis vel duot
250 pluribus concordet cum proposita diccione. Si autem hoc
non poteris invenire, saltem quere rem cuius nomen in
prima sillaba consonet proposite diccioni, quod potes per
conclusionem priorem, et supponatur quod sicut res se habet
quod per partes contingit memorari de toto et econtra et
255 per principium diccionis quandoque de ipsa tota et per
unum similem de altero simili vel per unum contrariorum de
reliquo et per quodlibet annexum aut quomodolibet pertinens
contingit de alio reminisci.

Hiis taliter expeditis restat de memoria oracionum
260 dicere talis autem conclusio premittatur. Quamlibet
oracionem propositam recitare hoc sequitur ex secunda:
benedictus deus qui pro rege anglie Berwicum fortissimum
et totam Scociam subiugavit. Pro prima ergo diccione si
noveris aliquem benedictum nomine vel eciam sanctum bene-
265 dictum abbatem pone in principio primi loci, et si habu-
eris aliquem dominum tibi notum qui absoluto nomine
dominus appelleter, pone eum vulneratum in facie tractum
per capillos laceratum vel aliter contrectatum per dexteram benedicti vel ponas ibi sanctum Dominicum vel
270 dominicanum imperatorem vel alium tibi notum tali nomine
vocitatum; pro tercia diccione et quarta, que sunt mona-
sillabe per conclusionem de sillabis operare vel pro qui
pone vaccam albissimam cum uberibus maximis valde rubeis
erectam super pedes posteriores cuius anteriorem pedem
275 dexterum sinistra sua tripudians teneat benedictus; vacca
vero vocatur qui in anglico boreali; vacca ergo in pede
anteriori sinistro perdicem teneat miro modo, que hanc

diccionem permemorie tue dabit. In secundi vero loci
principio colloces unum regem corona et ceteris magestatis
280 regie insigniis refulgentem, vel si bene noveris ullum
regem, aut aliquem vocitatum vel cognominatum regem, vel
qui in aliquo ludo fuerit rex ponas eum ibi et teneat in
dextera sua manu anguillam se plurimum agitantem, que
angliam tibi dabit; sinistra vero teneat ursum per caudem
285 vel pedem, qui in anglico duas primas sillabas huius diccionis Berwycum significet et per consequens totum nomen;
ex altera parte ursi veniat Sampson fortissimus vel leo et
percuciat illum ursum. Sic que fortissimum tibi figurabit,
exempli vero residuum in tercio loco similibus modis fiet
290 ponendo ibi aliquem vocatum Thomam dextera sua manu in-
curvantem ut bestiam vel aliquem stotum, vel aliquem sic
vocatum aut cognominatum, vel aliquem quem nosti in Scocia
se strenue habuisse; sinistra vero sua iugum mirabile
ponendo. Hoc de memoria auditorum. De memoria vero viso-
295 rum, ut de memoria scripture potest quilibet a simili se
iuvare. Nunc vertendus est stilus ad memoriam numerorum:
igitur pro uno constituas unicornem; pro duobus, Moysen
pro duobus cornubus scilicet vel duobus tabulis; pro tribus,
tripedem vel trinitatem ut in ecclesiis solet pingi; pro
300 quattuor, unum animalium Ezechielis quattuor habens facies;
pro quinque, Christum quinque vulneribus cruciatum; pro
sextem, angelum cum sextem alis; pro septem, agnum habentem
septem cornua vel oculos septem; pro octo, Octonianum imperatorem; pro novem, angelum albissima veste indutum habente
305 novem protracciones rubissi- (f. 256v) mas transversatiles:
tres superius, tres inferius, et tres in medio que tibi
significent novem ordines angelorum vel sic homo abscissus
pollicem altera manu alligans vulnus suum, tunc vero tantum
novem digiti remanebunt; pro decem [sic] cifra ponatur vel
310 chira et cetera secundem algorismi periciam operare. Qui
autem sciverit artem notoriam, huius artis summam perfeccionem
attinget.

Explicit tractatus Magistri Thome Bradwardyn de memoria
artificiali adquirenda. Deo gracias quod R. Emylton

4

The Legend of Good Women:
Some Implications

ROBERT WORTH FRANK, JR.

The *Legend of Good Women,*
if studied properly, can assist our understanding of Chaucer's art in several ways. One of the most important of these is that it forces on us an issue which, by our literary taste and training, we are reluctant to face or even unable to see. This is the fundamental importance of tale, of story, in the late Middle Ages and early Renaissance. Our passion today is all for other matters. If the modern novel is a cherished form, it is cherished as a rhetorical triumph. We admire it for style, for irony, for complexity of structure; we may also admire it for novelty of theme, for daring or outrageous material, even sometimes for truth or for subtlety of characterization, but not for story. Story is in some fashion necessary for the novel, but E. M. Forster's grudging, regretful acknowledgment of this necessity many years ago in *Aspects of the Novel,* his sigh, is ours also. "Oh, yes—oh, dear, yes—it tells a story." Story is the gross flesh that drags down and sometimes damns the bright soul of fiction.

But in the thirteenth, fourteenth, fifteenth, and sixteenth centuries a passion for story flamed up in the Western world. It is the period of great narrative collections. The explicitly religious or moral narrative collections that first come to mind are Caesar of Heisterbach's *Liber Miraculorum,* Jacobus de Voragine's *Legenda Aurea,* and the *Gesta*

Romanorum. Italy is of course the home of the greatest secular collections. The first of these was probably that compilation of *novelle* of unknown authorship called the *Novellino,* first printed at Bologna in 1525 but probably collected around 1280. There were also Boccaccio's *Decamerone* (ca. 1350); Giovanni Fiorentino's *Pecorone,* fifty *novelle* exchanged by a friar and a nun, written between 1378 and 1385; Sercambi's *Novelliero,* 155 *novelle,* written between 1385 and 1387; and Franco Sachetti's *Trecentonovelle,* dating between 1388 and 1395. Two more Italian collections followed in the fifteenth century and another two in the sixteenth. In the first half of the fourteenth century in Spain, there was Juan Ruiz, the Archpriest of Hita's *Libro de Buen Amor.* The list is merely illustrative, not exhaustive.

England is very much a part of this movement, and Chaucer plays a leading role. Within the space of two decades, there came the *Legend of Good Women,* the *Monk's Tale* (a collection, though a brief one, whether or not we see it as initially a separate project), the *Canterbury Tales,* and Gower's *Confessio Amantis.* Other collections followed, such as Lydgate's *Fall of Princes,* which, though an amplified translation of Laurence de Premierfait's expanded translation into French of Boccaccio's *De Casibus Virorum Illustrium,* should be placed in the same movement. To it we might add, near the end of the fifteenth entury, Caxton's translations of *Reynard the Fox* and *Aesop's Fables* (noting their Continental originals as two more items), and perhaps Henryson's *Fables.* For England and the Continent, the list could obviously go on.

The collections by Chaucer and Gower in England in the space of about fifteen or twenty years are a remarkable phenomenon. John Burrow has rightly, I believe, identified *narrative* as the characteristic genre of Ricardian poetry: "the voice of narrative prevails. . . . Perhaps no subsequent period is so dominated by the narrative voice." And before considering "something of the subtle literary artistry displayed in Ricardian narrative," he pays tribute to "its simpler qualities of sheer vigour and narrative conviction

. . . . They preserve a pristine energy in their narrative as few poets in the Renaissance or after have been able to do."[1] Burrow suggests they owe this to earlier minstrel traditions. This may be largely correct. But the great harvesting of story, going on over much of western Europe in these centuries, is the larger context in which Ricardian narrative must be placed. The primacy of story is not a local phenomenon. Clearly, story was a matter of the greatest importance. And the *Legend of Good Women* forces this on our attention, with implications that also must be attended to, in the very first statement of its *Prologue*:

> Than mote we to bokes that we fynde,
> Thurgh whiche that olde thinges ben in mynde,
> And to the doctrine of these olde wyse,
> Yeve credence, in every skylful wise,
> That tellen of these olde appreved stories
> Of holynesse, of regnes, of victories,
> Of love, of hate, of other sondry thynges,
> Of whiche I may not maken rehersynges.
> And yf that olde bokes were aweye,
> Yloren were of remembrance the keye.[2] (*LGW*, F 17–28)

If we go back to Chaucer's earlier work, we can find a few comments in a not dissimilar vein—his remarks in the opening of the *Book of the Duchess* on the book of fables which whiled away sleepless hours; his catalogue of "rounynges and of jangles" in the wicker cage of Rumor in the *House of Fame*; his concern for "the olde storie, in Latyn," in *Anelida and Arcite*:

> That elde, which that al can fret and bite,
> As it hath freten mony a noble storie,
> Hath nygh devoured out of oure memorie.[3]

And he tells the tale of Ceys and Alcione in the *Book of the Duchess* and summarizes the Dido-Aeneas story in the *House of Fame* before the more leisurely lyric and expository modes take over in those poems.

But the *Legend* for the first time insists that we attend to "olde appreved stories" that range widely over human experience—love and hate, holiness, reigns, victories. And the *Legend* is Chaucer's first collection of tales told, swiftly and economically, for story's sake: ten in all, if we count "Hypsipyle and Medea" as two tales, and originally the plan seems to have been for the *Legend* to be at least twice as long as what we have. For this fact alone the *Legend* deserves the critics' attention.

Few works, however, have been more badly served by criticism. The canard, sent out into the world by Skeat at the very beginning of modern Chaucer studies, and supported by Lounsbury, Tatlock, and Root, that the *Legend* bored its author almost before he began it, has paralyzed criticism of the *Legend* for eighty years.[4] The enormously greater variety, artistic success, and popularity of the *Canterbury Tales* in the twentieth century has seemed to corroborate those early scholars' judgment: that his boredom made him turn from the *Legend* to the Canterbury project. The truth of the matter, however, is exactly opposite: it is precisely because the project begun in the *Legend* fascinated Chaucer that he began the *Canterbury Tales*. That is, the telling of a series of tales proved to be so satisfying an experience that he spent the remainder of his life doing more of the same. He altered the frame device and expanded the range of tales, but essentially the *Canterbury Tales* continues what he first does in the *Legend.* If we can rid ourselves of the critical misconceptions about the *Legend,* perhaps we can begin to see it for what it is.

What does Chaucer do in the *Legend?* He tells stories. This seems so obvious that it is hardly worth mentioning, but it is what is most important about the *Legend* and most worth examination. It places the *Legend,* and Chaucer, in that great stream of storytelling that is a major fact of Western literature in the fourteenth century and for two centuries to follow. When we look at them as stories, what do we see? Here his older friend, Gower, is very helpful, for apparently he was doing exactly the same thing at almost precisely the same moment. We do not know whether Gower's example inspired Chaucer, or whether Gower advised him in his undertaking, or whether they started independently of one another and, one would guess, compared what they were doing as they worked away. But to look at the stories in the *Confessio* and the stories in the *Legend,* side by side as it were, is very instructive. They possess many elements in common, elements we must assume their authors wished and worked for. Many of these common elements, however, in Chaucer are the very qualities for which the *Legend* is belittled.

Most peripheral for our examination is the fact that these stories have a point: in Gower they are tied to a rather elaborate moral scheme which Gower takes seriously; in the *Legend* they are tied to a simple value scheme—women are true in love; men are usually false—which Chaucer takes lightly. For a story to have a moral, an explicitly stated moral, that is, is a fatal weakness in the eyes of modern critics. It is better for a story to have a point than not to have one, and a moral is a particular kind of point. When the point or moral of a story is clearly spelled out at the beginning (as is true of both the *Confessio* and the *Legend*), a specific advantage accrues: the reader or listener can concentrate more on the story, on the sequence of events. (Further, a particular pleasure or satisfaction is opened up—not in discovering the point, as in so much modern narrative, but in seeing how the story does in fact demonstrate or work out the purpose, the moral lesson, claimed for it.)

A more important characteristic shared by the tales that make up the *Legend* and the *Confessio* is the easy, unimpeded succession of events. The key word is "unimpeded." Nothing seems easier, but it is not so easy to achieve. The narrator must never linger, however great the temptation, in introducing a character, describing a scene, or reporting speech.

Gower's story of "Paulus and Mundus" in Book I of the *Confessio*[5] is told to illustrate the sin of hypocrisy. In Rome a duke, Mundus, lusts after a beautiful married woman,

Paulina, but his wooing is in vain. By means of gifts, he persuades two priests of the temple of Isis to tell Paulina that
because of her chastity the god Anubis is in love with her
and has prepared a room in the temple so that he may come
to her. She informs her husband, who bids her submit to
the god, and so she obeys. In the temple during the night,
Mundus, arrayed like a god, emerges from a secret closet,
persuades her that the child he will beget upon her will be
worshiped, and seduces her. In the morning, returning
home, Paulina meets Mundus, who informs her that he has
been Anubis' lieutenant in her bed. Overwhelmed with
horror and grief, she tells her husband. He vows revenge,
consults his friends, and on their advice takes his complaint
to the king. The two priests are executed and Mundus is ex-
iled.

The tale verges on the bizarre, but nevertheless it presents a variety of possibilities for expanded treatment. It
raises questions of character and psychology—of Paulina in
particular, but also of Mundus. Paulina's reactions on hearing the message from the priests, her reactions in the temple that night, her reactions after she learns the truth would
seem too dramatic to ignore. What of the priests? How
readily did they consent to this act of profanation? What
kind of person was the husband that he should agree, and
what were his reactions? None of these considerations is
relevant for Gower, who tells the tale in 300 lines. Paulina's
character is handled thus: she "was to every mannes sihte
Of al the Cite the faireste, And as men seiden, ek the beste"
(I, 766–68). Her beauty is described summarily: "This wif,
which in hire lustes grene Was fair and freissh and tendre of
age" (I, 778–79). When the priests tell her she is the chosen
of a god:

>   Glade was hire innocence tho
>   Of suche wordes as sche herde,
>   With humble chiere and thus answerde,
>   And seide that the goddes wille
>   Sche was al redy to fulfille,

> That be hire housebondes leve
> Sche wolde in Ysis temple at eve
> Upon hire goddes grace abide,
> To serven him the nyhtes tide. (*CA* I, 852–60)

To our taste this may seem a scandalous denial of artistic responsibilities. We must assume, however, that Gower was doing precisely what he wanted to do and what his audience wanted him to do. The priests leave her, she goes home, and her husband bids her obey. One unit of action follows another without pause. Eighteen lines after the priests have given Paulina their awesome news, it is night and she has gone to the temple. The events are everything. Characterization, reaction, scene (no dialogue between husband and wife on this occasion), description are as nothing. It is the story alone that matters. Two hundred years later, in Shakespeare's day, we must remember, Gower was still a storyteller whose name counted. We must acknowledge the power, the appeal of bald story.

In the *Legend*, we find the same sort of simple narration. If we look at the first legend, "Cleopatra," we are told a Roman senator named Anthony was sent out to conquer kingdoms and gain honor for Rome. At first he prospered. But Fortune was against him: he rebelled and came into conflict against Rome; wanting "another wyf," he was false to Caesar's sister, and came into conflict with Caesar himself. For the love of Cleopatra, he set the world at no value:

> Hym roughte nat in armes for to sterve
> In the defence of hyre and of hire ryght. (*LGW* 605–06)

Antony is characterized only by his possession of the chivalric virtues, Cleopatra only by the quality of beauty:

> He was, of persone and of gentillesse,
> And of discrecioun and hardynesse,
> Worthi to any wyght that liven may;
> And she was fayre as is the rose in May. (*LGW* 610–13)

After their marriage, Octavius sets out to destroy him "With stoute Romeyns, crewel as lyoun," (627) and Antony and Cleopatra go to meet him, "His wif and he, and al his ost, forth wente To shipe anon, no lengere they ne stente . . . " (632–33). The splendid sea fight, one of the few familiar passages in the *Legend,* follows. There is no betrayal; Antony simply loses the battle:

> Tyl at the laste, as every thyng hath ende,
> Antony is schent, and put hym to the flyghte,
> And al his folk to-go, that best go myghte.
> Fleth ek the queen, with al hire purpre sayl . . .
>
> (*LGW* 651–54)

Antony sees his cause is lost and kills himself in despair. There are no complexities of motive or feeling and there is no death scene:

> "Allas," quod he, "the day that I was born!
> My worshipe in this day thus have I lorn."
> And for dispeyr out of his wit he sterte,
> And rof hymself anon thourghout the herte,
> Or that he ferther wente out of the place. (*LGW* 658–62)

The remaining 40 lines of this poem of 120 lines are given over to Cleopatra's dedicated love for the dead Antony, which is the point of the narrative:

> But herkeneth, ye that speken of kyndenesse,
> Ye men that falsly swereth many an oth
> That ye wol deye, if that youre love be wroth,
> Here may ye sen of wemen which a trouthe!
>
> (*LGW* 665–68)

Cleopatra has workmen build a shrine of rubies and precious stones and has Antony's body embalmed and placed in the shrine. Next to it a pit is dug and filled with snakes, "all the serpentes that she myghte have, She putte hem in that grave." In fifteen lines, she explains that she had made an oath to experience whatever Antony did, whether weal or woe, and to that oath she is true:

> "And thilke covenant, whil me lasteth breth,
> I wol fulfille; and that shal ben wel sene,
> Was nevere unto hire love a trewer quene."
>
> *(LGW* 693–95)

Whereupon, "with ful good herte" she goes naked into the pit of adders. "And she hire deth receyveth with good cheere, For love of Antony that was hire so dere" (700–701).

I have deliberately chosen the first and probably the weakest of the legends.[6] Much is wrong with Chaucer's "Cleopatra," but it does what it sets out to do: One, it makes its point. Two, it tells a story expeditiously—from this point of view the famous sea battle may be a mistake. Three, it takes us into a momentous world: a great Roman rebels and incurs Caesar's enmity for love of a queen, whom he marries. Caesar comes to destroy him. In despair, the Roman kills himself. The queen buries him in a splendid tomb and, true till death, walks naked into a pit of serpents. We can read the newspapers a long time before we ever come across such story elements: power and kingdom lost, great generals and an Egyptian queen, exotic lands and an exotic death.

"But, but," you are spluttering, "what about the big scene, what did Antony feel and say before he died, where's the serpent of old Nile?" The questions are irrelevant. The story and its point are what matter. If the story moves a bit awkwardly—Chaucer spends too much time in some places, not enough in others—that is because what he does is not all that easy to do. Chaucer's tale does not have quite enough meat on its bones, though the brief recording of a story is a perfectly legitimate narrative activity—Gower himself often does just that and no more. It is a legitimate activity because until we have the story *in outline, at least,* we have nothing.

The famous ballade that appears in both *Prologues* to the *Legend* will illustrate the point. It consists of a litany of names: Absolon, Esther, Jonathas, Penelope, Marcia Cato, Isolde, Helen, Alceste, Lavinia, Lucrece, Polixena, Cleopatra, Thisbe, Hero, Dido, Laodamia, Phyllis, Demophon, Canace, Hypsipyle, Hypermnestra, Ariadne. Some names are identified by a phrase—"Phillis, hangynge for thy Demophon"—but many are not. Let us match this catalogue against another: Mabel, Patricia, Sally, Irma, Wilma, Audrey, Caroline. This second list has no resonances, echoes, or dramatic value (as the first list does), because there are no stories, or at least none that are generally known. The legends of Mabel, of Audrey, of Wilma have never existed, or if they have they are forever lost. For every name on the first list there is a story which even in fragmentary form flashes across the memory and illuminates the name. Without the story there is nothing: without the rape of Paris and the siege, betrayal, and fall of Troy, Helen is only another name.

What is the appeal of bare story, we may ask? As we all know, it almost always entertains. It entertains first because something happened, that is, it came to pass, it is an event. Events are the substance of life, of experience, and even of dream. We do not dream lyrics (except in the rarest instances); we do not dream essays or literary criticism or footnotes to scholarly articles. We dream *events,* however bizarre. Though life is something more, or something less, than constant events—one must allow for sleep and daydream and vacancy, though these too can be catalogued as events—events give our life such framework as it may possess. "That was the year that John was born, that we went to the mountains, that we bought our first car." The reality external to myself that is closest to myself is a human event, a human action, for of such happenings my own life is made, and though the event happened to you, or to him, it might have happened to me. Since story is reported or remembered events, I can identify with it. In the abstract, events form interchangeable modules. Particular reported events are part of the life of Dido, of Isolde, of Esther, but they might have been a part of mine. Every story is in some degree my story.

Paradoxically, however, story entertains also because the modules in a story have a more patterned arrangement than those ordinarily in my life. This patterned arrangement consequently fixes the attention, focuses and heightens it. Story diverts the mind from worry, from boredom, from blankness (i.e., from reality) by the simple device of setting the situation on a sequential track. By saying A (an event) we promise to say B (a related event), and our attention is directed to watch and wait for B, and then for C. Meanwhile we can forget our own lives in which ordinarily A (an event) is followed by T (a totally unrelated event) or by b (a related event but of such little consequence as to give no sense of pattern and to arouse no further expectations).

Story has another quality as well. It is a remembered action. It is an action, an event sufficiently out of the ordinary to make it memorable, remembered, and so repeated. Ordinary lives are not memorable in the events that compose them. We forget much of our own history; people listen with reluctance to most of what we tell them of it; and they forget most or all of what they have heard. But what happened to Cleopatra, a queen who died for love of a great Roman who lost a great battle, and died by letting snakes poison her, or what happened to Paulina, who was seduced by a Roman duke in the guise of a god, is worth remembering. If we see the appeal as feeding a hunger for sensationalism and nothing more, we are mistaken. The merely sensational explodes and dies. These are *remembered* events. When we hear them we acquire a dimension beyond our mortality. We are linked with others who have heard the story in the past and we share a human history. If extraordinary human events are not to be remembered, then all of human life is for naught. The memorable event makes an assertion about human experience.

Story is memorable also because it has significance. We search the events of our own lives for meanings, often in vain. We search the world of story as an additional body of data with more hope, looking for significance. The fact that here are events worth remembering suggests that they are much more likely to be meaningful. If a moral is already attached, then they are certifiably significant. Story apparently satisfied some of the same need for guidance, for clues to the conduct of life, in the late Middle Ages, that the proverb did. In times of social change and uncertainty, fable may have had social utility.

It is possible, I believe, to justify the telling of relatively simple stories, such as we have in the *Legend*. They must have events, sequence, memorability, meaning—but above all, events, action. The art of such storytelling is not our subject. What the *Legend* reveals, if we allow it its proper voice and weight, is the importance of story for Chaucer. He gives us there what he set out to give us, not quasi-novels, truncated *Troilus and Criseyde's,* failed *Knight's Tales,* but stories. They are not very complex, but complexity is not essential to a tale, indeed not always desirable. Simplicity is more often a virtue.

A more or less complex vision of experience may develop, as one simple narrative after another is unfolded. The sequence of tales in the *Confessio Amantis* creates a somewhat rigid but articulated and elaborate moral system—there by implication even if the explicit moral connective tissue were to be removed. Although the *Legend* is committed to an apparently simple statement about love (women are always faithful; men are usually false), the stories actually create, I believe, a sense of the variety and violence of love, its capacity to evolve in powerful and unexpected forms. Whatever the view of love, it is fundamentally an excuse for Chaucer to tell stories.

So also is the device of the *Canterbury Tales* an excuse for telling stories. This is the conclusion implied by the *Legend.* We have been talking so long about Chaucer's seeking for a satisfactory frame device, that we have come to think the frame the most important element in his final art. The evidence, however, suggests that the frame is important only as a way of telling stories. The device of the *Legend* enabled Chaucer to tell a number of stories of one kind, the device of the *Monk's Tale* enabled him to tell a number of stories of another kind, and the device of the *Canterbury Tales* enabled him to tell stories of all kinds.

Interesting implications flow from this overwhelming concern with storytelling in the last fourteen years of Chaucer's life. The view that the stories told in the *Canterbury Tales* illustrate the character of the teller or are only projections of the personality or the psychology of the teller[7] assumes, to my mind, an interest in psychology alien to fourteenth-century attitudes and without foundation in fourteenth-century culture. It certainly goes counter to the total preoccupation with the story that we see in Chaucer's last years. The pilgrims are there to make the stories possible; the stories are not there to make the pilgrims possible. The *Legend* is important evidence that story comes first.

The passion of so many men of talent and genius in the last centuries of the Middle Ages for casting their nets among the teeming schools of folk tale, jest, exemplum, legend, myth, history, and narrative of any form is a phenomenon we cannot ignore. As a product of their passion, the *Legend* demands our attention as story. We cannot question that Chaucer progressed to more complex treatment of story in the *Canterbury Tales,* but we should not ignore or condemn what he began with. "Whilom—once upon a time—" the master storyteller must begin by responding himself to the magnetic power of simple tale. The *Legend of Good Women* has that distinction.

THE PENNSYLVANIA STATE UNIVERSITY

FOOTNOTES

1. J. A. Burrow, *Ricardian Poetry: Chaucer, Gower, Langland and the Gawain Poet* (London: Routledge & Kegan Paul, 1971), pp. 47, 52.

2. *The Works of Geoffrey Chaucer,* ed. F. N. Robinson, 2nd ed. (Boston: Houghton Mifflin, 1957). All quotations are from this edition.

3. *Book of the Duchess,* 44–59; *House of Fame,* 1960; *Anelida and Arcite,* 10, 12–14.

4. I have reviewed these opinions and presented an extended counterargument in "The Legend of the *Legend of Good Women,*" *Chaucer Review,* 1 (1966), 110–33; and somewhat more briefly in *Chaucer and The Legend of Good Women* (Cambridge, Mass.: Harvard Univ. Press, 1972), pp. 189–210.

5. *The English Works of John Gower,* ed. G. C. Macaulay (Oxford: Clarendon Press, 1900), Vol. 1; also in *EETS,* es 81 (London, 1900).

6. A more detailed discussion in *Chaucer and the Legend of Good Women,* pp. 37–46.

7. The most extended treatment of this point of view is in R.M. Lumiansky, *Of Sondry Folk: The Dramatic Principle in the Canterbury Tales* (Austin: Univ. of Texas Press, 1964), passim.

5

The Question of Genre:
Five Chaucerian Romances*

ROBERT M. JORDAN

The taxonomy of literary forms is a hazardous business at best, and romance is a more troublesome form than most. Even when narrowing the field to medieval romance one is struck by the diversity of narratives which claim the name. Nor is the problem much simplified by the further qualification of "Chaucerian romance." Chaucer's practice seems to defy any but the loosest generic definition, which is customarily expressed in terms of tales of "knightly life and love."[1] The usefulness of such a definition is plainly limited. For example, the *Merchant's Tale* and the *Manciple's Tale* are not usually regarded as romances, although they deal with "knightly life and love," and on the other hand the Man of Law's tale of Constance and the Clerk's tale of Griselda are often regarded as romances despite the absence of knightly elements.[2] Moreover, the literary differences between, say, the philosophical and deeply emotional *Troilus and Criseyde* and the Squire's delicate and decorative tale of a magical bird's love-lament—both works belonging to the accepted canon

*A much abbreviated version of this paper was requested by the editor of *Yale French Studies* before publication of the Albany Conference papers was anticipated. That version appears in *YFS* , 51 (1975).

of romances—are so much more decisive than their similarities, that the generic designation seems gratuitous. And
certainly, to glance for a moment somewhat more widely,
the tie of romance that binds the Knight's richly textured
chivalric tale with, say, the Middle English *Sir Orfeo* is slim
indeed. One could cite innumerable anomalies of this sort,
both among Chaucer's own works and between them and
other so-called romances of the late medieval period, both
English and Continental.

A generic criterion based on subject matter, and only
loosely applicable at best, can provide for only the simplest
kinds of literary discriminations. Certainly such a criterion
does not provide the precision necessary to respond satis-
factorily to the questions about the art of narrative which
have been raised in recent decades by Auerbach, Booth, Ja-
kobson, and many others. New ways of looking at the elements of structure and style, and more precise terminology
for registering and analyzing them, seem to promise a
deeper understanding of narrative art than has resulted
from classification of subject matters. It still remains difficult to achieve general agreement on definitions of structure and style, but at least in dealing with medieval works
we are fortunate to have the example of medieval rhetoricians (to whom I shall return), who were less hesitant than
modern scholars to fix clearly the elements of style and
structure and distinguish them from subject matter.

As a literary criterion, content is relatively unsatisfactory
because it is finally reducible to non-literary terms. Content
is therefore more amenable to historical or anthropological
classification than to aesthetic analysis. This is true whether
we speak of manifest content, such as knighthood, love, or
war (be it matter of Britain, France, or greater Rome) or of
latent, thematic content, such as moral quest or life-renew-
al. Both kinds of content exist outside of language as well as
in it, and are therefore not uniquely answerable to definitive literary analysis. On the other hand, those attributes
which are more integral to the actions of writing and composing are likely to provide a more detailed account of the

literary and artistic character of narrative because they express those elusive, constantly shifting energies which constitute artistic expression. Chaucerian scholarship of the past two or three decades has reflected increased interest in the techniques of narrative, as distinct from its subject matter and the provenance of its themes. As a result of this change of focus, we can expect the old generic categories to lose some of their persuasiveness and utility as new forms of definition emerge more clearly.

My concern in this paper is the relationship between structural analysis and the traditional generic classification of the romances according to chivalric subject matter. The large question is whether or not structural analysis confirms a significant literary and artistic relationship among the several narratives traditionally grouped as romances: *Troilus and Criseyde*, the *Knight's Tale*, the *Squire's Tale*, the *Wife of Bath's Tale*, and in its special way, *Sir Thopas*. But for generic as well as historical orientation we turn first to twelfth-century France.

If the narratives of Chrétien de Troyes form the "paradigm" of romance,[3] that is, the model from which variations occur, mainly degenerative, certainly by the time the form found its way into fourteenth-century English it had lost much of its elegance and subtlety. The gap between even the best of the popular Middle English romances—such as *Havelok the Dane*—and *Cligès* or *Le Conte de la charrette* is wide indeed. Chaucer's exceptional practice, like that of the equally exceptional Gawain poet, is thus, historically speaking, decadent, in that it displays the sense of structural and stylistic resources characteristic of earlier romance, mainly French.

The revolution in literary attitudes and practices which took place in twelfth-century France exerted a decisive influence on the development of narrative poetry in general and romance in particular, including Chaucerian romance. Chrétien and his contemporaries reinstituted the classical conception of poetry as a thoughtful and sophisticated art. Leaning upon Horace's *De Arte Poetica*, Chrétien differentiated between mere vulgar storytelling and his own learned art. Near the beginning of *Erec et Enide,* Chrétien utilizes his learning to "conjoin" a subtle elaboration to a simple *conte d'aventure.* As Vinaver has pointed out, the poem was now to be regarded as a deliberately and artfully composed work of the mind. Vinaver stresses the rhetorical character of Chrétien's art, seeing it as an art of *composition* in the etymological sense of the term, that is, as the conscious construction of a whole out of many constituent parts:

> Since in his opinion it is reasonable that everyone should always endeavor to speak well and teach the right things, Chrétien de Troyes draws (*tret*) from a tale of adventure (*d'un conte d'aventure*) a very fine *conjointure (une mout bele conjointure),* whereby it may be proved and made known that he is not wise who does not use his learning so long as God gives him grace.[4]

Vinaver interprets "conjointure" as the poet's compositional method of dealing with the received material of the *conte* and at the same time elevating it, so to speak, to the stature of romance. Vinaver's perception of romance as *conte* and *conjointure* joined together, the interpretive elaboration superimposed upon the kernel story but not superseding or absorbing it, will prove very helpful in our examination of Chaucer's later practice.

It was not in Chaucer's nature to produce an artistic credo comparable to Chrétien's statement in *Erec et Enide,* though he scatters through his works a number of sidelong, humorous, and ironic allusions to his art. As for romance, certainly the word itself meant very little to him. Of its mere fourteen appearances in his works, nine either refer to the title "Romance of the Rose" or occur in the Chaucerian translation of that work. The remaining five associate the word with noble stories of olden times, that is, presumably, with simple *contes d'aventure.* With so little explicit help

from the poet, we must look to his romances themselves
for an idea of what the form meant to him.

The *Tale of Sir Thopas,* a sport among the Chaucerian romances, is the closest Chaucer came to an explicit assessment of the genre. This crushing and comical parody could
be described as the only Chaucerian romance cast in the
simple form of a *conte d'aventure.* The doughty knight Sir
Thopas "priketh thurgh a fair forest," hears the song of the
thrush, falls into love-longing, and dedicates himself in
quest for the elf-queen, for whose love he forsakes all other women. But plainly there is more to it than that. Ringed
with layers of irony and pretense, *Sir Thopas* sets up an artful *conjointure* of a special kind, mingling strands of self-
parody with parody of all the literary elements of contemporary English popular romance—prosody, rhyme, style,
pacing, characterization, etc.

The other romances show Chaucer to be, like Chrétien,
interested in probing traditional *contes* and elaborating
them for moral, philosophical, spiritual, and comic purposes. Also, and to a much greater extent than Chrétien,
Chaucer exploits the possibilities of his poetic medium for
verbal irony, stylistic variety, and aesthetic perspective. He
thus expands the areas of potential meaning by introducing
multiple viewpoints and in general exposing his received
materials as well as his art itself to a variety of interpretations, by no means always credulous and respectful. In approaching the large question of Chaucerian *conjointure,* I
shall follow the narrow road of compositional technique
and leave out of account many other determinants of the
character of narrative. I think it is proper to regard composition as a vital structural procedure, more vital indeed
than one might readily infer from the dry prescriptive character of both medieval and modern handbooks of composition. A study of Chaucer's practice can reveal a great deal
about his approach to romance and to narrative art in general.

The medieval rhetoricians devoted relatively little of their
teaching to explicit discussion of composition, or *dispo-*

sitio, apart from some rather perfunctory and obvious directions for where to begin (e.g., at the beginning or *in medias res*), how to begin (e.g., with a *sententia* or an *exemplum*), and how to end.[5] But in their exhaustive catalogues and hierarchical classifications of the techniques and varieties of amplification and abbreviation, and in their comprehensive enumeration of figures of speech and ornaments of style, these treatises manifest in their own form the "quantitative" compositional assumptions which underlie their teachings. In their expository, scholastic style, stressing comprehensive coverage of the total subject of rhetoric and at the same time sharply articulating each of the constituent elements and sub-elements, these handbooks reveal a preoccupation with the conscious art of construction. Their function is to display the choices available to the writer and to instill in him a sense of propriety in choosing materials, in shaping them, and in disposing them—almost in the manner of a builder—in proper relations with one another.[6]

Chaucer's many allusions to rhetoric and rhetorical teachings leave no doubt of his general orientation.[7] A comparative study of the compositional structure of the romances reveals how fully Chaucer followed the injunction of Geoffrey of Vinsauf to be varied and yet the same. Being deliberately elaborated or "conjoined" tales, the romances all observe the rhetorical imperatives of *amplificatio*. But they are so different in many structural features that the single generic term romance seems inadequate to define them.

Having referred briefly to *Sir Thopas* and its unique self-parodic form of *conjointure,* I shall now consider four of the other five romances, some in more detail than others. *Troilus and Criseyde* I shall deal with only indirectly, partly because it is too large and complex to yield to the kind of cursory treatment I would have to give it in this context, but also because many of the observations I make about the others, especially the *Knight's Tale,* will appear readily applicable to *Troilus.*

THE SQUIRE'S TALE

If *Sir Thopas* resembles a pure *conte d'aventure*, which Chaucer transforms into a parodic romance through an ironic form of *conjointure*, the *Squire's Tale* represents an entirely different approach not only to *conjointure* but to the basic *conte* as well. Simply put, the *Squire's Tale* lacks both plot and theme, and the question arises whether what remains can be legitimately regarded as romance or even as a narrative. Although only a fragment, the *Squire's Tale* proceeded far enough—about 700 lines—for Chaucer to have realized that it was leading nowhere.[8]

The absence of linear progression of action, together with the presence in profusion of lengthy disquisitions and descriptions, results in a compositional structure which juxtaposes neatly outlined rhetorical elements with one another in essentially static patterns. A narrative structure of this kind can be defined as configurational, or planimetric, as opposed to the more traditional form of narrative, which more fully exploits progression and sequentiality. In the terms of medieval rhetoric it can be said that the *Squire's Tale* observes the prescriptions of *amplificatio* to an extreme degree.

The *Squire's Tale* is divided by rubric into two parts; "Pars Tercia" barely gets under way before the interruption by Franklin and Host aborts the enterprise. Part One is almost entirely descriptive, providing individual sections of varying length to expatiate on each of the magical gifts brought to King Cambiuskan's court by the mysterious knight from the East. First the knight himself describes them in a series of four set descriptions of ten to fifteen lines each, following one upon the other: the steed of brass (115-30); the mirror of omniscience (131-41); the magic ring (142-55); and the naked sword (156-67). This entire presentation is neatly concluded with the simple statement, "and whan this knyght hath thus his tale toold, He rideth out of halle, and down he lighte." Then the gifts are again described, each in turn, this time in the third person, from the point of view of the press of amazed members of the court. These descriptions are more extensive than the first, conveying the reactions of the crowd to each marvellous object as well as direct description of the object. Forty-five lines are devoted to the horse, ten to the mirror, eleven to the sword, fifteen to the ring—again one following directly after the other (181–267). Following these, and concluding Part One, is another description, this one of the feast at court. This time the narrator articulates the change with a rhetorical *occupatio,* explaining that since only Lancelot could describe the jolly, subtle, and covert love-play taking place at this festive gathering, he himself will desist. He then delivers nonetheless a deft fifteen-line account of the sundry sensuous delights of the occasion, followed by a further passage on the wondrous brass horse. As a whole, then, Part One presents a series of individuated sections which, though sequential in verbal order, are essentially equivalent in their descriptive function, and hence produce a static, aggregative effect.

The elements of such a structure relate to one another somewhat in the manner of the items in a laundry list—by which metaphor I intend no disrespect to our text—in that they relate to one another by contiguity rather than by organic fusion, and yet the contiguous relations are not entirely random since all the items belong to the name at the head of the list. This kind of "inorganic" relationship governs the descriptive passages in Part One: they are individual and merely contiguous, and yet they are related as constituent elements of the courtly setting. A narrative structure such as this, lacking directional imperatives, is subject to capricious modes of development, and perhaps this is why Chaucer could not or would not complete the *Squire's Tale.* It is plain, nevertheless, that the magical gifts described in Part One will be the subject, though one would expect, simply on the indications of prominence and length of descriptive treatment, that the steed of brass would assume major importance. Such is not the case, however, for Part Two concerns only the magical ring. Allowing for the considerable degree of arbitrariness inherent in an inorganic ordonnance, we are still inclined to question Chaucer's artistic judgment in his choice of the ring as the subject of Part Two. I think he finally realized that the story of the ring was leading him astray, and at the close of Part Two he himself implies some humorous skepticism toward his narrator's expressed intention to return to relevance:

> But hennesforth I wol my proces holde
> To speken of aventures and of batailles,
> That nevere yet was herd so grete mervailles.[5]
> 　　　　　　　　　　　　　　　(V, 658–60)

He will return, that is, from a bird's love-lament to the true substance of a *conte d'aventure*, but finally the prospect proved less than irresistible, and after a gesture toward a Part Three Chaucer gave it up.

Part Two is taken up almost entirely with the love-lament of a falcon, whose language Canacee can now understand, thanks to the efficacy of the ring. The falcon's tribulations over her faithless tiercel constitute a rather attractive genre piece, but in this setting its interest is vitiated in direct proportion to its length (about 250 lines) and its remoteness from any perceptible main subject or thematic idea. But if our concern is to define the general structure of the narrative rather than to assess its particular effectiveness or quality in this instance, we may simply observe that the falcon's lament and Part Two as a whole display on a larger scale the same formal organization that is evident in the individually articulated elements of Part One. Throughout the narrative individuated parts are consecutively disposed, their number and size being determined not by internal, "organic" demands of the materials but by the poet's arbitrary choice, exercised independently in each instance. The narrative's weaknesses are thus not alleviated in Part Two. There is still no central strand of plot action, and this lack corresponds with the absence of a protagonist. No knight errant appears as the central figure (nor even a knight *amant* as in *Troilus*), and hence the customary series of sequential and more or less closely related adventures does not materialize as an organizing motif. Nor does King Cambiuskan assume a proprietary role comparable, say, to that of Theseus in the *Knight's Tale.* Hence the tale also lacks the larger thematic continuity which such a role could provide. For these negative reasons it is difficult to accept Robinson's opinion that "the *Squire's Tale* is a typical romance."[10] The tale does, of course, contain magical and exotic elements, generally regarded as characteristic of romance, but by the same token the absence of these would seem to deny the status of romance to *Troilus* and the *Knight's Tale.* The *Squire's Tale* does display certain chivalric values, but the absence of a compelling narrative context robs them of significance. It might be claimed that the *Squire's Tale* is a *conjointure* without a *conte,* but while we can appreciate a simple, unelaborated tale for what it is, a disembodied *conjointure* is meaningless. With respect to our effort to define Chaucerian romance, perhaps the most we can say for the *Squire's Tale* is that it clearly illustrates the difficulty of defining genre by subject matter alone. About the significance of its compositional structure we must reserve judgment until we have considered the other romances.

THE WIFE OF BATH'S TALE

Unlike the *Squire's Tale* and *Sir Thopas,* the *Wife of Bath's Tale* is built around a plot line of some integrity and coherence, which traces a young knight's quest for the answer to what it is women most desire, and culminates in his enlightenment at the hands of the Loathly Lady. In comparison to his treatment of the received *conte* in *Troilus and Criseyde* and the *Knight's Tale,* Chaucer's *conjointure* in the *Wife of Bath's Tale* is not aesthetically complex or extensive, nor is it morally or thematically arresting. Yet it seems to share with those tales a mode of narrative procedure, and it displays a binary relationship between *conte* and superstructure not clearly apparent in the *Squire's Tale*.

Like the other romances, the *Wife of Bath's Tale* is based upon an additive principle of composition. A series of largely self-contained and clearly articulated parts, often varying in size, style, and degree of relevance to the *conte*, are more or less loosely strung together to form an "inorganic" whole.

The opening twenty-five lines of the tale, ostensibly establishing the setting in King Arthur's time, in fact present an only remotely relevant (though engaging and delicately ironic) lament for the fairies, long since displaced in the landscape of Britain by "lymytours and othere hooly freres." The concluding thought of this section, that ladies can now walk without fear of attack from hidden incubi because now only friars lurk in the bushes (and they would do no more than "dishonor" a lady), alludes with archness and subtlety to a host of provocative questions, though these hover at the far periphery of the tale's subject. Thus the introductory passage as a whole is both attractive in its own right and tangential—almost irrelevant—to the main plot line of the tale. Plainly Chaucer's approach to his *conte* is leisurely and indirect. While one might strain to derive thematic relevance from this and other embellished passages, it seems more appropriate to understand and accept Chaucer's compositional method for what it is. The "inefficiency" of the tale is perhaps best measured by the amount of purely expository material it contains, only slightly if at all disguised as integral to the *conte*. The most conspicuous of such passages is the hag's sententious disquisition on gentillesse and poverty. This passage is quite long, comprising one hundred lines, or almost one-fourth of the tale. In its own right it is a lively and interesting treatment of two popular Boethian themes; and it is developed in its own right, without evident concern for subordination to its narrative context. Nor is it integrated in more than superficial fashion with the thematic imperatives of the story.

The opening of the hag's speech contains a gesture toward continuity in her reference to the preceding words of the knight, "But, for ye speken of swich gentillesse . . ." However, the knight had not been speaking of gentillesse—he had merely expressed his revulsion at her ugliness, her age, and her lowliness "of kynde." Nor does the long speech on gentillesse really direct itself to the knight; it is in fact addressed to the audience. Chaucer apparently wished to include such a discourse at this point. He composed it in accordance with its own rhetorical imperatives and inserted it here, along with the succeeding discourse on poverty.

Only slightly less conspicuously "digressive" is the story of Midas and his wife. In the form of a tantalizingly incomplete adaptation from Ovid, this narrative is inserted in the long summary account of the knight's unsuccessful year-long quest (before he encountered the hag on his way back to court). The summary itself, an amusing catalogue of feminine vanities—none of which happens to be the right answer to the question—is at least as engaging in its own right as in relation to the knight's quest:

> Somme seyde wommen loven best richesse,
> Some seyde honour, somme seyde jolynesse,
> Somme riche array, somme seyden lust abedde,
> And oftetyme to be wydwe and wedde. (III, 925–28)

Beyond this witty but gratuitous bit of antifeminism we are again disengaged from the knightly quest, and distanced even further from it, by the story of Midas, which develops an absorbing narrative life of its own. Ostensibly this story illustrates one of the enumerated feminine traits—the delight in being thought to be trustworthy—but the story develops its own substance and momentum, including a deftly compressed background account of Midas's love for his wife and his sensitivity about his physical deformity. Then the foreground action moves artfully into discourse between Midas and his wife and becomes sufficiently complex to include a shift of scene when the wife, unable to hold her tongue, hurries to the marsh and tells her husband's secret to the water.

The transition from the Midas story back to the main quest narrative typifies the structural mode of the tale. As if to assure explicit articulation of the separate parts even as he is joining them together, the poet capitalizes the point of juncture by bringing the narrator forward to present an interpretation, or gloss, of the Midas story as well as an explicit statement that that story is over. The return to the main narrative is abrupt, displaying little effort to smooth the edges or soften the disjunct movement:

> Heere may ye se, thogh we [women] a tyme abyde,
> Yet out it moot; we kan no conseil hyde.
> The remenant of the tale if ye wol heere,
> Redeth Ovyde, and ther ye may it leere.
> This knyght, of which my tale is specially . . .
>
> (III, 979–83)

Perhaps enough has been said about the ordonnance of the *Wife of Bath's Tale* to indicate its additive character, comprising as it does a number of discrete parts—disquisition, catalogue, a self-contained "mini" tale, etc.—which are loosely strung along the thread of the *conte,* and which often are related to it only by the thinnest of pretexts.[11] The inorganic mode of composition provides the poet with structural justification, even encouragement, for dilations and digressions. These occur in an almost improvisatory fashion (which, incidentally, accounts for much of the "naturalness" and vitality of Chaucer's style in general). As a result, narrative progression is spasmodic, the dilatory impulses frequently interrupting the underlying pattern of linear sequence. Such a structure admits of infinite variety of materials, the range depending upon the imagination and learning of the poet as well as his skill in *conjointure.* Is this the characteristic structure of Chaucerian romance?

THE KNIGHT'S TALE

Chaucer's other romances, though differing greatly among themselves in scale and substance, nevertheless display similar compositional traits. The *Knight's Tale* is in every way a more substantial poem than the *Wife of Bath's Tale*. Though it displays the same clearly articulated ordonnance, its mode of development is more closely akin to that of *Troilus*. Its solidity, depth, and endless interest are attributable in large part to the fact that the elements of compositional structure harmonize with the subject matter to form an artistic unity of rare consistency, in this respect even surpassing *Troilus*. The *Knight's Tale's* thematic concern with the significance of order and form in an unpredictable world is everywhere reflected in its own formal structure. The design of the poem has been amply demonstrated in a number of studies in recent years,[12] and here I wish to point out only a few aspects concerned directly with narrative composition.

Of the four explicit divisions of the poem, the first two deal with the Palamon-Emily-Arcite love triangle on the scale of human conflict between individuals, while in the latter half of the poem the conflict is elevated and expanded to the level of public ceremony, of which the tourney is both emblem and substance. There is more narrative movement, paradoxically, in the first half of the poem than in the parts concerned with the tourney, but as a whole the poem depicts surprisingly little action, and the mode of narration tends toward the static, formalized presentation of balanced sequences of episodes, speeches, and spectacles.

The poem as a whole deliberately exploits the symmetry inherent in the love triangle. In the first half the focal point shifts regularly between Palamon and Arcite. First Palamon falls in love with Emily:

> And so bifel, by aventure or cas,
> That thurgh a wyndow, thikke of many a barre
> Of iren greet and square as any sparre,

> He cast his eye upon Emelya,
> And therwithal he bleynte and cride, "A!"
> As though he stongen were unto the herte. (I, 1074–79)

Then Arcite, in a passage of equal size and impact:

> And with that word Arcite gan espye
> Wher as this lady romed to and fro,
> And with that sighte hir beautee hurte hym so,
> That, if that Palamon was wounded sore,
> Arcite is hurt as muche as he, or moore. (I, 1112–16)

The rivalry is cast in a broad philosophical context, and the narrative allots comparable passages to the rival claims, proceeding in a series of paired speeches culminating in the balanced *demande d'amour* which ends Part I:

> Yow loveres axe I now this questioun:
> Who hath the worse, Arcite or Palamoun?
> That oon may seen his lady day by day,
> But in prison he moot dwelle alway;
> That oother wher hym list may ride or go,
> But seen his lady shal he nevere mo. (I, 1347–52)

When the suitors are separated after Arcite's banishment and Palamon's escape, the alternation of narrative focus covers wider distances and the transitions seem more abrupt, as indicated by the frequently used formula, " . . . lete I now Arcite, And speke I wole of Palamon a lite" (1449–50). The result is a formalized succession of pairings. The rendering of the tourney is similarly structured, though the shifts between narrative focuses are confined within the area circumscribed by the circular form of the arena, and hence the divisions seem less emphatic than in the earlier parts of the poem, where the narrative often swings between scenes widely separated in fictional space.

The description of the arena illustrates the pattern very distinctly; it accords roughly equal treatment to each of the temples allotted to the opposing knights (on opposite sides of the arena) and to the lady in between. All three descriptions are self-contained paragraphs, neatly articulated by the narrator, and all are formed in the same two-part fashion: first a description of the richly decorated inner walls of the temple, and then a description of the god.

The tourney itself, a rather small jewel in the ceremonial setting, is narrated in similar fashion. The equality of sides having been verbally and visually established in roughly equal rhetorical units of brilliantly colorful description, a brief summary poises the narrative for the climactic action:

> For ther was noon so wys that koude seye
> That any hadde of oother avauntage
> Of worthynesse, ne of estaat, ne age,
> So evene were they chosen, for to gesse. (I, 2590-93)

The rhetorical signal given by the narrator echoes the trumpet sound on the field as the narrative moves with all due formality to the new phase of action:

> Now ryngen trompes loude and clarioun.
> Ther is namoore to seyn, but west and est
> In goon the speres ful sadly in arrest;
> In gooth the sharpe spore into the syde. (I, 2600-03)

The action is compressed into a brilliant fifty-line rendering (after some 700 lines of ceremonial preparation). Uncharacteristically, its conclusion, though marked decisively by Theseus' intercession ("Hoo! namoore, for it is doon!") is not accompanied by an equally abrupt rhetorical transition. The intensity of our involvement in the scene is not diminished until the death of Arcite, and then, almost as though to relieve the shock of that event, but also to effect a new focus and articulate the change, the narrator steps forward:

> His [Arcite's] spirit chaunged hous and wente ther,
> As I cam nevere, I kan nat tellen wher.

Therefore I stynte, I nam no divinistre;
Of soules fynde I nat in this registre,
Ne me ne list thilke opinions to telle
Of hem, though that they writen wher they dwelle.
Arcite is coold, ther Mars his soule gye!
Now wol I speken forth of Emelye. (I, 2809–16)

For its remaining 300 lines or so the poem reverts to a compositional structure which can contain in rough juxtaposition a sequence of diversified and individuated rhetorical elements: Egeus' solemn little homily on "Joye after wo, and wo after gladnesse" (2837–52); the rich descriptive narration of Theseus' preparations and the somber funeral procession (2853–2912); the dazzling and subtly comic description of the funeral pyre—an *occupatio* in which the narrator struggles helplessly and uselessly to compress an irresistible flood of details (2913–66); Theseus' majestic oration on the First Mover (2098–3089), followed by the brief knitting up of the plot, as Theseus, the dispenser of order, applies his own wise counsel to make a virtue of the necessity of Arcite's death.

This jostling mixture of passages which are startlingly diverse in tone, style, and thematic and narrative purpose (and which share the quality of structural autonomy) illustrates once again the variety and vitality attainable within an inorganic ordonnance. Together these passages form another element in the *Knight's Tale*, consecutive with the larger elements of the love contest and the tourney, all contained within the morally ordered world of Theseus and the rich structural configuration of Chaucer's poem.

Though description, exposition, and visual display are predominant features of the *Knight's Tale*, a linear progression is apparent nonetheless, not so firmly etched and compelling as that in *Troilus*, but certainly more so than that in the *Squire's Tale*. The comparative thinness of the latter, as we have observed, is due not only to the absence of a compelling linear logic but also to the lack of thematic development of its rhetorical components. The *Knight's*

Tale, in contrast, follows the linear imperatives of the developing love conflict between Palamon and Arcite to a climax in the tourney and a resolution in the fateful death of Arcite, followed by the marriage of Palamon and Emily. But more than that, it develops both the sensuous and the moral and philosophical possibilities inherent in the fictional structure. If the *Squire's Tale* is indeed "a typical romance," we are left wondering what properly to call the *Knight's Tale, Troilus and Criseyde,* and even the *Wife of Bath's Tale.*

THE FRANKLIN'S TALE

More fully than any of the Chaucerian romances, the *Franklin's Tale* exemplifies that preoccupation with the ethical problems of amorous relationships which is characteristic of French courtly poetry. One could readily say of its characters, as Vinaver has said of Chrétien's, "everything they do is related to a problem and its elaboration within the work, since it is with problems that courtly poetry is concerned, not with human realities."[13] Over a simple tale of ancient lineage, known to folklorists as "The Damsel's Rash Promise," Chaucer has woven a complex *conjointure* to probe and elaborate the ethical implications of "trouthe," "fredom," "franchise," and "gentillesse." For such an analytical purpose, perhaps verging on casuistry as it poses the closing question, "Which was the mooste fre, as thynketh yow," the principles of inorganic composition are very well suited. In a series of nicely articulated scenes and episodes Chaucer is able to delve—briefly or at length, as the occasion moves him—into a variety of problems more or less relevant to the basic story, but always germane to the courtly ethos and no doubt intriguing to Chaucer's courtly audience.

For example, following the economically narrated account of the courtship and marriage of Dorigen and Ar-

veragus (729–60), Chaucer offers a passage of the same
length on the vexed problem of love and sovereignty in
marriage. His solution, impeccably reasoned and elegantly
versified, is also humorously sententious. It is an artful disquisition in its own right, by no means essential to the progress of the *conte* and in fact damaging to narrative continuity, but perfectly fitting and relevant in the terms of
Chaucer's kind of narrative composition. Beginning in leisurely fashion, "For o thyng, sires, saufly dar I seye . . ."
(761) it goes on to offer irresistible observations such as the
following celebrated passage:

> Love wol nat been constreyned by maistrye.
> Whan maistrie comth, the God of Love anon
> Beteth his wynges, and farewel, he is gon!
> Love is a thyng as any spirit free. (V, 764–67)

Chaucer's subject is not the marriage, not the human relationship of Dorigen and Arveragus, but marriage-related
ethical problems. Hence the cryptic, one-line account of
the first year or more of the marriage, almost grudgingly included after a three-line, typically Chaucerian, double-
edged eulogy of the marital state:

> Who koude telle, but he hadde wedded be,
> The joye, the ese, and the prosperitee
> That s bitwixe an housbonde and his wyf?
> A yeer and moore lasted this blisful lyf,
> Till that the knyght of which I speke of thus,
> That of Kayrrud was cleped Arveragus,
> Shoop hym to goon and dwelle a yeer or tweyne
> In Engelond, that cleped was eek Briteyne,
> To seke in armes worshipe and honour;
> For al his lust he sette in swich labour;
> And dwelled there two yeer, the book seith thus.
> Now wol I stynten of this Arveragus,
> And speken I wole of Dorigen his wyf . . . (V, 803–15)

The formulaic articulation in these last two lines effects the transition with typical directness and introduces a long section devoted to Dorigen (814–1086). This in turn divides roughly in half. The first part depicts Dorigen in melancholy solitude, lamenting the absence of her husband and musing fearfully on the "grisly feendly rokes blakke" that obstruct his return. The second part depicts her in a social scene arranged by her friends to help relieve her melancholy. Here too an unambiguous transition is effected by use of a readily recognizable narrative formula:

> So on a day, right in the morwe-tyde,
> Unto a gardyn that was ther bisyde,
> In which that they hadde maad hir ordinaunce
> Of vitaille and of oother purveiaunce,
> They goon and pleye hem al the longe day. (V, 901–05)

The ensuing scene contrasts in every way with the preceding passage of attenuated melancholy. The *topos* of the garden and the timely allusion to the "sixte morwe of May" signal a courtly episode, and Chaucer fulfills this expectation in sensuous and sophisticated fashion. After the French style he depicts in delicate detail the sights and odors of that "verray paradys," in which occur dancing and singing and Dorigen's fateful encounter with the love-lorn squire Aurelius.

This section is concluded by a two-line intrusion of the narrator, commenting on the condition of Aurelius, who now lies in a swoon after addressing his passionate plaint to Dorigen. Then the next section, switching focus to the newly returned Arveragus, abruptly begins:

> Lete I this woful creature lye;
> Chese he, for me, wheither he wol lyve or dye.
> Arveragus, with heele and greet honour,
> As he that was of chivalrie the flour,
> Is comen hoom, and othere worthy men. (V, 1085–89)

From this point onward, somewhat more than half the tale, the narrative structure becomes increasingly complex as it encompasses the actions of the three main characters and several shifts of scene, including the detailed excursion of Aurelius to Orleans and back. We should note one passage in particular, which Chaucer seems to have fashioned with unusual care and which achieves a deep emotional intensity. This is the passage which begins (1239) with Aurelius' return to Brittany, accompanied by the magician who will attempt to remove the threat of the black rocks, thus fulfilling Aurelius' part of the bargain with Dorigen. It ends (1340) at the tale's point of crisis, as Aurelius, after deferentially reminding Dorigen of her promise, announces to her that the rocks are gone. Though this section begins with a conventional narrative formula, "Upon the morwe, whan that it was day" (1239), Aurelius' return to Brittany is invested with unusual significance by the formal language in which it is couched. The simple statement that it was "The colde, frosty seson of Decembre" (1244) is elaborated both by specific astrological allusions ("Phebus wax old . . . in Capricorn adoun he lighte") and generalized homely touches ("And 'Nowell' crieth every lusty man"). The movement to the climactic confrontation is carefully timed and deliberately paced. At the center is "this subtel clerk" working his magic, which Chaucer describes in astrological detail, not without the touch of skepticism which assures the awesomeness of the result:

> So atte laste he hath his tyme yfounde
> To maken his japes and his wrecchednesse
> Of swich a supersticious cursednesse. (V, 1270–72)

The detailed description of the clerk's calculations separates two allusions to the anxious state of Aurelius and at the same time attenuates the sense of dreadful anticipation and verifies the reality of the scene. The section concludes climactically as Aurelius, "with dredful herte and with ful

humble cheere," delivers his formal plaint to the astonished Dorigen:

> "In yow lith al to do me lyve or deye,
> But wel I woot the rokkes been aweye."
> He taketh his leve, as she astoned stood;
> In al hir face nas a drope of blood. (V, 1337–40)

The special quality of this scene is partly inherent in the
conte, which determines that a lady be required to fulfill
the terms of a rash promise. But the manner in which Chaucer disposes and elaborates the elements of the story creates a depth of human poignancy not necessarily present in
the *conte* itself and rarely encountered elsewhere in Chaucer's own poetry. We might detect in this passage a strain-
ing toward a new kind of fictional depiction of human situations. Structurally speaking, the internal rhetorical demar-
cations between narrative parts seem to be giving way, resulting in a swiftness of movement and a fuller emergence
of the action from its background and narrative frame. But
still the outer limits of the section, in accord with the prevailing compositional pattern, remain firm and clear, the
elaborated return of Arveragus (1239) and Aurelius' with-
drawal from the astonished Dorigen (1339).

But the sense of personal emotion is not sustained far
beyond this point. The denouement analyzes the resulting
ethical dilemma in a manner for which the inorganic ordonnance of the narrative is especially well suited. Briefly, the
denouement unfolds in this fashion. First, Dorigen's soli-
tary plaint to Fortune (1355–1456) expounds in fervent language, enhanced by examples from history and legend, the
depth of the dilemma of a woman torn between irreconcil-
able moral claims. This is followed by a sequence of con-
frontations in which the characters dramatize and finally re-
solve the stated dilemma. Dorigen faces Arveragus and
confesses her woe to him, and his response produces
another poignant moment, but only a moment:

"Trouthe is the hyeste thyng that man may keoe"
But with that word he brast anon to wepe . . .

(V, 1479–80)

The truth Arveragus means, of course, is truth to her promise to Aurelius. And thus is prepared her sorrowfu encounter with Aurelius. Aurelius, moved by the "fredom" of Arveragus as well as the "trouthe" of Dorigen, releases her from her promise. This scene is matched by that in which the clerk in a comparable act of "fredom" releases Aurelius from his debt of a thousand pounds for the clerk's necromantic services. The rhetorical neatness and the ethical propriety of this resolution are effectively abetted by the capacity of the narrative structure to accommodate such a configuration of elements. We see, then, that through this structure Chaucer is able to deal individually with a variety of problems germane to the courtly ethos and more or less relevant to the basic *conte* of the Damsel's Rash Promise.

The mode of narrative organization we have been describing is by no means uniquely Chaucerian, though Chaucer brings to it unique gifts of language, mind, and personality. His practice is in fact governed by the rules of rhetoric and grammar which were the commonplaces of humane education in the Middle Ages: rhetoric governing the disposition of verbal elements and their ornamentation, and grammar governing their interpretation, or the extraction of meaning. Among the great narrative poets after Chrétien, certainly Dante and Boccaccio partook of the learned tradition, and Chaucer is of the same mold. What finally distinguishes Chaucerian romance from popular Middle English romance, and aligns it with the intellectual tradition, is its capacity to develop meaning from its received materials. But lest this point be misunderstood or misapplied, we should emphasize the difference between romance and allegory. As I hope my comments on Chaucer's romances have made clear, the essence of the form is variety of allusion and multiplicity of focus, even occasionally to the point of incongruity and incoherence, as the ostensible point of a story may be forgotten, ignored, or contradicted. Despite the efforts of some critics, influenced by medieval biblical exegesis, to reduce every Chaucerian narrative to an allegory of Christian redemption, the facts of literary analysis seem to bear out Vinaver's point that "romance by its very nature favours variety rather than consistency."[14] The proper means for a consistent expression of ideology, whether courtly or Christian, would be allegory or lyric. In a Chaucerian romance, on the other hand, it is more accurate to speak of meanings than of *the* meaning.

If Chaucer's romances, despite their manifest differences in scale, tone, depth of treatment, and even subject matter (though all contain some form of chivalric adventure), are nevertheless linked together by common structural techniques and a common method of elaborating basic materials, we may have found corroboration in structural terms for the traditional generic grouping according to subject matter. Unfortunately, such a claim would be unsupportable, for the disconcerting reason that it apparently applies to *all* Chaucerian narrative. I think it can in fact be demonstrated that the same principle of inorganic composition, giving rise to a similar variety of works which are themselves internally digressive and diffuse, governs the fabliaux, the saint's lives, the exempla, and other less readily classifiable genres in the canon. Only the short lyrics and the dream visions appear to follow somewhat different compositional patterns, though the dream visions, despite or perhaps because of their essential impulse toward exposition and display, are likely to possess a greater rather than a lesser affinity with inorganic narrative. Finally, then, so far as romance is concerned, we seem to be faced with two taxonomic alternatives, neither one entirely satisfying: either all of Chaucer's narratives are romances—that is to say, narratives composed in the learned tradition appropriated to story-telling by twelfth-century French courtly poets—cr the Chaucer canon contains no such genre as romance, in any meaningful sense of the term.[15] In either case the term romance would seem to retain little critical value. If, as I am suggesting, the narrative structures used by Chaucer do not observe the generic boundaries formulated by post-medieval scholarship, our proper study must be narrative structures, not genres.

THE UNIVERSITY OF BRITISH COLUMBIA

FOOTNOTES

1. J. Burke Severs, "The Tales of Romance," in *Companion to Chaucer Studies,* ed. Beryl Rowland (Toronto: Oxford Univ. Press, 1968). p. 229. See also A. C. Baugh et al., *A Literary History of England* (New York: Appleton-Century-Crofts, 1948), p. 173.

2. L. H. Hornstein, "Eustace-Constance-Florence-Griselda Legends," in *A Manual of the Writings in Middle English 1050–1500,* ed. J. Burke Severs, I, Romances (New Haven: Connecticut Academy, 1967), pp. 120–32.

3. See Peter Haidu, "Realism, Convention, Fictionality and the Theory of Genres in *Le Bel Inconnu,*" *L'Esprit Créateur,* 12 (1972), 37–60.

4. *The Rise of Romance* (Oxford: Clarendon Press, 1971), pp. 36–37. The revolution in the status of poetry was late in reaching England. Chaucer was a first-generation beneficiary, as P. M. Kean, *Chaucer and the Making of English Poetry,* vol. I, *Love Vision and Debate* (London: Routledge & Kegan Paul, 1972), pp. 23–24, has shown.

5. A contrary view of the prominence of explicit discussion of composition in medieval rhetoric is argued by Douglas Kelly, "Theory of Composition in Medieval Narrative poetry and Geoffrey de Vinsauf's *Poetria Nova,*" *Mediaeval Studies,* 31 (1969), 117–48. Whatever the extent of explicit discussion of *dispositio,* it is clear that the rhetoricians regard writing as the art of skillfully disposing the elements of language. Geoffrey of Vinsauf recommends his precepts as a means of molding the writer's material, "like the molding of wax;" the techniques of amplification and abbreviation and the ornaments of style enumerate the materials

of an art whose nature is, by definition, compositional—or "dispositional"—rather than "creative" or "expressive" in the modern sense of those terms. A comprehensive guide to the rhetorical texts and the tradition is James J. Murphy, *Medieval Rhetoric: A Select Bibliography* (Toronto: Univ. of Toronto Press, 1971).

6. These quantitative presuppositions are not exclusive to rhetoric and poetics but underlie medieval aesthetics in general. I have tried to draw the literary implications of medieval aesthetic theory in *Chaucer and the Shape of Creation: the Aesthetic Possibilities of Inorganic Structure* (Cambridge, Mass.: Harvard Univ. Press, 1967), pp. 29–43. The definitive study of medieval aesthetics is Edgar de Bruyne, *Etudes d'esthétique médiévale*, 3 vols. (Bruges: De Tempel, 1946). For a striking derivation of general principles via analogies between verbal and plastic structures, see Erwin Panofsky, *Gothic Architecture and Scholasticism* (Latrobe, Pa.: Archabbey Press, 1951).

7. The rhetorical basis of Chaucer's art is explored by Robert O. Payne, *The Key of Remembrance: A Study of Chaucer's Poetics* (New Haven: Yale Univ. Press, 1963).

8. While the point is not directly relevant to the question of romance, there is some disagreement about Chaucer's intentions in producing this fragmentary tale. Joyce E. Peterson, "The Finished Fragment: A Reassessment of the *Squire's Tale*," *Chaucer Review*, 5 (1970), p. 66, has recently argued that the tale is as complete as Chaucer intended it to be. Reasoning mainly from "dramatic" principles, she argues that the Franklin "interrupts the Squire by *pretending* to think him finished." Earlier studies along the same line, stressing Chaucer's ironic humor in providing the youthful Squire with a wonderfully flawed narrative include John P. McCall, "The Squire in Wonderland," *Chaucer Review*, 1 (1966), 103–09; and Gardiner Stillwell, "Chaucer in Tartary," *RES*, 24 (1948), 177–88. More germane to generic and structural concerns are the following: D. A. Pearsall, "The Squire as Story Teller," *UTQ*, 36 (1964), 82–92; Robert S. Haller, "Chaucer's *Squire's Tale* and the Uses of Rhetoric," *MP*, 62 (1965), 285–95.

9. *The Works of Geoffrey Chaucer*, ed. F. N. Robinson, 2nd ed. (Boston: Houghton-Mifflin, 1957). All other Chaucer quotations are also taken from this edition.

10. *Works*, p. 717.

11. In a discussion of oral delivery as a determinant of the discontinuity of much medieval narrative, A. C. Spearing, *Criticism and Medieval Poetry*, 2nd ed., rev. (New York: Barnes & Noble, 1972), p. 26, cites the *WBT* as an example of a story that "changes shape and focus halfway through, the beginning apparently being

forgotten by the time the end is reached." As Spearing indicates, the *WBT* is not unique in this respect, either among Chaucer's works or among medieval narratives in general.

12. Studies particularly relevant to the aesthetics of the poem—its stylistic, structural, and rhetorical features—are Charles Muscatine, "Form, Texture, and Meaning in Chaucer's *Knight's Tale*," *PMLA*, 65 (1950), 911–29; and William Frost, "An Interpretation of Chaucer's *Knight's Tale*," *RES*, 25 (1949), 289–304. For a detailed structural analysis see Jordan, op. cit., pp. 152–84. An interesting "structuralist" study is Frederick Turner, "A Structuralist Analysis of the *Knight's Tale*," *Chaucer Review*, 8 (1974), 279–96.

13. *The Rise of Romance*, p. 31.

14. *The Rise of Romance*, p. 32. See also Spearing, op. cit., pp. 25 ff.

15. R. S. Haller, loc. cit., speaking from a somewhat different standpoint, regards romance as one of the "pseudo-genres" of the Middle Ages, along with Breton *lai* and Arthurian tale, in contrast with the authenticity of epic.

6

St. Nicholas
and Saintly Allusion

ANN S. HASKELL

Allusion of all kinds, whether historical, animal, or botanical, is a standard rhetorical device; moreover it is a time-honored area of Chaucerian scholarship, as the footnotes to any edition adequately attest. Much still remains to be researched, using a veritable gamut of approaches, from traditional to avant garde. This paper will deal with saintly allusion and Chaucer's flexible use of it, illustrated by the allusions to St. Nicholas in the *Prioress' Tale* and in the *Miller's Tale*.

Though congregations would regularly hear the legends of the major saints repeated year after year at the celebration of their feast days, and would hear amusing or shocking anecdotes in homily or sermon, the men and women of the Middle Ages—even the isolated and illiterate—would also be permanently influenced by the visual representation of the heroes of the Church in ecclesiastical art, in wall painting, in sculpture, in images, in processions, as well as (for the richer and more literate) in illuminated horae and breviaries.

Iconographical representation of saints frequently features a single and typical object—a flower, an animal, or a tool—associated with the saint, which subsequently becomes a shorthand symbol to recall a whole incident or motif. In the churches, both "lewed" and lettered could thus comprehend entire lives of saints with the aid of individualizing attributes, which would otherwise have required lengthy explanations. The whole fearsome story of St. Erasmus' martyrdom could be evoked from the windlass shown in his hand—never mind that his bowels wound around the instrument had once been only rope! The story of St. Denis' decapitation was recalled by the head he always bore in his hands, and St. Uncumber's beard reminded men of her struggle to remain chaste. The breasts held by Agatha and the beehive of Ambrose likewise became symbols of complete legends. These symbols or icons are presented in the literary pictorialism of Jean Hagstrum and, more recently, John B. Bender,[1] and may appear straightforwardly or (with Chaucer) "up-so-doun," as in the *Summoner's Tale,* where Chaucer has used an ironic inversion at either end.[2]

A good example of how art extends the significance of words, summoning new backgrounds to weave ironic associations, occurs in the *Miller's Tale,* if I may anticipate my later comments, in the legend of the three rescued by St. Nicholas from death in pickling tubs. Here is a clear and obvious parallel. In the *Miller's Tale* (I, 3636–42). Alison, John, and who but *Nicholas,* sitting in their three vats, present a scene highly suggestive of the most popular of the St. Nicholas icons, the three men in tubs. Though the three-men-in-a-tub, with its nursery rhyme tone, is not rare, three figures in three individual tubs are encountered with some frequency in the iconography of St. Nicholas. For instance, there is an excellent late fourteenth century example of St. Nicholas with three figures in separate tubs by Gentile da Fabriano.[3] This icon, probably influenced by the three resuscitated from pickling tubs, or possibly by the legend of the pious infant St. Nicholas standing in his bathtub to praise God, in all likelihood evolved from the legend of the three falsely accused men or the legend of the three clerks. Nevertheless, the scene of the three naked figures, wearing pious expressions, rising from tubs around the elegant bishop-saint, must have been evoked in the minds of the medieval audience by the comically parallel scene of the tub trio in the *Miller's Tale,* wearing only their expressions of fatigue and adultery.

Though the saints were outranked by many other members of the Church Triumphant, their relationship with medieval men was more personal and less awesome than that of, say, the Archangels or the Holy Trinity. Having once been human themselves, saints might be presumed to understand human needs and frailties, and as such, were valued friends at the heavenly court.[4] The saints' afflictions were those of the flesh—St. Appolonia's omnipresent toothache and St. Erasmus' perpetual bellyache—and saints were invoked according to the particular bailiwick of misery over which they presided.

Chaucer's allusions to saints are generally to the purely factual or "historical," such as the "hooly blisful martir" of the *General Prologue,* or the various saints (referred to ninety-seven times) in the *Parson's Tale.* These allusions will not be discussed here. But the historical accuracy of a saint's vita is less important than the legend which surrounded him in the mind of Chaucer's audience. More interesting to the reader, therefore, are Chaucer's allusions to what may be called "referential" saints. These are the saints to whom in the Middle Ages a mass of miscellaneous legend and myth became attached, and whose lives and miracles were popularized both in story and in stone. Thus the simple mention of a name would, by a kind of instant conditioned response, quickly conjure a host of ideas and associations now lost to modern readers reared in other traditions. In any work of Chaucer, whether a fabliau, romance, exemplum, or even a saint's life itself, a saint's name might provide increased depth of perspective to the context of the whole work.[5]

Saints might be introduced into the text by means of oaths, straightforward references, or word play (parono-

masia) or puns—for example, the juxtaposition of "St. Ro-
nian" with "runian" in the Pardoner's headlink (VI, 310).
That the saints' legends are prone to twists, puns, irony,
and the like, heightens the possibility of finding such word
play in the Chaucerian references.[6] To go one step further,
a critic may find a complete double exposure of incidents in
a saint's life, corresponding to the incidents of the tale—the
saintly reinforcing and adding subtlety to the secular.[7]

It is not surprising that Chaucer refers to St. Nicholas, for
he was one of the most popular saints in Christendom. Almost every English village had its St. Nicholas church, for
there were over 400 ancient dedications to the saint,[8] many
of which must have included Nicholas representations in
sculpture, stained glass, or other graphic forms. Further,
these were infrequently single scenes, but were more likely
to be encountered as series of incidents from his legends
or, if single, composites of several legends.[9] And the 527
Latin hymns incorporating his legends would have insured
a knowledge of St. Nicholas by the medieval Christian.[10]

But Nicholas is a very complex saint, so complex indeed
that he has recently been removed from the church calendar. During some periods in the Middle Ages, St. Nicholas
and St. Mary actually vied with one another for popularity;
and they have been considered counterparts of one another, St. Mary as heavenly intercessor and Nicholas as earthly
general helper.[11] This counterpartite scheme of homage is
present also in the *Prioress' Tale*. In addition, St. Nicholas is
a good example of how, in the words of Northrop Frye, "in
Christianity the saints play so prominent a role in absorbing
local gods."[12] St. Nicholas becomes inextricably fused with
Poseidon, and ends up as the patron saint of sailors. But he
is also the patron of schoolboys and clerks, of brides and
young girls, as well as of apothecaries and perfumers. To
study the possible allusions to Nicholas in Chaucer's tales
one has to draw on all this involved mass of myth and legend.

St. Nicholas is mentioned by name only once in the *Prior-*

ess' *Tale,* but the saint's life provides a mirror-parallel to
that of the "litel clergeon:"

> But ay, whan I remembre on this mateere,
> Seint Nicholas stant evere in my presence . . .[13]
>
> (VII, 513–14)

Legends of St. Nicholas have obvious affinities with the tale
told by the Prioress. For example, one of the many legends
of St. Nicholas, that of the kidnapped son, appears in several versions (including the Son of Getron and the legend of
Basilios), and is clearly parallel in motif and fable. The story
basically is as follows:

> During St. Nicholas celebrations a boy, judged to
> be seven years old[14] and, sometimes, the only son
> of a widow, is stolen by heathens and taken to
> serve their ruler. Even among the heathens the
> child continues his praise of God and eventually
> beseeches St. Nicholas for aid. After his mother's
> piteous lamentations during his absence, he is re-
> turned to his home (in one version, singing).[15]

One version has the child rescued from a prison where he
has been put following a beating for praising St. Nicholas.[16]
And a different, though related, legend of St. Nicholas concerns three sons of a poor, weeping widow, murdered by a
son of Satan (who can therefore be construed as a Jew),[17]
who are resuscitated and returned to their mother by St.
Nicholas.[18]

The main elements of the basic story of St. Nicholas are
comparable to Chaucer's tale of a seven-year-old boy, the
only son of a widow, murdered amidst an alien people because of his faith, delivered to eternal life (although in most
analogues restored to earthly life)[19] by the Virgin Mary, the
object of his particular worship. While I am not suggesting
that the Nicholas story is a direct ancestor to the *Prioress'*

Tale, the several versions of the Nicholas legend and the tale share the same bone structure and show a family resemblance.

Apart from the general parallelism of the legends themselves, perhaps the most fully explored aspect is the connection of St. Nicholas with the Feast of the Holy Innocents; consequently I will not pursue this.[20]

As patron of schoolboys, Nicholas was praised for his diligence in study, especially as a child.[21] In the stanza in which the Prioress specifically mentions St. Nicholas, she states that the early learning of the widow's little son is attributable to his character, "For sely child wol alday soone leere" (VII, 512). This precocity, she continues, always reminds her of St. Nicholas, "For he so yong to Crist dide reverence" (VII, 515). That his precocity should refer specifically to the incident in his legend in which he is supposed to have abstained from the breast on fast days,[22] as is always pointed out by editors of the tale, is an unnecessary assumption. The abstention legend is a commonplace event found in the canons of several saints.[23] A more distinctive legend of St. Nicholas is that in which he is reputed to have stood in his bath for two hours immediately following his birth.[24] Since graphic representations of this scene depict the newborn saint with hands clasped in prayer and eyes rolled heavenward, this can certainly be considered the earliest instance of piety in his life.[25] An allusion to Nicholas' fasting at the breast is more appropriately attributed to a second passage:

> But by the mouth of children thy bountee
> Parfourned is, for on the brest soukynge
> Somtyme shewen they thyn heriynge. (VII, 457–59)

There are other details in the Prioress' story of the murdered child which suggest the legend of St. Nicholas of Myra. For example, there is reference to the boy's "body sweete" (VII, 682) and to his "tombe of marbul stones cleere" (VII, 681). While sweetness is not the property of any single saint, the legend of St. Nicholas' manna, with its pun on *myrrhe* and *Myre* ("Myra," of which he was bishop), was famous,[26] and for this reason the pilgrimage to his tomb at Bari became well known. The scent and healing power of the manna were such that Nicholas was the patron saint of both apothecaries and perfumers.[27] And the "greyn" (VII, 662) also is reminiscent of the Nicholas legends, for spices—this one probably cardamon, the "grain of paradise"—are mentioned continually as symbols of the saint.[28] What is particularly interesting about the use of "greyn" in the *Prioress' Tale* is that Chaucer has also used it in connection with another sweet St. Nicholas-related character in the *Miller's Tale*.

In addition to legends, the elements of which are comparable to those of the *Prioress' Tale*, the Nicholas canon includes other stories which concern Jews, the most familiar known as "The Image of St. Nicholas" and "The Jew and the Dishonest Christian."[29]

Although the "Image of St. Nicholas" is a typical conversion story, which might account for a lenient view toward the Jew, "The Jew and the Dishonest Christian" does not emphasize conversion in any of the versions and in none is the plot dependent on it. While one critic would cite these legends as evidence that Christians believed the Jews really admitted the truth of Christianity (and hence that the Jews therein are presented as pious Christians-to-be, rather than as disparaged Jews), there are numerous stories of Jewish converts who are presented maliciously prior to their change of faith.[30] In the legend of "The Jew and the Dishonest Christian," the Jew is represented in his most contemptible role, the stereotyped moneylender. For this reason one would expect the attitude of stock medieval repugnance. But the Jew is not depicted as a pariah; he is, in fact, treated sympathetically. The comment on the Prioress and her tale of full reprisal "by the lawe" is therefore formidable.

The affinities of some of St. Nicholas' legends to the *Prioress' Tale* are, then, pronounced; and we can see the Jewish overtones in the saint's canon of legends. Let us turn now to the implications of the St. Nicholas references in relation to Chaucer and the Prioress.

There has been much speculation concerning possible anti-Semitism in the literal level of the tale. Discussion has included the Jews who are condemned for the murder of the little clergeon, the St. Hugh of Lincoln incident, and the pro- or anti-Semitic feelings of fourteenth-century English society in general.[31]

The reference to St. Nicholas, much like the reference to St. Loy in the Prioress' description in the *General Prologue,* serves as a pulse check for the entire tale. By its very nature, the Nicholas reference calls for a dualistic examination—"a look beyond what seems to be to what is"—for the allusion, like the tale in which it is embedded, is two-sided. It is on the one hand a benign reference to a kindly patron of children, Father Christmas; on the other, to the most complex saint in Christendom, not only the protector of children but the entire *kindergegen*[32] (courtship, procreation, childbirth), alleviator of poverty (even sexual),[33] patron of sailors, prisoners, men of all work, and even, it seems, the Jews, all examined in de Groot's psychoanalytic study of the Nicholas legend.

That Chaucer knew no Jews, as has been contended, is contrary to plausibility; it is highly improbable that he did not know some. First of all, the very occupation of Chaucer's father makes ignorance of Jews remote, for residence in the Vintry would have guaranteed young Chaucer's contact with sailors,[34] including those from Spain, where there had as yet been no expulsion and where Jews had a flourishing late medieval culture.[35] As a child Chaucer might have heard the stories of anti-Jewish atrocities, such as those of the 1349 St. Valentine's Day massacre at Strasbourg and the many others that followed the Black Death all over Europe, since the epidemic was often blamed on Jewish well-poisoning.[36] Though Chaucer was a young child when these events took place, the tales of 1349 were probably long remembered and frequently repeated, since the toll in lives was so heavy. Chaucer's own family lost several members in that year.[37]

References to Jews in connection with the Black Death would have been unfavorable, and Chaucer undoubtedly encountered the "diabolical and grotesque stage-Jew" who lived on in England after the 1290 expulsion.[38] He had ample opportunity to compare the mythic Jew with the real life counterpart. Chaucer's early and continuing presence in the royal households assured his contact with Jews, presumably of the highest calibre. In post-expulsion England numerous Jews were summoned to attend the king and members of the royal family and aristocracy. There are records of physicians and other professional Jews coming to England in a steady flow from about 1310 on.[39] There is even that persistent report from such scholars as Cecil Roth, that there were enough Jews in fourteenth-century England to warrant a post-expulsion expulsion.[40]

Chaucer's contact with Spain seems an especially important source of Jewish knowledge. The record of his presence in Navarre in 1366 is particularly significant.[41] While it is possible that he was simply passing through on an overland pilgrimage to the shrine of St. James of Compostella,[42] the political involvements of England in Spain at that time make the likelihood remote, or at least secondary.[43] Chaucer's presence at the court of Pedro I of Castile is quite possible. Not only were the Jews still relatively undisturbed in most of Spain, but were especially promoted in Don Pedro's court. Pedro's chief adviser was a Jew, as were numerous others in high office.[44] Further, it will be recalled, John of Gaunt married Pedro's daughter Constance, to whom Chaucer's wife Phillippa became lady-in-waiting.[45] Reference to Chaucer's Spanish experience appears in his account of the "wikked deeth" of Pedro in the *Monk's Tale* (VII, 2375–90).[46]

As Raymond Preston has observed, defense of the Prioress' naiveté, in the face of several popes' edicts of toleration, rests on the shakiest of ground.[47] For Chaucer, knowledgeable regarding Jews, to have portrayed her as disregarding church doctrine is incriminating indeed. Nowhere else is his writings does he treat the Jews disrespectfully; only through the mouth of the Prioress do they become "cursed." And that she should be made to refer to St. Nicholas is especially ironic, since he is a saint not of revenge, but of compassion. Though his legends deal with murder—including even the butchering of young boys—he is never vindictive. He never blames, pronounces guilt, or levies punishment, as did the Celtic saints. The Prioress' reference to a saint so completely divergent in point of view is a hallmark of Chaucerian irony. That the Jews in the tale were seized and bound (VII, 620) and, without benefit of hearing, tormented (VII, 628), sentenced (VII, 629), drawn by wild horses (VII, 633), and hung "by the lawe" (VII, 634) is, indeed, "shameful deeth." The final irony lies in the Prioress' supplication to "God so merciful" to pray for us, "we synful folk unstable."

I should like to turn now to a very different use of the same legend, the allusions to St. Nicholas in the *Miller's Tale.* Men and women have always been named after saints, and since Nicholas was, as we have seen, one of the most popular saints in the entire Christian calendar, it is not unexpected that Chaucer would so name the "hende clerk" of the *Miller's Tale.* But our curiosity can extend further.

The obvious reason for Chaucer's choice of name was that Nicholas was the patron saint of clerks.[48] Of his many legends, the most relevant here runs essentially as follows:

> Three clerks came to an inn, asking for a night's lodging. While they slept, they were murdered by the innkeeper and his wife. Soon after, St. Nicholas also came to the inn, where he requested fresh meat. At the innkeeper's declaration that he

had none, the saint revealed his knowledge of the murdered clerks, the innkeeper and his wife repented, and the three clerks were resuscitated.[49]

Further, the legend of St. Nicholas is so rich and the tale of the Miller so intriguing it is difficult to believe Chaucer's sense of satire let him develop the allusion to this saint no further than the facile stage of occupational aptness. Beyond the easy choice of a name for a clerk, the similarity between Nicholas the saint and Nicholas the clerk is clearly satiric. We learn from the *Golden Legend,* for example, that the saint "spent his nights in prayer, denying his body and forgoing the company of women."[50] The contrast with the Miller's Nicholas is spectacular. Not only are the characters of the two Nicholases themselves comparable satirically, but the host-guest relationships in which they are involved invite comparison as well.

After the statement on how "this clerk was cleped" (I, 3199), the tale contains a description of Nicholas and his room. We learn that the chamber was:

> Ful fetisly ydight with herbes swoote;
> And he hymself as sweete as is the roote
> Of lycorys, or any cetewale. (I, 3205–07)

Further, he is referred to as "this sweete clerk." That the clerk should emit such sweetness and that his dwelling should likewise be perfumed is especially fitting for a namesake of St. Nicholas. As we have seen, one of the traditional stories of the saint is the miracle of the sweet oil that issued from his tomb and, in some variations, of the sweetness that emanated from the body itself.[51]

Following the description of the clerk, the *Miller's Tale* includes a portrait of Alisoun, a bride (I, 3221), only eighteen years old (I, 3223). Once again the material recalls St. Nicholas. This saint is the patron of brides and young girls, especially of the bourgeoisie, such as Alisoun, fitting "For any lord to leggen in his bedde, Or yet for any good yeman to wedde" (I, 3269–70).[52] These patronages were earned through the very popular legend of the three maidens, referred to variously as the "Charity of St. Nicholas," the Dowry," or *Tres Filiae:*

> A father who had fallen into financial difficulties, since he could not otherwise provide for them, was faced with the choice of prostitution or starvation for his three young daughters. The good St. Nicholas, hearing of their plight, anonymously donated dowries to the girls on three successive nights by tossing bags of gold coins through their window.[53]

As well as occurring in the literary references to the saint, this legend had wide circulation in the graphic arts and in drama.[54] Alisoun's portrait contains the specific icons of the dowry legend of St. Nicholas. There is, for instance, a "purs of lether" (I, 3250). The purse is one of the most frequently encountered symbols for Nicholas and is usually seen in a group of three, either as actual purses or, as they evolved, gold balls, eventually adopted as the sign of the pawnbroker.[55] Another hint of the dowry legend is Chaucer's use of gold coins in his description of Alisoun:

> Ful brighter was the shynyng of hir hewe
> Than in the Tour the noble yforged newe. (I, 3255–56)

And another possible implication of the legend, with its anonymous donor, is that Nicholas, clerk, "Of deerne love . . . koude and of solas; And therto he was sleigh and ful privee" (I, 3200–01). This may be a satiric echo of St. Nicholas' life, since the holy man was loath to expose his generosity, preferring to bestow his gifts unobtrusively. The father of the three young women in the story had to lie in wait, ready to seize the benefactor, since the young saint had failed to stop when called.[56]

Alisoun's portrait contains other reminders of St. Nicholas, such as the legend of the sweet manna—"Hir mouth was sweete as bragot or the meeth" (I, 3261)—and apples, the symbol of fruit evolving from the golden balls as more appropriate for the saint in his role as Father Christmas.[57]

Almost all legends of St. Nicholas fall into one of two categories: those which are variations on the rescue or resuscitation of three people, or those which concern the sea. In the *Miller's Tale* the accumulation of allusions to the latter type begins when the young bride is described as "Long as a mast" (I, 3264). The nautical motif increases as the discussion of the imminent flood and the preparations for it proceed (I, 3516–3600). St. Nicholas is especially well known as the patron saint of sailors and was invoked by sea travelers against tempest and general calamity at sea.[58] The legend from which these patronages arose is found in several variations, but the salient aspects are the same in all of them:

> Nicholas, on his way to the Holy Land by ship, was entreated to save the crew when a tempest arose. He banished the storm and saved the ship. Later a sailor drowned and was restored to life by the saint.[59]

In the description of Absolon, too, there are reminders of the Nicholas legend, satiric though they may be. The allusion to sweetness is again evident. There is the statement that Absolon swings the censer, perfuming the parish wives on holy days (I, 3340–41). And his gifts to Alisoun include sweet drinks (I, 3378), suggesting Nicholas' several patronages in the wine industry.[60] The description recalls the vignette of the three maidens, so often represented in art, with St. Nicholas as a young man, standing on tiptoe in the full of the moon under the young girls' bedroom window, the father in the background, looking quite unhappy.[61] Absolon stands in the full of the moon under the window of Alisoun's room, in which there is also a chagrined old man, her husband. Absolon's gifts include more St. Nicholas images: wine, wafers and money. The food suggests the gifts of the Christmas tradition, the saint's attribute of bread,[62] his patronage of the wine industry, and money, again recalling the dowries.

There are additional St. Nicholas allusions used in connection with Absolon. For example, the sweetness is stressed in the passage:

> . . . he cheweth greyn and lycorys,
> To smellen sweete, er he hadde kembed his heer.
> Under his tonge a trewe-love he beer. (I, 3690–92).

A bit further he calls Alisoun "hony-comb, sweete Alisoun . . . my sweete cynamone" (I, 3698–99). There is another window scene (I, 3695 ff.), and more imagery reminiscent of the icons of the St. Nicholas legend: gold (I, 3779), a bag full of coins (I, 3780), and a golden ring (I, 3794).

The culmination of the third window scene, at the tale's end, is not only a neat binding up of Chaucer's two episodes, but a juncture for the combination of the two main St. Nicholas legends. In addition to the dowry legend, the scene is a reminder of the saint's invocation against tempest and catastrophe at sea, with the repetitive "water, water." Further, Nicholas' burned "toute" recalls the saint's invocation against fire, earned by his restoration to health of a burned child by making the sign of the cross over it.[63] It also hints at the story of Nicholas' having thwarted a scheme to burn the church in Bari (in which his relics were contained), by his persuading pilgrims, victims of Satanic demons, that the oil with which they planned to anoint the church was an incendiary agent.[64]

A further reminder of the Christmas tradition and St. Nicholas occurs at the end of the *Miller's Tale*. There are two references not to *Noe's,* but to *Nowelis* flood (I, 3818, 3834), which suggest the saint in his role as Father Christmas, the gist of "Nowelis flood" being "Nicholas' flood."

In addition to the images or situations in the *Miller's Tale* which are, either straightforwardly or satirically, comparable to the St. Nicholas legends, there are fleeting images which, taken together, form an appropriate backdrop for the larger parallels. For example, the mention of Satan (I, 3750) and the following references to the forge (I, 3762), hot coulter and fireplace (I, 3776), suggestive of the devil, are reminiscent of some of the literary and graphic representations of St. Nicholas. In depicting a legend of butchered children served up as meat for humans (and ultimately restored to life by Nicholas), artists presented the murderer as the devil,[65] and in a number of his written legends, Nicholas contends with the devil.[66] Immediately following these diabolic references, and within the same scene—that of the blacksmith shop—are the more familiar St. Nicholas attributes of gold and a bag of coins.[67]

Most signal of all the allusions to St. Nicholas in the *Miller's Tale*, however, is that previously mentioned of the three-men-in-a-tub and Alisoun, John, and Nicholas, sitting in their three vats.

Though the Nicholas allusions in the tales told by the Prioress and the Miller draw on exactly the same canon of legends, the uses to which the poet puts that common material in two very different contexts are in striking contrast. The analysis of specific allusions is as old as literary criticism, but the discovery and determination of the patterns of those allusions in Chaucer are far from complete.

STATE UNIVERSITY OF NEW YORK AT BUFFALO

FOOTNOTES

1. Jean Hagstrum, *The Sister Arts* (Chicago: Univ. of Chicago Press, 1958); John B. Bender, *Spenser and Literary Pictorialism* (Princeton: Princeton Univ. Press, 1973).

2. John V. Fleming, "The Summoner's Prologue: An Iconographic Adjustment," *Chaucer Review*, 2 (1967), 95–107; and see my chapter 10,

on St. Thomas, in *Essays on Chaucer's Saints* (The Hague: Mouton), forthcoming.

3. "San Nicolo Resuscita Tre Fanciulli" by Gentile da Fabriano (b. 1370). Bicci de Lorenzo's representation of the same subject, along with his painting of the dowry legend, is conveniently available in Allardyce Nicoll, *World Drama* (New York: Harcourt Brace, 1949), facing p. 161. And see Louis Réau, *Iconographie de l'art chrétien* (Paris: Presses universitaires de France, 1959), III, pt. 2, 980, 984 (hereafter cited as Réau); Francis Bond, *Dedications of English Churches* (London: Oxford Univ. Press, 1914), pp. 298, 325; R. L. P. Milburn, *Saints and their Emblems in English Churches* (London: Oxford Univ. Press, 1949), pp. 190–91. For influences, see Réau, 977; and [Abbé] Jules Laroche, *Vie de saint Nicolas* (Paris: J.-F. Féchoz, 1886), p. 375.

4. Milburn, op. cit., p. xv.

5. Helen C. White, *Tudor Books of Saints and Martyrs* (Madison: Univ. of Wisconsin Press, 1963), p. 29.

6. E.g., Paull F. Baum, "Chaucer's Puns," *PMLA*, 71 (1956), 225–46; and "Chaucer's Puns, A Supplementary List," *PMLA*, 73 (1958), 167–70; Helge Kökeritz, "Rhetorical Word-Play in Chaucer," *PMLA*, 69 (1954), 937–52; Norman D. Hinton, "More Puns in Chaucer," *AN&Q*, 2 (1964), 115–16; Thomas Wynne Ross, *Chaucer's Bawdy* (New York: Dutton, 1972).

7. St. Olaf (Holofius) is the patron saint of bakers, who have mistaken his name for "whole Loaf," and the *vin* in St. Vincent's name has earned him the patronage of the wine industry.

8. Bond, op. cit., p. 237; Milburn, op. cit., p. 190; Anna B. Jameson, *Sacred and Legendary Art*, 8th ed. (London: Longmans Green, 1879), II. 451 (hereafter cited as Jameson).

9. Réau, 980–88; Jameson, II, 461.

10. G. M. Dreves, C. Blume, and H. M. Bannister, *Analecta Hymnica Medii Aevi*, 55 vols. (Leipzig, 1886–1922; rpt. New York: Johnson and Johnson, and Frankfurt am Main: Minerva, 1961).

11. Mary S. Crawford, *Life of St. Nicholas* (Philadelphia: Univ. of Pennsylvania, diss., 1923), p. 12; Adriaan D. DeGroot, *Saint Nicholas: A Psychoanalytic Study of his History and Myth* (The Hague: Mouton, 1965), pp. 161–62.

12. Northrop Frye, "Literature and Myth," in *Relations of Literary Study* (New York: Modern Language Association of America, 1967), pp. 32–33.

13. References to the *Canterbury Tales* are from *The Works of Geoffrey Chaucer*, ed. F. N. Robinson, 2nd ed. (Boston: Houghton Mifflin, 1957).

14. Karl Meisen, *Nikolauskult und Nicholausbrauch im Abendlande* (Düsseldorf: L. Schwann, 1931); discussed by DeGroot, op. cit., pp. 39–40.

15. DeGroot, op. cit., pp. 121–22; Jameson, II. 463–64; Crawford, synopsis of Wace's version, op. cit., p. 32; Karl Young, *The Drama of the Medieval Church* (Oxford: Clarendon Press, 1933), II, 351–60, and (Mombritius' Latin text) 492–95.

16. Jacques de Voragine, *La Légende dorée*, ed. M. G[ustave] B[runet] (Paris: C. Gosselin, 1843), I. 47.

17. Joshua Trachtenberg, *The Devil and the Jews* (New Haven: Yale Univ. Press, 1943), pp. 20–22, 42; Norman Cohn, *The Pursuit of the Millennium*, rev. ed. (New York: Oxford Univ. Press, 1970), p. 75.

18. Jameson, II, 454–55, 460.

19. Robinson, *Chaucer*, p. 734.

20. Marie Hamilton, "Echoes of Childermas in the Tale of the Prioress," *MLR*, 34 (1939), 1–8.

21. *Légende dorée*, I, 41–47. See also Jameson, II, 451–52; Réau, 978.

22. Réau, 976.

23. C. Grant Loomis, *White Magic* (Cambridge, Mass.: Mediaeval Academy of America, 1948), p. 23.

24. Jameson, II, 461; Réau, 976. 982; *Légende dorée,* I, 41.

25. Jameson, II, 461; Laroche, op. cit., p. 41.

26. *Légende dorée*, I, 45; Réau, 977, 987–88.

27. Émile Mâle, *The Gothic Image*, trans. Dora Nussey (New York: Harper, 1958), p. 329; Laroche, op. cit., p. 222.

28. DeGroot, op. cit., p.20.

29. Réau, 985–86; *Légende dorée*, I, 45–46; Crawford, op. cit., p. 31; DeGroot, op. cit., pp. 119–20, 124; Jameson, II, 462–63.

30. E.g., Trachtenberg, op. cit., pp. 47–50. Note that Jameson, II, 462, in reporting the legend of the Image of St. Nicholas, calls the Jew parenthetically "an irreverent pagan."

31. Raymond Preston, "Chaucer, His Prioress, The Jews, and Professor Robinson," *N&Q*, 206 (1961), 7–8; Cecil Roth, *A History of the Jews in England*, 2nd ed. (Oxford: Clarendon Press, 1949); and Florence Ridley, *The Prioress and the Critics*, Univ. of California Publ., English Studies, 30 (Berkeley: Univ. of California Press, 1965). See also R. J. Schoeck, "Chaucer's Prioress: Mercy and Tender Heart," *Bridge*, 2 (1956), 239–55.

32. DeGroot, op. cit., p. 108.

33. DeGroot, op. cit., p. 161.

34. Martin M. Crow and Clair C. Olson, *Chaucer Life-Records* (Austin: Univ. of Texas Press, 1966), pp. 1–12.

35. Americo Castro, *The Structure of Spanish History*, trans. Edmund L. King (Princeton: Princeton Univ. Press, 1954), pp. 466 ff.; P. E. Russell, *The English Intervention in Spain and Portugal in the Time of Edward III and Richard II* (Oxford: Clarendon Press, 1955), pp. 9–10: "Anglo-Castilian trade was important to both countries and merchants and seamen of both countries were well acquainted with each other's ways. Chaucer's

shipman naturally knew 'every cryke in Britayne and in Spayne.' Spanish wine from Lepe (near Ayamonte) had, as the Pardoner explained, special qualities which were appreciated—if not approved—in Fleet Street and in Cheapside."

36. Trachtenberg, op. cit., pp. 97–108.

37. Crow and Olson, op. cit., p. 4.

38. Montagu Frank Modder, *The Jew in the Literature of England* (Philadelphia: Jewish Publ. Soc. of America, 1939), p. 15. See also Harold Fisch, *The Dual Image, The Figure of the Jew in English and American Literature* (New York: Ktav Publishing House, [1971]).

39. Roth, op. cit., p. 132; Modder, op. cit., p. 12.

40. Roth, op. cit., p. 132. Roth must be used with caution.

41. Crow and Olson, op. cit., pp. 64–65.

42. Crow and Olson, op. cit., p. 65.

43. Russell, op. cit., Chapters 1–3; *Chaucer's World*, comp. Edith Rickert (New York: Columbia Univ. Press, 1948), p. 325.

44. Castro, op. cit., p. 471; Russell, op. cit., p. 21, fn. 2.

45. Crow and Olson, op. cit., p. 65, fn. 2; and Chapter 5, pp. 67–93.

46. Professor Harriet Goldberg has suggested to me the speculation whether Chaucer's contact with Spain had not also brought contact with Spanish literature, particularly whether he knew the epic *El Cid*. The episode concerning Jewish moneylenders, Requel and Vidas, deceived in a transaction by the Christian Cid, has affinities with the St. Nicholas legend of "The Jew and the Dishonest Christian." As in the saint's legend, the Jews in *El Cid* are presented without derogatory overtones and as victims of an unjust act. Castro, op. cit., p. 472, fn. 11, however, has excused the Cid's behavior as "an act that may be taken for the *vox populi*."

47 Preston, loc. cit., 7. One must remember, however, that there was always a wide gap between precept (the popes' edicts) and practice (the actual treatment of Jews in towns and villages).

48. *The Reader's Encyclopedia,* ed. W. R. Benét (New York: Crowell, 1955), pp. 975, 981; Young, op. cit., II, 329, 490.

49. Young, op. cit., II, 324–37.

50. *Légende dorée,* I, 42.

51. Mâle, op. cit., p. 329; Réau, 977–78, 979.

52. Jameson, II, 57; *Reader's Encyclopedia,* p. 980.

53. Réau, 982–83; *Légende dorée,* I, 41–42.

54. Young, op. cit., II, 311–24, 488–90. This episode is shown both on the South Porch and in stained glass at Chartres.

55. Milburn, op. cit., p. 191; H. P. Brewster, *Saints and Festivals of the Christian Church* (New York: Frederick A. Stokes, [1904], p. 13.

56. *Légende dorée*, I, 42; Young, op. cit., II, 314–15, 322.

57. Bond, op. cit., pp. 325, 298; Réau, 980.

58. Réau, 979.

59. *Légende dorée*, I, 42; Jameson, II, 60, 63, 68.

60. Réau, 979.

61. A. N. Didron, *Christian Iconography or The History of Christian Art in the Middle Ages*, trans. E. J. Millington and Margaret Stokes (London: H. G. Bohn, 1891), II, 368; Jameson, II, 59–60.

62. Otto Wimmer, *Handbuch der Namen und Heiligen* (Innsbruck: Tyrolia Verlag, 1956), p. 369.

63. Sabine Baring-Gould, *The Lives of the Saints*, rev. ed. (Edinburgh: J. Grant, 1914), XV, 65.

64. *Légende dorée*, I, 43; Réau, 987.

65. Jameson, II, 61, 65.

66. E.g., Laroche, op. cit., p. 62.

67. Another hint of the St. Nicholas legend occurs in the carpenter's worrying about the clerk's long stay in his room. John says of Nicholas, "He shal be rated of his studiyng" (I, 3463). St. Nicholas, the patron saint of scholars and school boys, "was distinguished . . . for his gravity and his attention to his studies" (Jameson, II, 59).

7

The Transformation
of a Frame Story:
The Dynamics of Fiction

CHARLES A. OWEN, JR.

The *Canterbury Tales* started out as a collection of stories. Whatever else was in Chaucer's mind when he began the imaginary journey from Southwark, I think we can agree on that. Some of the contradictions in the work are evidences of growth, and the direction of growth was from the conventional metaphor of pilgrimage as life, from a relatively inert collection of varied stories, to a drama of contrasting visions with the added aesthetic stimulus of a storytelling contest.[1]

Let us begin at the end—with the *Parson's Prologue*. It has long been recognized that here we have one of the obvious contradictions. The Host calls on the Parson for his tale:

"Now lakketh us no tales mo than oon . . .
For every man, save thou, hath toold his tale."
(I, 16, 25)

Critics have seen the reduction from four tales to one as a political retrenchment of old age and diminished energies. Chaucer saw the impossibility of completing his ambitious plan, he felt moreover the imminence of death; he brought both his lifework and his life to an end by stepping out from behind his fiction and asking forgiveness for all that makes him interesting to us. The pilgrimage in this reading never quite reached Canterbury before the metaphor became too real and the vision "Of thilke parfit glorious pilgrimage That highte Jerusalem celestial" (I 50–51) displaced in Chaucer's mind the Prioress, the Pardoner, and the Wife of Bath, the Knight, the Squire, the Clerk, the Franklin—yes, and the Parson too.

Against this generally accepted and plausible explanation[2] we can pit only certain internal relationships within the *Canterbury Tales,* and what I hope is a more sensitive reading of the evidence.

First, a small but significant point: Are the pilgrims still on their outward journey? Have they not yet reached Canterbury? Literally they are entering "at a thropes ende" and it was "foure of the clokke."[3] The Host says:

> "Fulfilled is my sentence and my decree;
> I trowe that we han herd of ech degree;
> Almoost fulfild is al myn ordinance." (I 17–19)

Are we to assume that the Host's idea was for the pilgrims to ride to Canterbury together and then break up, or that they were to amuse themselves with stories on the outward journey and ride back to the Tabard in silence? What about the night in Ospring, less than ten miles from Canterbury, referred to by the Canon's Yeoman (G 588) when he and his master overtake the pilgrims at Boughton under Blee? Must we assume that it took the pilgrims from early in the morning until after four in the evening to ride those last five miles between Boughton and Canterbury?[4]

There is also the question of the Manciple, whose name is written over an erasure in the Hengwrt manuscript, and whose tale has been linked to the *Parson's Prologue* by such eminent Chaucerians as Robert Pratt and Wayne Shumaker.[5] The town of Bobbe-up-and-down (H 1–3) is still a mystery, but the Blee Forest on the London side of Canterbury sufficiently locates it. It must be between Boughton and Canterbury. The fact that Chaucer knew this village (and we do not) suggests a detailed knowledge of the road and an interest in placing the pilgrims on it that contrast with the vagueness of the "thropes ende" in the *Parson's Prologue*. That there is both distance and time between the Manciple's performance and the Parson's is further indicated by the drama of the *Manciple's Prologue*. When Chaucer has the Manciple replace the drunken Cook as storyteller, he eliminates the possibility of a connection with the *Parson's Prologue*. The Host could hardly say, "For every man, save thou, hath toold his tale," (I 25) if the cook were still waiting for his turn.

One further point is worth considering—the dramatic, thematic, and formal relationships between the framework of the *Man of Law's Tale* and the *Parson's Prologue*. These framing passages share three techniques with each other— two of them found nowhere else in the *Canterbury Tales*— the method of telling time, the preparation for a prose tale, and an encounter between the Host and the Parson. The dramatic connection between the two includes the Parson's response to the Host's request for a tale in the *Man of Law's Epilogue*, "*Benedicite!* What eyleth the man, so synfully to swere?" (B 1171); the accusation by the Host of Lollardry and the intervention of another pilgrim, originally the Wife of Bath,[6] to avert the danger of heretical preaching, "He wolde sowen som difficulte, Or springen cokkel in our clene corn" (B 1184–85); and the long silence of the Parson as he witnesses the secularization of the pilgrimage, with the Host presiding over the game of storytelling.

Finally forced to call on the Parson by the rules of his own game, the Host addresses him in a condescending way— the familiar "thou" throughout, the inquiry as to his rank, and the suggestion that he tell "a fable anon, for cokkes

THE OUTWARD JOURNEY TO CANTERBURY *(Read down)*

Plan III	Plan II	Plan I	Route	m.
FIRST NIGHT				
Prologue	Prologue	Prologue	Tabard	0
A–Knight Miller Reeve Cook	B¹ – Man of Law (Constance)	B¹ – Man of Law (Melibee) Wife of Bath (Shipman's Tale)	St. Thomas Watering Greenwich / Deptford	2 5
SECOND NIGHT			Dartford	16
	B² – Shipman Prioress Chaucer (Sir Thopas) Chaucer (Melibee) Monk Nun's Priest			
			Rochester	30
			Sittingbourne	40
THIRD NIGHT			Ospring	47
	G – Second Nun Canon's Yeoman		Boughton Blee Forest	50
			Harbledown(?)	55
			Canterbury	57
FOURTH NIGHT				

THE RETURN JOURNEY FROM CANTERBURY *(Read up)*

m.	Route	Plan I	Plan II	Plan III
		SIXTH NIGHT		
57	Tabard		[Drama of Host and Wife at Tabard]	[Prize-awarding Supper, etc.]
55	St. Thomas Watering			
52	Greenwich / Deptford	I –Parson	I – Parson	I – Parson
41	Dartford			
			Franklin Squire Merchant E-F – Clerk	
27	Rochester			
		FIFTH NIGHT		
17	Sittingbourne			
10	Ospring		Pardoner C – Physician	
7	Boughton Blee Forest		Summoner Friar D – Wife of Bath	
2	Harbledown (?)		H – Manciple	
0	Canterbury			
		FOURTH NIGHT		

bones," being only three of the barbs in his gloating remarks.[7] Implicit is a certain sense of triumph at the success of his plans, at the way the storytelling rather than any religious purpose has made the journey memorable, in short at his having supplanted the Parson as spiritual leader of the group. The Parson's response is at first angry as he turns down the Host's suggestion "al atones," quotes St. Paul on the dangers of fiction, and turns to the pilgrims ("you") with his offer of "Moralitee and vertuous mateere" (I 38). Before he has finished, the Parson has emerged from his long and silent frustration with a triumphant proposal. He will use the very instrument of the Host's power over the pilgrimage; he will take advantage of the antipathy felt on both sides that makes him the last speaker; he will transform with "his myrie tale in prose," long after the external incentives in the martyr's shrine are past, the pilgrims' experience and show them:

> ". . . the wey in this viage
> Of thilke parfit glorious pilgrimage
> That highte Jerusalem celestial." (I 49–51)

Those who would rob the pilgrimage of its return journey are denying the Parson much of his triumph and the poet his skill at preparing an end. The orchestration is impressive. Nature and man both contribute. The sun is setting. Four distinct voices—the Host's the Parson's, the pilgrims in concert, and the poet's—sound the valedictory. The consecration through art, "To knytte up al this feeste and make an ende," (I 47) is projected. Even the Host is converted and addresses the Parson respectfully:

> "Sire preest," quod he, "now faire you bifalle!
> Telleth," quod he, "youre meditacioun.
> But hasteth yow, the sonne wole adoun;
> Beth fructuous, and that in litel space . . ." (I 68–71)

This preparation for an ending was never, I think, con-
summated. The treatise on penitence known as the *Parson's Tale* picks up the main image of the *Parson's Prologue*
and fuses it with a passage from *Jeremiah* to make an impressive opening into its subject matter. But nothing else in
the long and systematic work suggests a fulfillment of the
inspiration in the *Prologue*. When we come to the *Retraction* with which it ends, the address "to hem alle that
herkne this litel tretys or rede" and the reference to the
Canterbury Tales, coming as it does in the midst of a list—
". . . the book of Seint Valentynes day of the Parlement of
Briddes; the tales of Caunterbury, thilke that sownen into
synne; the book of the Leoun; and many another book, if
they were in my remembrance . . ."—both contradict the
final rubric; they could hardly be more explicit in indicating
that the *Canterbury Tales* is a separate work, coming into
his remembrance with the other secular poems for which
he is asking forgiveness. That this treatise served as source
for passages in several of the *Canterbury Tales,* especially
for the *Pardoner's Tale* and the *Merchant's,* marks it as earlier than those works and suggests that there was a period,
after Chaucer had started the *Canterbury Tales* but before
he had composed some of the most striking ones, when he
not only abandoned work on his masterpiece but repented
having started it.

These implications that tend to show the dramatic sequence—*Man of Law's Introduction—Man of Law's Epilogue . . . Parson's Prologue*—to be an early framework
for the *Canterbury Tales* as a whole are strengthened by a
number of other considerations. The *Man of Law's* framing
passages involve two changes in the assignment of stories.
The Man of Law originally told a tale in prose, perhaps the
Melibeus later assigned to Chaucer.[8] The Wife of Bath, who
reveals herself unmistakably in the vaunt, "My joly body
shal a tale telle And I schal clynken you so mery a
belle . . ." (B 1185–86), originally told the tale of the Wife
of St. Denis, later assigned to the Shipman.[9] Thus the com-

position of two great blocks of tales is placed later in the development than the sequence involving Host and Parson. The B² (VII) fragment, which has the pilgrims passing Rochester in the *Prologue to the Monk's Tale,* starts with the original *Wife of Bath's Tale* now assigned to the Shipman, includes the *Melibeus* as Chaucer's second tale, and ends with the *Nun's Priest's Tale* (involving another change in plan, the reduction of the Prioress' three priests to one). The other block is, of course, the series of tales influenced by the Wife of Bath, now removed from connection with the *Man of Law's Epilogue,*[10] with her marital autobiography fully developed, telling a tale that permits her to combine the quest for power with the quest for love, and to transform herself vicariously into everything that a young man could desire in a wife and mistress.

We have still to consider one of the most important implications of the *Parson's Prologue.* The drama of Host and Parson that reflects the inherent conflict of storytelling and pilgrimage, of "solaas" and sentence, finds its resolution in the Parson's understanding that the two can be fused, that the highest "solaas" inheres in the most meaningful fiction. The Parson's word was apparently the final one. We look in vain for references to any supper at the Tabard, to any anticipation of reunion between the Host and his wife Goodelief, to any judgment by the Host as to the best story. On the contrary, such considerations are repeatedly ruled out. The Host speaks of the fulfillment of his "sentence" and "decree," "Almoost fulfild is al myn ordinaunce." (I 19) The Parson will "make an end"; the pilgrims as a group assent:

> For, as it seemed, it was for to doone,
> To enden in som vertuous sentence . . . (I 62–63)

The conclusion contemplated in the *Parson's Prologue* puts emphasis on the story as the vehicle of meaning. The drama that prepares it involves two pilgrims in a relatively simple relationship. The image that dominates the ending is the conventional one of life seen as pilgrimage with its goal salvation.

It might be well to recapitulate the particulars of this early frame material for the *Canterbury Tales* and stress the implications before going on to further considerations. The *Introduction* to the *Man of Law's Tale* prepares us for a tale in prose. It has the Host telling time by the comparison of the length of a shadow with the height of the object causing it; it gives the date but specifies no place on the road; it has the Host admonishing the pilgrims that they have wasted a quarter of the day and reminding the Man of Law of his agreement to tell a story; it has the Man of Law assenting with some emphasis on his sense of obligation and commenting at length on his difficulties in choosing a suitable narrative. Everything here suggests the beginning of the storytelling, just as the *Parson's Prologue* marks the end. The *Epilogue* to the *Man of Law's Tale* reinforces this suggestion by providing us with the motivation that will be seen in the *Parson's Prologue* to have been tacitly at work throughout the tales. The simple question uttered by the Parson, extending beyond a single line by the length of a Latin blessing, epitomizes his displeasure and his displacement, storytelling substituted for religious purpose, until the very end of the pilgrimage. Then, at the hour determined by the same trigonometry of shadows, as the sun sets and they reach a "thropes ende," the Parson undertakes to give their journeyings, both real and imaginary, on the road, in their lives, and in their stories, a sacramental meaning. The prose tales at beginning and end set off the dramatic and thematic connections between the two, to give what had seemed episodic the unity of a continuing conflict, resolved at the moment of recognition in the reversal wrought by the Parson. This structure gives meaning to the collection of stories. It envisages a single story from each pilgrim, no contest beyond the one decided in the Parson's unwritten tale, no dramatic aftermath at the Tabard.

If it were the Parson who was originally to give a meaning to the collection of stories, it was the Wife of Bath who was to transform the collection into drama, and the Host who was to add the dimension of aesthetic judgment to the stories. The two great blocks of tales already referred to, the one beginning with the *Shipman's Tale* and ending with the *Nun's Priest's,* the other associated with the Wife of Bath and including the *Pardoner's Prologue* and *Tale,* as well as the series from the *Clerk's Tale* to the *Franklin's,* provide us with the evidence for the second stage in the development. The Wife of Bath plays a considerable role in both of these blocks. It is her original tale that as *Shipman's Tale* starts off the long fragment. This tale was originally linked by a part of her *Prologue* to what was probably the beginning of the storytelling.[11] She performed originally for the Parson the role the Miller was later to play for the Monk—that of pushing aside the narrator designated by the Host. The *Shipman's Tale* has a characteristic attributable to none of the other stories presumed by what evidence we have to be early, with the single exception of the *Manciple's.* It projects a point of view at variance with Chaucer's. We cannot determine whether Chaucer's portrait of the Wife suggested the kind of tale he would have to write for her, or whether the fabliau was already in his mind when he delineated the portrait of its narrator. For what was almost certainly the first time in Chaucer's career as a poet he was ventriloquizing as a storyteller. The implicit cynicism of this story, where the interchangeability of sex and money underlies the propriety and orthodoxy of an unruffled surface, cannot reflect Chaucer's view. To reinforce our sense of the distance between the poet and the narrator Chaucer gives us the woman's intrusion into her own fiction at the beginning, the evident delight of the teller in the skill and blatancy of the intrigue, and the inverted moral at the end with its playful fusion of the money and sex that dominates the tale:

Thus endeth now my tale, and God us sende
Tail'ynge ynough unto oure lyves ende. Amen
(B 1623–24)

No one can mistake the delight Chaucer took in his fabliaux, the freedom the dramatic structure gave him (as it
has given others since) to develop his art beyond the limits
normally drawn by morality. Not just the speech of a single
character, but the *Weltanschauung* of the entire story,
could now be the subject of imitation. The surprise is that
with his gallery of varied characters he made so little use of
this freedom in the early years of the work on the tales.
Apart from the *Shipman's Tale,* only the *Manciple's* reflects
this freedom. And the *Manciple's* is a far tamer instance
than the story about the Wife of St. Denis. Instead, we have
a gallery of good women in the early tales, women good in
a broader sense than the heroines of his "Seintes Legend of
Cupide"—Prudence, Virginia, Griselda, Constance, probably also Canace and Dorigen. If Germaine Dempster's dating is correct (and I think it is),[12] it was some years before
Chaucer again breathed that heady air, returned to his great
fiction, and saw the full possibilities of the drama of
conflicting visions it made possible. The Wife of Bath again
played a leading role. She refused, as it were, to tell the story originally assigned her. As her autobiography grew in
Chaucer's imagination, as her expertise in marriage fleshed
itself out in the three old and "goode" husbands, the two
young and "badde," Chaucer found the vision of sex and
money as interchangeable too narrow and limited for this
magnificent virago of a woman, whose discovery even of
love could not change the stridency of her voice and views,
especially if she was to have only one chance to tell a story.

Meanwhile, with the stories that attached themselves to
what was now to be the *Shipman's Tale,* the Host was developing his penchant for literary criticism, with results almost as momentous for the *Canterbury Tales* as the growth

in Chaucer's conception of the Wife of Bath. The *Prioress'*
Tale moves the Host so deeply that he feels the need for
"myrthe," and picks on Chaucer, whom he apparently regards as a sleeper among the pilgrim narrators. The ensuing
stories are cunningly designed to expose the Host both as
man and critic. His interruption of *Sir Thomas* and his autobiographical response to the *Melibee* are equally ill-con-
ceived. If he has failed to see the skill and the humor in the
parody of popular romance, he has also derived from the
prose allegory the one moral it will not sustain—that a man
can find outside himself, in Goodelief in the Host's case,
the source of the evil in his life.[13] The impudence of his
address to the Monk draws on the company the threat of
a hundred tragedies, and when the Knight interrupts, the
Host chimes in with some muddled comment and, without
realizing it, sets himself up as rival to the greatest poet of
his generation, "And wel I woot the substance is in me If
any thing shal wel reported be." (B 3993–94) The challenge
of writing the *Canterbury Tales* by Harry Bailly has yet to be
taken up. The Nun's Priest, who tells the final tale in this
longest of fragments, caps the literary interest to which all
the stories contribute, by tripping momentarily over an an-
ti-feminist interpretation of his own fiction. Recovering
himself, he mocks the medieval demand for morals:

> But ye that holden this tale a folye,
> As of a fox or of a cok and hen,
> Taketh the moralite, goode men . . . (B 4629–30)

He draws finally from the Host a repetition of the impudence earlier visited on the Monk, a sexual innuendo that
the tale itself does everything possible to rule out. Meanwhile, the Host has made clear in his offer of second
chances to the interrupted pilgrims that they will not have
three more opportunities, and in pointing out Rochester as
he calls on the Monk, has tied this fragment to a definite
place on the road, a little past the midpoint of the outward
journey, on what (as Tatlock has pointed out) must be the

second day of the pilgrimage.[14] The literary interest, so prominent an element in these stories, will suggest to Chaucer some time in the future the extra dimension of a storytelling contest, with the Host as judge and a meal at the Tabard as prize.

The series of tales, in three separate fragments influenced by the Wife of Bath, shows the dramatic interest at its most intense. The Wife not only becomes a more complex and interesting character, but she signally reveals a great deal beyond what she intends or is even aware of. Inadvertent self-revelation adds a third kind of significance to the literal level and the author's purpose in telling the story. The Wife has chosen a story that repeats the miraculous discovery of love she experienced but didn't recognize with her fifth husband, to add to the feminist and wish-fulfillment meanings her story also embodies. From the patterns of the series of tales following the *Wife of Bath's* emerges a final level of meaning that suggests the anagoge of the exegetes—meaning that is never consciously willed but that comes into being as the amalgam of what men will, the kind of meaning only an objective vision such as God's or a reader's can appreciate. The marriage group, interrupted but the more impressive for being the final of the Wife's influences on the pilgrims and their tales, provides such a level of meaning. The anagogical implications of such a sequence might be abstracted as a universal predisposition to order in God's creation, which gives inevitable meaning to man's choices. The one choice a man cannot make is to mean nothing by his choices.

Chaucer's work on the *Pardoner's Prologue* and *Tale* and the marriage group shows the elements of his basic fiction interacting to create the drama of conflicting visions. The portraits of Friar and Summoner, which belong themselves perhaps to this period of development,[15] figure in the tales which the two men tell as a kind of double ground which the surface events adorn. Each extends the other's portrait to devastating effect; each expresses himself in his own fiction. The suavity of the Friar concludes in prayer for the

Summoner. But the Friar overextends himself by touching on the hellish torments that await his rival. The Summoner, infuriated by the skill with which the Friar has shown him sending himself to hell, takes the opening his enemy has given him and subjects him three times to excremental discharge, first in the hell the Friar has claimed expert knowledge of, then in the house of the sick and irascible Thomas, and finally at the hub of Squire Jankyn's wheel. The annihilation of his rival which each man purposes does not occur. What does occur is a kind of total exposure, effected by an energy of observation and art that everywhere surprises and delights.

Chaucer avoids repeating or systematizing his relationships. The Pardoner's performance, unlike the Friar's and Summoner's, serves as gloss on his own portrait. His confession distinguishes itself from the Wife's by his professional histrionics, by the acknowledgment of villainy that he expects will defuse his self-exposure, and by formal acrobatics that he hopes will distract his auditors from seeing his all too painful incapacity. He gives an example of his preaching to show how skilled an operator he is. The sermon is itself an exemplum containing the sermon material which spawns further exempla. But the gold that is death at the center of his fiction escapes the control of this formal leger-de-main. The bell tolls for him as well as for his dead revellers. The Host gives the Pardoner's efforts an inadvertent *coup de grace,* as his penchant for virile banter, already exercised in varying degrees on Chaucer, the Monk, and the Nun's Priest, finds its most vulgar expression and its most vulnerable victim.

The relationship between the portraits and the tales is perhaps most surprising in the case of the Merchant. Nothing in the *General Prologue* prepares us for the extraordinary revelations of the *Merchant's Prologue* and *Tale.* Here we see the potential for the unexpected that the combination of pilgrimage and storytelling made possible, a potential exploited in a wholly different way when the Canon and his Yeoman overtake the pilgrims five miles from Canterbury. The Merchant's bitterness over his two-month marriage does not contradict what the portrait shows us; it does not even change the general impression of selfish disregard for any but his own narrow interests. On the other hand, it justifies the most radical combination of narrative materials Chaucer has yet attempted. From the mock epithalamion to the final scene in the garden, in its contradictory rhetorical extravagances and its mealy-mouthed euphemisms, the *Merchant's Tale* serves as indirect confession—the blindness of the narrator reflected in the blindness of January, the only alternative to his own unhappiness as husband the fate suffered by his hero in the garden, which confirms the Merchant's introductory reflections on the lot of husbands:

> "We wedded men lyven in sorwe and care.
> Assaye whoso wole, and he shal fynde
> That I seye sooth, by Seint Thomas of Ynde,
> As for the moore part, I say not alle.
> God shilde that it sholde so bifalle!" (E 1228–32)

The exception is presented in the interests of accuracy—January, the happy husband—merely confirming the bitter cynicism about marriage, expressed both as self-castigation and as authorial intrusion into the tale. Sight and blindness are equally ineffectual in preventing the inevitable fate of husbands:

> For as good is blynd deceyved be
> As to be deceyved whan a man may se. (E 2109–10)

That the large block of tales inspired by the Wife of Bath was intended in the years around 1396 for the homeward journey is suggested not only by the fact that they could easily have been attached to the other stories, if Chaucer had wanted them there—negative evidence to be sure—but is also indicated by the contradiction in the implications of the time-and-place-references in the D (III) and E–F (IV–V) fragments, with the passing of Rochester in the *Monk's Pro-*

logue, and the night in Ospring pointed to unmistakably in
the *Canon Yeoman's Prologue.*[16] Even more persuasive, because both indirect and positive, is the response of the
Host to the *Merchant's Tale,* associated with his detailed
description of his wife after the *Melibeus,* but very different
in its caution and its implications for the future:

> "Ey! Goddes mercy!" seyde oure Hooste tho,
> "Now swich a wyf I pray God kepe me fro . . .
> But doutelees, as trewe as any steele
> I have a wyf, though that she povre be,
> But of hir tonge, a labbyng shrewe is she,
> And yet she hath an heep of vices mo . . ."
>
>   (E 2419–29)

At this point discretion begins to influence the Host's volu-
bility. He admits regretting his marriage and at the same
time recognizes a motivation for silence it would be "to
nyce" to ignore:

> "And cause why, it sholde reported be
> And toold to hire of somme of this meynee,—
> Of whom, it nedeth nat for to declare,
> Syn wommen konnen outen swich chaffare . . ."
>
>   (E 2435–38)

In Rochester, more than halfway to Canterbury, the Host
feels no need for caution as he described his wife's incite-
ments to violence. Less than a hundred lines after the
Host's cautious self-censorship in the *Merchant's Epilogue,*
the Squire refers to the fact that it is "pryme" (9 a.m. in our
parlance), probably indicating the day after the Wife stimu-
lated so many of the pilgrims to their varied responses.
Very little time and space, and those diminishing, remain
before the reunion of Harry Bailly and his wife at the Tabard. The passage proclaims itself not only as belonging to
the homeward journey; it suggests that Chaucer was thinking beyond his original conclusion; that the reality of his

pilgrims was demanding a more dramatic and lively ending; that the pilgrimage to Jerusalem celestial, while still to be expressed, was the Parson's and no longer Chaucer's exclusive sense of the meaning of his collection of tales. Here again the Wife of Bath intrudes and influences the work of her creator. We can only guess what she put in Chaucer's mind to have her do and say when she and Goodelief meet and compare notes at the Tabard.

Toward the end of his work on the two great blocks of tales, another idea was apparently modifying Chaucer's conception of the work as a whole. At the end of the marriage group, the Host in calling on the Franklin, tacitly changes the conditions of his "game":

> "What Frankeleyn! pardee, sire, wel thou woost
> That ech of yow moot tellen atte leste
> A tale or two, or breken his beheste." (F 696–98)

Again, in the G (VIII) fragment, after the early *St. Cecilia* has been pressed without alteration into service as the *Second Nun's Tale*, the pilgrims are overtaken by the Canon and his Yeoman, and the Host asks the Yeoman of his master, "Can he oght telle a myrie tale or tweye, With which he glade may this compaignye?" (G 597–98) Suggesting more than the single tale for each pilgrim—this single tale not only explicit in the *Parson's Prologue*, but implicit when the Shipman takes over a perfectly good "Wife of Bath's Tale"; and when the Host gives Chaucer and the Monk, interrupted for what he considers good reason in their first efforts, a second chance—and increasing the scope of his work sent Chaucer back to a reconsideration of his beginning. Since his substitution of the *Constance* for the prose tale originally told by the Man of Law, and his detachment of the Wife of Bath from her original position in this sequence, only additional portraits in the *Prologue* had drawn his attention to this part of his work. The Monk, the Friar, and the churls had some obvious connections with the two big blocks of tales. But the erratic course of Chaucer's invention had left the beginning relatively undeveloped. Now a whole series of new ideas and modifications of old coalesced in Chaucer's mind—the *Palamon and Arcite* as *Knight's Tale;* the three churls and their fabliau triptych as balance; the variety of motives producing pattern, meaning, value; the four stories for each pilgrim; the telling of stories, which had already superseded the mere collection of stories, becoming a storytelling contest, and the pilgrimage ending not with the Parson's overt morality, but with the irony of the Host as judge and literary critic, as well as the already prepared-for drama of the Host as husband; the use within the stories of the kind of portraits developed in the *Prologue;* heroes with epithets in fabliaux, "hende" Nicholas, "deynous" Symkin, and Perkyn "revelour"; frequent references to time and place as a means not just of keeping the stages of the pilgrimage distinct, but of giving as many dimensions as possible to the literal existence of the pilgrims.

In revising *Palamon and Arcite* for its position as *Knight's Tale,* the first of the series, Chaucer has the Knight refer to the prize to be awarded five days later on their return to the Tabard:

> I have, God woot, a large feeld to ere,
> And wayke been the oxen in my plough.
> The remenaunt of the tale is long ynough.
> I wol nat letten eek noon of this route;
> Lat every felawe telle his tale aboute,
> And lat se now who shal the soper wynne . . .
>
> (A 886–91)

Only in the A (I) fragment do we get reference to the prize supper and the storytelling as a contest. The competitive instinct motivates the drunken Miller to try to "quite the Knyghtes tale;" it also leads him to mock the language and repeat the rhyme of this noble pilgrim in his response to the Reeve:

> "I have a wyf, pardee, as wel as thow;
> Yet nolde I, for the oxen in my plogh,
> Take upon me moore than ynough
> As demen of myself that I were oon . . ." (A 3158–61)

as well as to mock some elements of the *Knight's Tale* in the structure of his own.[17] In apologizing for the churls' tales, Chaucer tells the reader to "turne over the leef and chese another tale" if he doesn't want to read of "synne and harlotries":

> For he shal fynde ynowe, grete and smale
> Of storial thyng that toucheth gentillesse
> And eek moralitee and hoolynesse. (A 3178–80)

The assurance can be the better given since the material he refers to is already there, not just in conception but in fact. Chaucer's attitude as expressed in the *Miller's Prologue* stands in subtle contrast to the rejection of tales "that sounnen into synne" in the *Retraction*.

Finally, the Cook acts on the assumption that he will have another opportunity to get his revenge on the Host. He merely threatens a tale about "an hostileer," "But netheless I wol not telle it yit; But er we parte, ywis, thou shalt be quit." (A 4361–62) He proceeds with "A litel jape that fil in oure citee," (A 4343) inadvertently completing a number of patterns. his delight at the *Reeve's Tale* contrasting with the Reeve's annoyance at the Miller's and the Miller's desire to correct impressions of love in the Knight's, and the three men cooperating on their earthy trilogy of life in town, in village, in city, each descending a little lower on the moral scale, from sexual attraction to casual coupling to prostitution, as they show the dangers of "herbergage" in the balance against the idealism of the Knight's chivalric lovers. The complexity of what Chaucer finally envisaged defies conjecture. Those who would deny the finality of this segment must see the development of the *Canterbury Tales* as a gradual diminishment, not a sudden one; now the storytelling contest is abandoned, now the number of tales is reduced, now the homeward journey and the return to the Tabard are eliminated, and finally whatever does not touch "gentillesse And eek moralitee and hoolynesse," including (one assumes) all the finest poetry of the English Middle Ages, is retracted.

Instead, what we see in the *Canterbury Tales* is a concept of the work as a whole that develops from simple to complex, from the traditional to the originally dramatic. What starts as a collection of varied stories, with the pilgrimage invoked at the end as a transforming and unifying image, through the interaction of prologue and stories, becomes a drama of conflicting visions, becomes in the end a storytelling contest with its final scene no longer the *Parson's Tale* begun at a "thropes ende," but a feast of celebration and judgment at the Tabard. There, where the pilgrims first become a community, the promise of a meeting between Alisoun and Goodelief portends only a slightly less serious exposure of the Host than the choice he will make of "The tales of best sentence and moost solaas." (A 798) Chaucer's final vision communicates itself to us as it did to its first readers,[18] as it did to Dryden—"Here is God's plenty."

THE UNIVERSITY OF CONNECTICUT

FOOTNOTES

1. This paper presents in different terms and with new evidence the theories developed in my previous articles, especially "The Development of the *Canterbury Tales*," *JEGP,* 57 (1958), 449–76; and "The Twenty-Nine Pilgrims and the Three Priests," *MLN,* 76 (1961), 392–97. See also Chapter 11, "The Design of the *Canterbury Tales*," with its appended bibliography, in *Companion to Chaucer Studies,* ed. Beryl Rowland (Toronto: Oxford Univ. Press, 1968). All quotations are from *The Works of Geoffrey Chaucer,* ed. F. N. Robinson, 2nd ed. (Boston: Houghton

Mifflin, 1957). Line references, however, follow the Chaucer Society's lettering of the fragments (A–I), not the Robinson numbers.

2. The most sophisticated presentations of the theory are to be found in Wayne Shumaker, "Chaucer's *Manciple's Tale* as Part of a Canterbury Group," *UTQ*, 22 (1953), 147–56; Ralph Baldwin, *The Unity of the Canterbury Tales*, Anglistica, 5 (Copenhagen: Rosenkilde and Bagger, 1955), p. 84; and E. Talbot Donaldson, *Chaucer's Poetry: An Anthology for the Modern Reader* (New York: Ronald Press, 1958), pp. 947–49. See also Robert Dudley French, *A Chaucer Handbook* (New York: F. S. Crofts, 1927), pp. 334–35; Robert Kilburn Root, *The Poetry of Chaucer* (Boston: Houghton Mifflin, [1922]; rpt. Gloucester, Mass.: Peter Smith, 1957), pp. 152–53, 288; William Witherle Lawrence, *Chaucer and the Canterbury Tales* (New York: Columbia Univ. Press, 1950), pp. 147–57; D. S. Brewer, *Chaucer* (London: Longmans, 1960), pp. 177–78, 188–89; 3rd ed. (1973), pp. 151–54, 161; and Paul Ruggiers, *The Art of the Canterbury Tales* (Madison: Univ. of Wisconsin Press, 1965), p. 40.

3. For arguments in favor of placing the *Manciple's Tale* and the *Parson's Prologue* on the homeward journey, see Robert K. Root, "The Manciple's Prologue," *MLN*, 44 (1929), 493–96; Charles A. Owen, Jr., "The Plan of the Canterbury Pilgrimage," *PMLA*, 66 (1951), 820–26.

4. *The Tale of Beryn*, written as a continuation of the *Canterbury Tales* shortly after Chaucer's death, describes the pilgrims arriving in Canterbury in the morning, in consonance with the suggestions in the *Canon's Yeoman's Prologue* that they reach Boughton at an early hour after spending the night at an inn which must be in Ospringe.

5. Robert A. Pratt, "The Order of The Canterbury Tales," *PMLA*, 66 (1951), 1144, finds "insufficient evidence for separating IX and X." Shumaker, loc. cit., fn. 2.

6. First pointed out by Pratt, loc. cit., 1154–57.

7. See Owen, *PMLA*, 67. 824–25; Baldwin, op. cit., pp. 92–95; Robert M. Lumiansky, *Of Sondry Folk* (Austin: Univ. of Texas Press, 1955), pp. 239–45; and Charles A. Owen, Jr., "The Earliest Plan of the *Canterbury Tales*," *Mediaeval Studies*, 21 (1959), 205–10.

8. A suggestion first made by Furnivall, rejected by Skeat, *The Complete Works of Geoffrey Chaucer* (Oxford: Clarendon Press, 1894–97), 3. 406, and supported strongly by John S. P. Tatlock, *The Development and Chronology of Chaucer's Works*, Chaucer Soc. (1907), pp. 188 ff. Tatlock's position has been accepted by most of those who have written on the development of the *Tales*.

9. W. W. Lawrence, "Chaucer's *Shipman's Tale*," *Speculum*, 33 (1958), 56–68, is definitive on this question.

10. The *Epilogue* of the *Man of Law's Tale* and the *Wife of Bath's Prologue* still fit together without "shake or bind." See Owen, *JEGP*, 57, 452; and Robert A. Pratt, "The Development of the Wife of Bath," in *Studies*

in Medieval Literature in Honor of Albert Croll Baugh, ed. MacEdward Leach (Philadelphia: Univ. of Pennsylvania Press, [1961]), pp. 45–47.

11. See Carleton Brown, "The Man of Law's Headlink and the Prologue of the Canterbury Tales," *SP,* 34 (1937), 8–35; and my own comments in *Mediaeval Studies,* 21. 202–10.

12. Germaine Dempster, "A Period in the Development of the *Canterbury Tales* Marriage Group and of Blocks B² and C," *PMLA,* 68 (1953), 1142–59.

13. See Charles A. Owen, Jr., "The *Tale of Melibee,*" *Chaucer Review,* 7 (1973), 267–80.

14. John S. P. Tatlock, "The Duration of the Canterbury Pilgrimage," *PMLA,* 21 (1906), 478–85.

15. Eleanor Prescott Hammond, *Chaucer: A Bibliographical Manual* (New York: Macmillan, 1908), pp. 254–58, says the Summoner must have been conceived at the same time that the characters were created.

16. Fragment D has the reference to Sittingbourne in the threat of the Summoner, line 847, apparently referred to as having been carried out in the last line of his tale, D 2294. In Fragments E–F the reference is to "pryme" (F 74), apparently the next morning. There is simply no space for the tales of E–F after D on the outward journey.

17. William Stokoe, "Structure and Intention in the First Fragment of the *Canterbury Tales,*" *UTQ,* 21 (1952), 120–27; and Charles A. Owen, Jr., "Chaucer's *Canterbury Tales:* Aesthetic Design in Stories of the First Day," *English Studies,* 35 (1954), 49–56.

18. The evidence points to Hengwrt as being the first manuscript collection of the *Tales.* The first readers of the *Canterbury Tales* apparently had the readings of the links restored where they had been altered to fit an order established before the links came to hand, and more significant, had the tales illuminated with portraits of the pilgrims telling the tales rather than with scenes from the stories, when the Ellesmere MS. was produced.

8

Getting Around
the Parson's Tale:
An Alternative
to Allegory and Irony

CAROL V. KASKE

What place is accorded secular literature in medieval thought? This still unsolved but in some quarters burning question has exercised the minds of many critics and cultural historians of recent decades, such as, in different ways, E. R. Curtius, D. W. Robertson, and most recently, Judson Allen, who are anxious to read medieval literature "with the same spirit that the author writ." It is of concern to Chaucerians, because Chaucer chose to end his *Canterbury Tales* with a very unliterary sermon, followed by a retraction of some of the earlier tales. This sermon, the *Parson's Tale*, seems to contradict most of the earlier tales with statements like "the love of every thyng that is nat . . . doon principally for Goddes sake, although that a man love it lasse than God, yet is it venial synne" (X, 366). Is the *Parson's Tale*—is Christianity itself—relevant for the secular tales, and if so, how? If it is so relevant as to be normative, as Professor Robertson believes,[1] and as one might well conclude a priori from the Christian character of medieval culture, it reduces most of the other tales, celebrating more temporal values, to ironic descriptions of sin or, in rare cases such as the moralization of the *Clerk's Tale* by its teller, to allegorical descriptions of Christian virtue. The inability of most Chaucer critics to accept this interpretation often drives them to the opposite extreme—that of seeing the *Canterbury Tales* as a mere anthology, subtitled "God's Plenty" and selected simply for aesthetic contrast. Effective though the work is on this level, to inquire no further is valid neither heuristically nor historically. Universal negations are by their very nature provisional, and they lead to fewer discoveries than does the assumption that a thing exists if only we could find it. Speaking historically, for a moment, such autonomy does not seem to have been granted to art in the Middle Ages,[2] nor does the reputation of this work as at least a magnificent fragment with a clear beginning and end seem to allow for so rudimentary a unity. There is, however, another alternative: "In my Father's house are many mansions"; not all morality, even in the Middle Ages, was that of charity and cupidity which Robertson sees, nor the Parson's *contemptus mundi,* nor even a fully Christian morality; nor, conversely, is Christianity so monolithic that some doctrines, such as God the Creator, cannot be treated on their own, independent of the system.

Although not a Chaucerian, I want to suggest a way which Chaucerians might try of taking account of an author's announced Christianity without making it the ironic or allegorical moral of everything in the work. Granting that medieval literature tends to conceal its moral in allusions, one still could stick closer than does Robertson to the actual words of the text and bring in no more of the Christian system than a given text clearly alludes to. To put it another way, if an author fails to express a Christian doctrine which is relevant to his subject, it might, I admit, be a conspicuous omission which cries out to be filled via indirection, but it might also be a simple omission, a limitation of the world view the author is trying to convey. Taking this approach will at least have the advantage of singling out the author's or teller's distinctive brand of Christianity and morality. My hypothesis is that one would find in medieval literature a mode, akin to "point of view" in post-Jamesian fiction, which tells literal truth so far as it goes, but which deliberately gives only the first round of a debate—the part knowable by reason or by experience, omitting whatever Christian doctrine would say on the subject. In the course of the present essay, I will give a brief history of this limited perspective as employed in some of Chaucer's sources, especially the *Consolation of Philosophy* and its literary heirs. My purpose is to show the presence of this mode in some secular tales of Chaucer from several different angles, each of which could form an essay in its own right: from the social classes of their tellers, from the recurrences of the experience-vs.-authority and the "I'm-no-theologian" formulae; from their indebtedness to other works of limited perspective; and from the extremism of their adversary, the *Parson's Tale*, especially when compared both with its own relevant source and with various other treatments of one particular topic.

Two topics which were debated in the twelfth through fourteenth centuries, the late Father Dunning tells us, were destiny vs. free will, and marriage—the one a doctrinal problem, the other a moral one; and Chaucer reflects that debate.[3] Destiny is treated in the *Knight's Tale,* the *Man of Law's Tale* (as I will argue), and the *de casibus* tragedies of the *Monk's Tale*—implicitly, in fact, in all the tales of misfortune, which we might loosely christen the Misfortune Group. Marriage is of course treated in the so-called Marriage Group, with many incidental contributions from other tales, for example, *Melibee.* The importance of the two debates for the *Canterbury Tales* is signaled by the travesties of them, as well as of Chaucer's other favorite *quaestio,* the validity of dreams, inserted into the *Nun's Priest's Tale* (destiny, VII, 3234 ff.; marriage, the scenes with Pertelote).

Chaucer indicates that there are two valid ways of looking at these two topics by applying to them his experience-vs.-authority formula, for example, "Experience, though noon auctoritee Were in this world, is right ynough for me . . ." What you have just heard is of course the voice of the Wife of Bath presenting the introductory tale in the Marriage Group; the formula itself is first invoked by Theseus in the *Knight's Tale* in relation to predestined death-days (I, 3000-01). All the uses in the *Canterbury Tales* pertain either to death and the afterlife (*KnT, FrT,* III, 1517 ff.) or to marriage, and in every one of these cases, some validity is claimed for experience.[4] Despite his continual citing of authorities, both sober and spoofing, Chaucer seems to be, for his time, remarkably empirical. From the point of view of experience, misfortune emerges as but an arc of the cycle of generations and a limit such as is appointed to each thing by God's "chain of love" (Theseus in *KnT*). From the point of view of authority (which includes revelation) we are taught to see misfortune as but the preparation for the endless bliss of a Christian heaven *(SecNT, PrT, ParsT)*. We learn that marriage, from the point of view of experience, should be an equilibrium of reciprocal servitude and lordship held together by bed-joy which in turn depends largely on the sexual attractiveness of the wife (*FranklT,* supported by *WBP, WBT* and, negatively, by *MerchT* and *ClT*). From the point of view of authority, it should be a man-dominated union of virtuous hearts, sacramentally mirroring that of Christ and the Church, reducing the deadly sin of lechery to venial sin *(ParsT,* supported by *ClT* and *MLT,* and by *SecNT* and *Mel.* except for the moderate dominance of the wife in them).

I hope to show that this dichotomy of authority and experience is reflected in contrasts between certain Christian and non-Christian tales in the Marriage and Misfortune Groups. Further study might also show, although my case does not depend on it, that the entire procession is divided by social class into what Chaucer would call *lerned* and *lewed*—in both senses of the word, as it usually turns out—educated and noneducated tellers. The learned, so far as I can see, tell stories whose moral is drawn from authority, for example, the saints' legends *(MLT, PrT, SecNT)* and the Monk's sad stories of the death of kings, while the *lewed* tell stories whose moral is drawn from experience—i.e., it is not predictable in advance but must be deduced from the facts of the tale, as for example, in the stories which involve a *question d'amour (KnT, WBT, FranklT)*. While the disclaimer of learning on the part of the Nun's Priest might seem incongruous with his learned social class, it is obviously just another example of Chaucer's ironic *occupatio* in view of the esoteric discussion which follows it (VII, 3234 ff.).

Now two works which Chaucer translated, parodied, and plagiarized—both "best-sellers" too in the Middle Ages generally—were the *Roman de la Rose* and Boethius' *Consolation of Philosophy;* and almost the same world view which I see in Chaucer's secular tales can be seen even more clearly in them. That Boethius deliberately limited his discussion to "pauca quae ratio valet humana de divina profunditate" (IV, pr.6), although he was "without doubt a Christian," was recognized as early as 1918 by E. K. Rand and H. F. Stewart and has been authoritatively restated by Pierre Courcelle.[5] In the Middle Ages too, Courcelle maintains, "les esprits les plus pénétrants" such as Conrad of Hirsau, for example, note that "vir iste totus catholicus Fortunam tociens in hoc opere ponit et testimoniis divinis litteram elegantem vacuam ostendit";[6] and John of Salisbury remarks that "Verbum non exprimat incarnatum."[7] Far from faulting Boethius, they both explain that he persuades by reason alone in order that even Jews and pagans might receive, in John's words, "congrua cuique medicamenta." As Dante might have put it, Boethius' Lady Philosophy is a Virgil without a Beatrice.[8] This limitation of perspective, being a process of omission rather than of inclusion, is not the same as syncretism, exemplified by, say, Ficino. Nor is it a giving of only one side of a debate with the Christian side implicitly evoked as a corrective, for a second and corrective voice is already given, answering a voice of unreason (the fictional Boethius).

Another medieval work of a perspective so limited (omitting mention of Christ or heaven) that it was sometimes attributed to the pagan author Seneca, is the brief but influential *Formula vitae honestae* by St. Martin of Braga (d. 579), which states its limitations in its Preface:

> Quem idcirco tali volui vocabulo superscribi, quia non illa ardua et perfecta quae a paucis et egregiis deicolis patrantur instituit, sed ea magis commonet quae et sine divinarum scripturarum praeceptis naturali tantum humanae intelligentiae lege etiam a laicis recte honesteque viventibus valeant adimpleri.[9]

There is a similar problem about the relation to Christianity of the *Roman de la Rose*—that other favorite of Chaucer and his age; and I believe it can be similarly solved, providing an alternative to the allegorical and ironic readings of that poem by such critics as Clement Marot in the sixteenth century and D. W. Robertson and his followers in the twentieth.[10] As for the personal Christianity of the poem's authors, we have no grounds to doubt that of Guillaume de Lorris, and that of Jean de Meun is well attested. Yet their most normative character, Reason, never cites the Bible (nor does any speaker, on those sexual topics which are the book's main concern; in contrast, the digression against mendicants cites Scripture on every page); in fact, her one use of the word "Scripture" means Boethius.[11] Reason disapproves of clerical celibacy as being against Nature.[12] Her survey of sexual and other kinds of love never discusses marriage and condones premarital sex so long as the "maiden" manages to become pregnant:

Mais coment que la besoigne aille,
Qui veaut d'amours joïr senz faille,
Fruit i deit querre e cil e cele,
Quel qu'ele seit, dame ou pucele. . . . (4545–48)

The other, less normative speakers are even less Christian
with regard to sex. Some critics have taken the literal at face
value and hailed Jean de Meun, at least, as the forerunner
of modern naturalism; but straightforward utterance and
total endorsement of such sentiments seem to have been
impossible in the Middle Ages without much more opposition than Jean is known to have actually encountered.[13]
How else, then, can we take such statements? Fleming si-
lently passes over these lines, or else he could not maintain
as he does that Reason is associated with "Divine Sapience,
or the Second Person of the Trinity" (p. 114, note the resur-
gence of allegory in subtler guise), and that her sexual eth-
ics is "Augustinian" (p. 116) and "thoroughly familiar" to
any thirteenth-century reader (p. 117). It is tendentious to
dilute them as Dahlberg does, by translating "dame ou pucele" as "lady or girl" and by stressing the help which Reason concedes that God's grace might give to the frustrated
celibate. Tuve recognizes such unchristian notes in Reason's character, but ascribes them to dramatic irony, saying
that the Christian perspective is omitted so conspicuously
that it is actually evoked as a corrective. But if Reason is
wrong—the highest and most comprehensive speaker—
then everybody in the poem is wrong, which hardly seems
likely; and the norm can only be found between the lines
and in self-betraying asides, which is what Reason's comment about God's grace becomes in this interpretation.

One ironist who points us in what I take to be the right
direction is Thomas D. Hill, who convincingly argues that
the perspective of Reason falls short of Christianity insofar
as she is ignorant of the Fall, which makes her advice
impracticable.[14] Indeed, as Winthrop Wetherbee declares,
"like the Nature of the *De Planctu*, Raison cannot think in

theological terms at all," even though she is the daughter of God.[15] If this is indeed Reason's only limitation vis-à-vis Christianity, there remains another explanation of her unchristian sexual morality, in which irony plays only the smallest of roles, though some sort of humor inevitably pervades this, just as it does any philosophical discussion of sex. It is that Jean's Reason is speaking on the subject of sex under the same limitation as Boethius' Lady Philosophy, whom she continually echoes and sometimes quotes by name, and with the same validity. Jean de Meun, like Chaucer, translated the *Consolation of Philosophy;* and he must have been one of "les esprits les plus pénétrants" who recognized its limitation of perspective; for his prologue, advertising the work to his king, has no Christian references and stresses the work's appeal to reason. Besides reason, the *Consolation* appeals also to experience, says Jean[16]—an appeal which we have found to be prominent and coordinated with authority in Chaucer. In the *Roman* too there are characters who base their advice on their own experiences—the Friend and the Duenna; and though less normative than Reason, they are frequently proved right by events. Therefore it would seem that experience, like reason, has a degree of validity independent of revelation. Under this interpretation, we simply do not know what the historical Jean de Meun personally believed about premarital sex or clerical celibacy, though it was probably something closer to the dogma of the church, but we do know that the good points of the former and the bad points of the latter seemed to him worth mentioning as one ingredient of the truth.

If setting the work in this kind of oblique relation to Christianity explains the *Consolation* and much of the *Roman de la Rose,* it might also help explain some works of Chaucer which owe so much else to them, thus freeing us alike from the burden of finding Christian truth everywhere or the disappointment of accepting the *Canterbury Tales* as a mere anthology. Chaucer's own translations of Boethius and of the *Roman,* at least of the one Fragment (A) ascribable with any probability to him, preserve their not distinctively Christian flavor.[17] In the *Canterbury Tales,* the secular speakers are a full step nearer the earth than is Lady Philosophy, in that, as we have seen, Chaucer's revelation (which retains its status as the highest of authorities) is contrasted not with reason (unless Dame Prudence in *Melibee* is reason) but only with experience.

Another difference is that we do of course have at least one Beatrice, though not a very enticing one—the Parson—along with the secular speakers, which addendum makes the work call to mind the *Divine Comedy.* But a Beatrice does not negate a Virgil. In the Middle Ages, Gilson assures us, reason and philosophy were enjoined by such thinkers as Dante and Aquinas upon anyone who was capable of pursuing them; and they had a right to be heard even when they seemed to disagree with theology, though among all but extreme Averrhoists they bowed to theology in the final verdict.[18] That Dante recognized both the validity of reason and its difference from revelation is obvious to every reader, most notably in the large role played by his Virgil. Singleton has discriminated the two viewpoints, and nowhere more tellingly than when he identifies Virgil's perspective with that which Green, Stewart and Rand, and Courcelle have found in the *Consolation.* Beatrice sometimes seems like "Lady Philosophy, that Lady who had brought comfort to Boethius" and sometimes like Sapientia or Holy Wisdom. When Dante has crossed the river Lethe and left Virgil behind, "she is seen in a splendor surpassing by far the natural light, and her name must rather be Wisdom, Sapientia, in the fullest Christian sense of the word" (pp. 126–27). "In the *Convivio,*" Singleton goes on (as in the minds of Christianizing readers of Boethius' Lady Philosophy), "no clear distinction is drawn" between Filosofia and Sapienza; rather they are interchangeable names for the same personage. In the *Comedy,* however:

> clearer lines of distinction are drawn. . . . When Beatrice comes to Virgil in Limbo [*Inf.* II, 76 ff.], we

see her through his eyes (since he is reporting the
event there), we know her in his perspective and
by his *light.* Virgil's is the perspective of ancient
thought which did not know Christ; Virgil.
. . . does not therefore see Beatrice in meanings
which are peculiarly Christian. . . . When we see
Beatrice through his eyes we see her within the
limits of his awareness as a pagan, in terms which
in no way exceed the frame of an ancient *pagan*
notion. Indeed, must we not also note that Virgil's
"point of view" is respected by Beatrice herself
when, addressing him in Limbo, she refers to the
man to be helped as "l'amico mio e non della
ventura"?[19]

I have quoted at such length because the passage provides
a model of the kind of relationship which I want to posit between the secular tales of misfortune and the *Parson's Tale.*
If they can be shown to have a Boethian perspective, then
we can assume that they too, like Dante's Virgil, have a certain validity.

One way in which a speaker tells us his perspective is limited to reason or experience but nevertheless valid is by the
disclaimer, "I am not a theologian," "I am not a divine."
This is not an incriminating admission, not an ironic givea-
way like "Allas! allas! that evere love was synne!"; for we
are all called out of sin, but we are not all called to be theologians—as the Wife of Bath unconsciously illustrates.
Dante's Virgil, for example, expounds to him free will vs.
one kind of destiny "as far as reason sees here" and refers
him for the rest to Beatrice because it "is matter of faith"
(*Purg.* XVIII, 46–48, cf. 73). In the *Roman de la Rose,* an infe-
rior but still not vicious speaker, Genius, condemns clerical
celibacy and then protests:

Je ne sai plus de la besoigne;
Viegnent devin que en devinent,
Qui de ce deviner ne finent. (19626–28)

Coming now to the *Canterbury Tales,* the Knight protests, "'I nam no divinistre,'" and hence disclaims knowledge of where his hero's soul went after death. The Wife of Bath twice similarly protests, "Men may divine and glosen, up and doun . . ." and "Glose whoso wole, and seye both up and doun That they were maked for purgacioun . . . The experience woot wel it is noght so" (III, 26, 119–24). These speakers lack the perspective of revelation, but the sentiments they express are not reprehensible, not even the Wife's teleology of the sexual organs, and I see no other grounds for holding this limitation against them. Two other disclaimers of theological knowledge are that of the Nun's Priest, whose incongruity was explained above as ironical except as a sign that he has a part in the two debates, and that of the Parson, which will be similarly explained below.

In the secular tales about misfortune, though not in the Marriage Group, there seems to be another hallmark of a point of view skewed like that of the *Consolation* away from theology and toward some substitute like reason or experience: the avoidance of the idea of heaven in favor of the here and now. Boethius' *Consolation* seldom appeals to "immortality of the soul" and to heaven, and then not as consolations in themselves but only as a step in proving something else; and Philosophy explicitly refuses to appeal to the punishment of the wicked in the afterlife, even though she firmly believes in it (IV, pr. 4). The afterlife—heaven, hell, and its devils—is a topic, according to the *Friar's Tale* (III, 1504–20) and especially the Prologue to the *Legend of Good Women,* of which man in this life normally has no experience, so that he is here regrettably thrown back entirely on the authority of revelation.

The first of the *Canterbury Tales,* the *Knight's Tale,* as R. M. Lumiansky and others have shown, is pervasively Boethian;[20] it goes to some lengths to avoid mentioning heaven—because, I propose, it is written from the point of view of experience. True, the *Knight's Tale* is set in pagan times, but historicity alone fails to account for this limitation, for Chaucer was not averse to making his speakers unrealistically Christian if he wanted to, like Pluto and Proserpina in the *Merchant's Tale*. In any case, the question remains, why did Chaucer choose to begin with a pagan tale? The Knight's refusal to tell where his hero's soul went after death—a departure from the source (*Teseide* XI, 6)—seems to me very significant, even though similar fussy interruptions are a favorite rhetorical quirk of his:

> His spirit chaunged hous and wente ther,
> As I cam nevere, I kan nat tellen wher;
> Therfore I stynte—I nam no divinistre:
> Of soules fynde I nat in this registre,
> Ne me ne list thilke opinions to telle
> Of hem, though that they writen wher they dwelle.
> Arcite is coold, ther Mars his soule gye. (I, 2809–15)

The Knight will not tell about the afterlife for two reasons: 1) he has never been there ("As I cam nevere"), in other words, he has had no experience of it; and 2) he excludes written authorities on the subject. This agnosticism on the part of the Knight—a layman, it is true, as we have noted, but personally a devout Christian—would be incredible in the youngest catechumen. It must therefore signify a deliberate limitation of somebody's perspective to that of reason and experience. Perhaps the words "of soules find I nat in this registre" screen the Knight as teller from the charge of this vincible ignorance by feigning a pagan source, presumably Statius' *Thebaid* quoted in the epigraph. What Chaucer rejected from his real source, Boccaccio's *Teseide*, at this point, is a picture of Arcite's soul in the eighth sphere, presumably the equivalent of heaven (XI, 1–3). He employed it instead for the rather Christian ending of the *Troilus*. Clearly, then, he regarded it as valid but too Christian for this tale.

Theseus, the tale's *raisonneur,* is on this topic of the afterlife no wiser than the teller. His climactic speech 200 lines later consoling Palamon and Emelye for the death of

Arcite, almost half of which is added to the source, appeals to what "is preved by experience." It ignores heaven, the main Christian consolation for death, in preference for sentiments from Boethius' *Consolation.*[21] I also believe, though I cannot elaborate it here, that a similar limitation of perspective might explain the omission of heaven from that Boethian but curiously unconsoling *consolatio,* the *Book of the Duchess.*

Conversely, in the Christian tales, heaven is important. It is invoked as a consolation for death in the *Second Nun's Tale,* when Cecile encourages her brother in the face of martyrdom:

> Men myghten dreden wel and skilfully
> This lyf to lese, myn owene deere brother,
> If this were lyvynge oonly and noon oother.
> But ther is bettre lif in oother place,
> That nevere shal be lost, ne drede thee noght,
> Which Goddes Sone us tolde thurgh his grace. . . .
> By word and by myracle heigh Goddes Sone,
> Whan he was in this world, declared heere
> That ther was oother lyf ther men may wone.
>
> (VIII, 320–25, 330–32)

The *Canterbury Tales* ends, as we would predict, with a portrayal of heaven, occupying the last paragraph of the *Parson's Tale* (X, 1075-80); in fact, the Parson from his *Prologue* on stresses "Jerusalem celestial," along with its opposite. The *Knight's Tale* and the *Parson's Tale* thus contrast as philosophy and theology, giving us a Virgil at the beginning of the *Canterbury Tales* to match the Beatrice at the end.

The end of the *Canterbury Tales* is, however, a long time to wait for a Christian complement to the *Knight's Tale.* The learned and ostensibly religious Monk would have been a likely teller for such a tale, and we would certainly expect him to stress heaven as a remedy for the misfortunes he records, but Chaucer satirically inverts this expectation for him, like all others,[22] and allots the next Christian tale of misfortune to the lay but learned Man of Law. In the *Man of Law's Tale,* placed by its prologue very early and thus near to the *Knight's Tale,* Chaucer's quite different strategy was to add things such as prayers to his source to make it *more* Christian, as Edward Block has shown.[23] On the basis of this, it would seem, as R. E. Kaske has suggested to me,[24] that the *Man of Law's Tale* is intended as a Christian complement to the *Knight's Tale.* They contrast significantly on the subject not precisely of heaven but of causation, especially causes of misfortune, in other words, destiny. The causes in the *Knight's Tale* are the Boethian ones—Providence, Fate or Destiny, Fortune or "aventure or cas," and Nature, especially that natural agent of destiny, the stars, sometimes personified as planetary gods. In the *Man of Law's Tale,* the stars play a large part in the first misfortunes of the heroine, as they do in the *Knight's Tale;* but her preservation in this and all later misfortunes is traced to the direct and often miraculous intervention of God, Christ, and Mary; and all her misfortunes bring her into contact with pagans whom she proceeds to convert to Christianity. Thus while the basically pagan astrological causation is reaffirmed, distinctively Christian causes of events unknown to Lady Philosophy are added on the authority of Revelation. The Christian tales of misfortune (see also the *SecNT* and the *PrT*) complement the secular, Boethian tales *(KT, MkT).*

We have been speaking mostly of misfortune and its cause, destiny; let us now turn our attention to that other topic whose fourteenth-century controversy is reflected in the *Canterbury Tales,* marriage. The *Roman de la Rose* had already applied the dictates of a Boethian reason, along with those of experience, to the topic of sexual relations. (Marriage itself was pushed to one side—in my opinion, because the French authors felt it was too much in the province of revelation.) In Chaucer's Marriage Group, the two main questions debated are rulership and sex, both propounded in the *Wife of Bath's Prologue* and developed in her tale: 1) "Who should rule?"—which is an aspect of

feminism vs. anti-feminism, and 2) "Is a woman's sexual attractiveness more important, or her character?"—which is
an aspect of the question, "What is the importance of sexual pleasure?"[25] I shall poll the debaters on these issues and
then focus on the *Parson's Tale*.

Just as the Knight was the experiential *raisonneur* of the
Misfortune Group, correcting such Fortune-dominated
speakers as his own heroes or his fellow-pilgrim the Monk,
so the Franklin is usually recognized to be the experiential
raisonneur of the Marriage Group, correcting, for example,
extremists like the Wife of Bath and the Clerk. Whether his
was to have been as structural a place as the Knight's in the
sequence of the tales, it is impossible to say; but it was
clearly a late one. His tale both parallels the *Knight's Tale*
and contrasts with the *Parson's Tale* in that, as Kathryn
Hume has shown, its setting is pagan and its alleged source,
a Breton lai, belongs to a *genre* characterized by non-Christian morality.[26] On the rulership question, his solution
seems based on experience: he is a family man; and his solution owes much to the advice of the Friend, one of the
two voices of experience in the *Roman de la Rose*. As to its
validity, as Donald Howard has noted (p. 232), this "bourgeois compromise" is the synthesis to which the debate
naturally leads:

> . . . freendes everych oother moot obeye,
> If they wol longe holden compaignye.
> Love wol nat been constreyned by maistrye.
>
> . . . .
> Wommen, of kynde, desiren libertee,
> And nat to been constreyned as a thral;
> And so doon men, if I sooth seyen shal.
>
> . . . .
> Heere may men seen an humble, wys accord;
> Thus hath she take hir servant and hir lord,
> Servant in love, and lord in mariage.
> Thanne was he both in lordshipe and servage.
>
> (V, 762–94)

It is reasonable and comprehensive, as is indicated by the tone and by the balanced though modest rhetoric. The troubles recounted in the rest of the tale do not undercut but rather test and vindicate, as Gertrude White has most recently pointed out, the viability of this equilibrium.[27] True, the Franklin lacks in the *General Prologue* the obviously normative personal traits which the Parson has in such a superlative degree; but he is a "Saint" (I, 340) in the same way as Sancho Panza's "saint," The Man in the Green Overcoat, in *Don Quixote, Part II.*

Though valid within the world of the poem, then, the Franklin's opinions about marriage are very different from those of the Parson. On the rulership question, the Parson counters him with: "how that a womman sholde be subget to hire housbonde, that telleth Seint Peter . . ." (X, 930). On the underlying issue of feminism vs. anti-feminism, I must admit that the Parson is remarkably noncommittal, at most condescending, thus branding as extreme from any point of view the Valerians and Theophrasts of irate husbands such as Jankin and Melibee. Another possible norm here would seem to reside in the power to counsel but not to master her husband won by the wife Dame Prudence in the *Tale of Melibee* (VII, 1055–1115). The tediousness of *Melibee* is of course self-mockery of its teller, Chaucer the pilgrim, but there seems to be no mockery of its content (which I would characterize as religious but syncretic). Not that *Melibee* is always the norm either; its authorities simply balance off those of the Parson.

On the question of sexual pleasure, our Virgil of love votes "yes": "O blisful artow now, thou Dorigen, That hast thy lusty housbonde in thyne armes" (*FranklT*, V, 1090–91). The Parson says, "for thre thynges a man and his wyf flesshly mowen assemble . . . scarsly may there any of thise be without venial synne, for the corrupcion and for the delit" (X, 939–42). In further contradiction of the Parson, Dorigen and Arveragus are oblivious of progeny, the Parson's main justification of the conjugal act (X, 939–41). (Whereas Jean de Meun thought reason demanded procreation but only revelation enjoined marriage, Chaucer seems to have relegated procreation to the province of revelation and derived marriage from reason and experience.)

On the related question—"Is a woman's sexual attractiveness or her virtue more important?"—another set of challengers step forth from the ranks of the learned and the *lewed*. The Wife of Bath—whose function seems to be more to propound questions than to give answers—dramatizes in her tale the dilemma that beauty and virtue are inversely related, up to the *dea-ex-machina* ending. The Man of Law, who is, as explained above, another spokesman for religious authority, coyly concurs with the *Wife of Bath's Tale* that wives chosen for their virtue will inevitably be less suited, whether in desire or desirability, for the bed:

> They goon to bedde, as it was skile and right;
> For thogh that wyves be ful hooly thynges,
> They moste take in pacience at nyght
> Swich manere necessaries as been plesynges
> To folk that han ywedded hem with rynges,
> And leye a lite hir hoolynesse aside,
> As for the time,—it may no bet bitide. (II, 708–14)

He not surprisingly opts for virtue. Those who perceive his alliance with the Parson will also not be surprised to learn that his heroine's virtues feature the Parson's favorite, submission to man's rulership (II, 267–87). On the other side, Dorigen, the heroine of the *Franklin's Tale*, is "oon the faireste under sonne" (V, 734).

In addition, the tales whose moral is drawn from experience often dramatize without comment how disappointingly the Parson's marital precepts work out in practice. On the topic of sexual pleasure, in line 941, the Parson says the wife has especial merit "that yeldeth to hir housbonde the dette of hir body, ye, though it be agayn hir likynge and the lust of hire herte." The Merchant's picture of May enduring the advances of January—and this is before her fall to Damian, when she still has our sympathy—is an effective if nondiscursive refutation of this authority from the point of view of experience. The fact that sexual pleasure is muted when the male dominates the marriage as well as when he selects a wife on grounds of virtue alone, is tacitly conceded by the *Clerk's Tale,* where, as R. E. Kaske puts it, "one hears of Walter's and Griselda's children with something like surprise."[28] Had Chaucer believed that the Christian picture of marriage summed up in the Parson's *Remedium Contra Peccatum Luxurie* was the all-sufficient last word on the subject, he would have made the experience recounted in the other tales more confirmatory of it.

On the topic of marriage, then, the Beatrice-figure and the Virgil-figure, the Parson and the Franklin, disagree. This is a sharper dichotomy than we have yet seen in Chaucer's predecessors and in the Misfortune Group, where Christianity either was omitted or was added as a complement. There the need of such a higher vantage-point was felt, in that Theseus' Boethian consolations (which fall short of even Philosophy's highest consolation, virtue for virtue's sake) seem rather meager. The grandeur which the medieval hierarchical view of the universe leads us to expect from the religious viewpoint shines forth in lines like "thilke parfit glorious pilgrymage That highte Jerusalem celestial." But in the parts of the Parson's treatise that contribute to the Marriage Group we do not have this feeling. And we do have another *raisonneur* who systematically contradicts him.

The theory that Chaucer saw no truth in the *Parson's Tale,* or inserted it for the "hoolyness" that comes of "dotage," must by its very nature be tabled as a last resort. Another approach which has been tried, without convincing results, is to somehow find Christian truth between the lines of the *Franklin's Tale;* but this is unnecessary, because it is theoretically possible (though Averrhoistic) in the Middle Ages, as Gilson says,[29] to admit a legitimate disagreement with revelation—a kind of double truth—especially on a matter not of faith but of morals. Two literary affirmations of double truth, according to Father Denomy, are the *De Amore* of Andreas Capellanus and, with some qualification, Chaucer's own *Troilus*.[30] In the *Canterbury Tales,* I will argue, Chaucer maintains the double perspective to the end by making his palinode too extreme for belief. Another possible example is *The Owl and the Nightingale.* I have recently argued that the *Faerie Queene* is another;[31] recognized examples are Spenser's *Fowre Hymnes, Don Quixote, Faust,* and *The Ring and the Book.* Background statistics of this sort can prove only the possibility of an interpretation, and for this, I think mine are sufficient.

That the contradiction is not a correction from a higher vantage-point, is confirmed by the Parson's parallel condemnations of belletristic literature in his *Prologue.* Within the world of a poem, a speaker who rejects poetry cannot have the whole truth. When the Parson rejects "fables" on the authority of Paul to Timothy (X, 32), he disapproves of the entire *Canterbury Tales* up to this point. Robertson's watering-down of this condemnation, that the fables condemned must have been those devoid of an edifying moral, simply has no basis in the text. The Parson means just what he says, for he abandons all semblance of fictional narrative and holds forth in straight exposition. Besides, in the exegesis to which Robertson appeals, Paul's condemnations of fables are only rarely taken as literary judgments of any sort; usually they are read quite properly in the context as referring to apocryphal gospels and superfluous doctrines;[32] hence the background evidence is not so overwhelming as to compel us to distort the text. Similarly, the Parson disapproves of verse, in which all but one of the other tales are written. Finally, the *Parson's Tale* leads right into Chaucer's retraction, in which "the maker of this book" apparently disapproves of almost the entire *Canterbury Tales.* (Whether he is Chaucer the pilgrim or Chaucer the author, and if so, whether of the *Parson's Tale* only or of the *Canterbury Tales,* is not clear.) The retraction forms one fragment, textually, with the *Parson's Tale.* It apparently refers back to it as "this litel tretys," since Chaucer never uses the word to refer to poetry, only to works like the *Tale of Melibee* and the *Astrolabe.* The retraction pushes Christianity too far, even for Robertson (who treats it summarily and I believe tendentiously, p. 369, fn. 179). These extreme literary judgments can themselves be explained if we follow Baldwin, Donaldson,[33] and others in seeing the retraction as part of the *Parson's Tale* and then follow me in seeing the unit so formed as but one of two equally valid but equally limited contradictory viewpoints. This literary extremism, furthermore, points to an extremism in the Parson's morality.

On the topic of marriage, I hope to show that Chaucer did not wholly agree with his Parson, and hence that his contradictions of earlier tales are not complements or corrections from a higher viewpoint. Father Dunning, E. Talbot Donaldson, and Judson Allen have all got around the Parson's morality by proving it to be grimmer than the general climate of fourteenth-century opinion.[34] But they could only argue at one remove from the text because they lacked that clue to an author's intention, a principal direct source, now happily discovered by Siegfried Wenzel for the relevant part of the *Parson's Tale,* the *Remedium contra Peccatum Luxurie.*

First, the Parson adds to his source (which Wenzel calls *Postquam* for want of a title) both the experience-vs.-authority tag (X, 924) and, somewhat surprisingly, the disclaimer of theological knowledge (X, 957; Wenzel does not comment specifically on this line; but if he had had a source for it, he surely would have mentioned it).[35] These seem to be added more as badges of the Parson's participation in the debate than as characterizations of his viewpoint; for clearly, authority weighs more than experience in his thinking, as is confirmed by his "text," (apparently also added to the source) which reads in part, "stondeth upon the weyes, and seeth, and axeth of olde pathes (that is to seyn, of olde sentences)."

In regard to his morality, the Parson strengthens the case for male rulership of the home. He duly translates from the source "God ne made nat womman of the foot of Adam, for she ne sholde nat been holden to lowe," but adds "for she can nat paciently suffre" (X, 928), a weaker-vessel argument adapted from his ultimate authority, I Peter 3. True, he has omitted the source's characterization of woman as man's enemy, *"hostis,"* but only to picture her as a child. Similarly, the Parson has added a passage (X, 931) reinforcing the subjection of a woman to her husband from the legal side and by an appeal to reason.

The Parson outdoes his source in condemnation of sexual pleasure. He adds what Donaldson calls "the special virtue of joylessness" in the marriage bed (X, 941), so disappointingly exemplified in Constance and especially in May. Most striking of all, though, he adds a condemnation of sexual pleasure so unqualified that it not only opposes the Franklin but goes beyond late medieval moralists such as Aquinas and Dan Michael of Northgate to an extreme which Father Dunning labels "quasi-heretical" (p. 93): "and trewely, scarsly may ther any of thise [motives for intercourse] be withoute venial synne, for the corrupcion and for the delit" (X, 942). To document a further change, I will quote all the relevant statements from the source, asking the reader to compare them with the lines of Chaucer cited in parentheses. Since comparing is enough of a mental gymnastic without translating, I will in this case quote my own translation, referring the reader for the Latin to Wenzel's convenient parallel texts:

> In this regard it should be understood that a wife is known for four reasons: either for the sake of procreating offspring (= X, 939).
>
> or of rendering the marriage debt, or of avoiding incontinence, or of fulfilling lust (= X, 940).

In the first case it is able to be meritorious, in the
second similarly (= X, 941),

and in the third, although venial sin is a con-
comitant (= X, 942).

In the fourth we must distinguish whether he
knows his wife with marital affection, albeit lustful-
ly, to this extent it is venial; if, however, his lust is
so great that he does not discern whether it is his
wife or another woman, it is deadly sin (= X, 943).

Through changes in the third and fourth "maneres," the
Parson extends the range of sin, both venial and mortal,
and restricts the range of merit. The Parson's labeling of the
motive of pleasure as a mortal sin here and in X, 904 is
classed by Noonan as the "rigorist" view, less prevalent
than that which labeled it, provided it was not pursued to
excess, a venial sin (pp. 250–52). As Wenzel comments,
"the discussion in *Postquam* of the possible sinfulness of
intercourse in married couples is more sophisticated,
lenient, and, as it were, 'modern' than in Chaucer" (p. 452,
n. 10). An author who adapts a source not to harmonize
with but to contradict the rest of his own work, probably
has in mind some such double perspective as I am suggesting.

Professor Wenzel's overall comment on Chaucer's
changes is that "the traditional pessimistic view of women
and marriage that appears in *Postquam* is considerably
toned down" (p. 451). He is reasoning from the omission of
condemnations of marriage and the shortening of the
praise of virginity. He is thus talking about gross omissions,
which admittedly his readers are in no position to estimate
without the manuscripts. As he describes them, however,
those could have been merely a sharpening of focus towards the subject of the Marriage Group rather than a ton-
ing-down. I am talking about the small additions in the
blocks Chaucer does translate. In these, it is true, we found
that the anti-feminism is slightly reduced. Pessimism about

marriage, however, is either retained and intensified or re-placed by idealistic rigor, so that the contrast with the other tales is actually heightened.

The present essay has tried to set the Knight and the Franklin in a separate but equal relationship to the Parson by showing that they contrast sharply with him; that they both speak from a limited perspective which has its own va-lidity and pedigree; and that the Parson's views on marriage are portrayed as unduly extreme in comparison with other speakers and with his source. The Parson as a speaker who is idealistic but limited despite his climactic place is compa-rable to the Hermit Contemplation at the climax of the edu-cation of Spenser's hero Red Cross. Like the Parson, Con-templation rejects the poem he appears in; he warns Red Cross that he must ultimately give up love and fighting be-cause they are transitory and lead to sin (*FQ* I.x.62), where-as Spenser himself has declared these to be the subject of his whole poem—"Fierce wars and faithful loves shall mor-alize my song" (I Proem i.9). The *Knight's Tale,* the *Frank-lin's Tale,* and other secular tales are likewise paralleled and in fact specifically cited and imitated by the later, more sec-ular books of the *Faerie Queene.* Chaucer and Spenser as writers of poems structured around pluralism draw clear battlelines and then refuse to take sides. They "really be-lieved" their idealistic speakers no more and no less than they did the limited voices of experience.[36]

CORNELL UNIVERSITY

FOOTNOTES

1. D. W. Robertson, Jr., *A Preface to Chaucer* (Princeton: Princeton Univ. Press, 1962), hereafter cited as Robertson, pp. 328n.; 336; implicit in 376.

2. Professor Robertson was right to insist upon this, just as he was to argue that the meaning of medieval art was more likely to

be implicit. Cf. E. R. Curtius, *European Literature and the Latin Middle Ages,* trans. Willard R. Trask (London: Routledge & Kegan Paul, 1953), p. 469, "How can the poet fit into society? . . . In the Middle Ages there was yet no concept of an autonomous 'culture.' " For example, whereas the sixteenth-century critic George Puttenham could preface his *Arte of English Poesie* (1589) with a defense of poetry as an honest recreation and a thing morally indifferent (ch. ix), the medieval *accessus ad auctores,* according to Judson Allen, appealed for justification exclusively to the moral value of poetry ("Allegory and the Form of the World: The Hidden Agenda of Literary Criticism," to appear in a collection of essays from the Seminar on Medieval and Renaissance Symbolism and Allegory of the Modern Language Association, ed. P. Aloysius Thomas). This critical commonplace has recently been amended by Glending Olson, "The Medieval Theory of Literature for Refreshment and its Use in the Fabliau Tradition," *SP,* 71 (1972), 291–313, but to an extent which would render autonomous only Chaucer's overt fabliaux, presumably those of the Miller, Reeve, Friar, Summoner, and Shipman, none of which is important to my case. The degree of moral emphasis this leads me to assume in works like the *Canterbury Tales* is comparable to that generally expected in a Victorian novel. Curtius contributes chapters on the poet as philosopher and as theologian (11 and 12) and Excursuses VII–XII.

3. T. P. Dunning, "Chaucer's Icarus-Complex: Some Notes on His Adventures in Theology," in G. I. Duthie, ed., *English Studies Today,* Series 3 (Edinburgh: Univ. Press, 1964), pp. 89–93, henceforth cited within text. The topic of "Providence, Predestination, and Destiny" was specifically and (for the greater part of the fourteenth century) freely debated at Oxford, pp. 89–91; the value of marriage was a perennial and less erudite topic of debate; it became crucial in the twelfth century with certain heresies which rejected the institution altogether, p. 93. When Dunning goes on to class those "many neo-Augustinian canons and theologians" who labeled the conjugal act a sin, as "quasi-heretical," he speaks loosely, since according to John T. Noonan, Jr., *Contraception* (Cambridge, Mass.: Belknap Press, 1965), *all* "canons and theologians" were "neo-Augustinian"; that is, they viewed sexual pleasure as a "defect" and the exclusive pursuit of it, even between married folk, as either a mortal sin (the "rigorist" view) or a venial (the milder and more prevalent view), pp. 131, 138, 250–252. Henceforth cited within text.

4. I find five occurrences in the *Canterbury Tales: KnT,* I,

3000–01; *WBP*, III, 1–2, 119–24; *FrT*, III, 1517 ff.; in attenuated form in *MchT*, IV, 2237–76; *ParsT*, X, 927. Another elaboration of the formula is the opening passage of the Prologue of the *Legend of Good Women*, reluctantly acknowledging authority on the topic of the afterlife (which we shall find relevant to the topic of destiny). All quotations are from *The Works of Geoffrey Chaucer*, ed. F. N. Robinson, 2nd ed. (Boston: Houghton Mifflin, 1957). Chaucer's attitude in such passages has been called "skeptical"; see Mary Thomas, *Medieval Skepticism and Chaucer* (New York: William Frederick Press, 1950); and Sheila Delany, *Chaucer's House of Fame: The Poetics of Skeptical Fideism* (Chicago: Univ. of Chicago Press, 1972), pp. 23–24 et passim. Henceforth cited as Delany.

5. E. K. Rand and H. F. Stewart, eds., Boethius, *Theological Tractates and Consolation of Philosophy*, Loeb Library (Cambridge, Mass.: Harvard Univ. Press, and London: William Heinemann, 1918), p. xi: "If it is asked why the *Consolation of Philosophy* contains no conscious or direct reference to the doctrines which are traced in the *Tractates* with so sure a hand, and is, at most, not out of harmony with Christianity, the answer is simple. In the *Consolation* he is writing philosophy; in the *Tractates* he is writing theology." See also Richard H. Green, ed. and trans., Boethius, *The Consolation of Philosophy* (New York: Bobbs, Merrill, 1962), p. xv. Pierre Courcelle, *La Consolation de Philosophie dans la tradition littéraire* (Paris: Études augustiniennes, 1967), to be quoted below. Nevertheless, scholars such as H. R. Patch and D. W. Robertson have persisted in Christianizing the *Consolation*, e.g., *Preface*, pp. 104, 364, 501; *The Tradition of Boethius* (New York: Oxford Univ. Press, 1935), pp. 6, 12, 18–19, 120, et passim. For example, Courcelle has to refute M.-T. D'Alverny's contention that Lady Philosophy's initial expulsion of the Muses of poetry is a rejection of secular literature in favor of Christian and to restate the obvious point that it is a rejection of emotional literature in favor of rational, pp. 34–35. C. S. Lewis agrees with Rand, Stewart, et al.; moreover, he disposes of the resulting anomaly of a Christian consoling himself for an approaching execution with "pauca quae ratio valet humana": he denies the relevancy of that biographical fact, since the work speaks of misfortune in general, not specifically of execution, *The Discarded Image* (Cambridge: University Press, 1967), pp. 76–77.

6. "This thoroughly Catholic man mentions Fortune so many times in this work and instead of the divine testimonies exhibits an empty literary word," *Dialogus super Auctores*, ed. R. B. C.

Huygens, Collection Latomus, 17 (Berchem-Brussels, 1955), p. 46, lines 63 ff.

7. "He does not express the incarnate Word," i.e., name Christ, *Policraticus*, VII, xv, 672b–c, ed. Clement Webb (Oxford: Clarendon Press, 1909), II, 155. Courcelle summarizes: "Les esprits les plus pénétrants du XIIe siècle avaient déjà fort bien compris et admis la position philosophique du chrétien Boèce. Ils n'adoptent nullement l'*interpretatio christiana* mise à la mode depuis Alcuin et Remi d'Auxerre; mais, contrairement à Bovo et d'autres, ils ne reprochent pas non plus à l'auteur de la *Consolation* de se placer sur le seul plan rationnel," pp. 343–44.

8. Dante's Virgil alludes to the *Consolation,* e.g., *Inf.* II, 61, 76–78, cf. VII 67 ff.; and Charles S. Singleton has shown that Virgil's "limited perspective" is associated by Dante with Boethius' perspective, "Lady Philosophy or Wisdom," in *Dante Studies II* (Cambridge, Mass.: Harvard Univ. Press, 1958), pp. 126–31. Henceforth cited within text.

9. "In regard to this, I want it to be superscribed with such an expression [*Formula vitae honestae*] because it teaches not those arduous and perfect things which are accomplished by a few outstanding worshippers of God, but it admonishes rather those things which are able to be fulfilled even without the precepts of divine scripture by the natural law of human intelligence only, even by laymen who live rightly and honestly," *Martini Episcopi Bracarensis Opera Omnia,* ed. Claude Barlow (New Haven: Yale Univ. Press, 1950), p. 237, also in *PL,* 72, 23, under the name Martinus Dumiensis. It is explicitly cited by Dante, *Convivio,* III, 8, citing 4, 33; and *De Monarchia,* II, 5, citing 5, 3. Chaucer's *Melibee* cites it, VII, 1070–71 (B[2], 2260–61) as "Senec"; VII, 1177 (B[2], 2367) as "the book," though Chaucer may have known it only indirectly through his main source, Renaud de Louens, which includes both citations.

10. A commentary by Molinet and a preface attributed to the influential sixteenth-century poet Clement Marot, both appended to redactions of the *Roman,* allegorized the Rose *in bono* in such a way that everything in the romance turns out to be allegory of Christian virtue: Jean Molinet, *Romant de la rose moralisie cler et net* (Verard, 1500), other eds. 1483; 1503; 1521; Clement Marot, supposed ed. and modernizer, "Exposition morale," prefixed to *Le Roman de la Rose dans la version attribuée à Clement Marot,* ed. Silvio F. Baridon and Antonio Viscardi (Milan: Instituto Editoriale Cisalpino, 1954), pp. 90–92; other eds. 1526, 1529, 1531, 1537–8. This allegorical approach is rejected by Rosemond Tuve, *Allegorical Imagery: Some Medieval Books and Their Posterity*

(Princeton: Princeton Univ. Press, 1966), pp. 233–331, et passim, in favor of the more modern ironic approach; but Marot and Molinet exemplify the extra-literal impulse behind all Christian interpretations of the *Roman;* for even Tuve and other Christian ironists continue to add further allegories to the anatomical and personification-allegories so obvious in the poem. For other readings which make Christianity the unspoken norm of the satire, see Charles Dahlberg, trans., *The Romance of the Rose* (Princeton: Princeton Univ. Press, 1971); Charles Dahlberg, "Macrobius and the Unity of the *Roman de la Rose*," *SP*, 58 (1961), 573–82; Robertson, pp. 91–104, et passim; and John V. Fleming, *The Roman de la Rose: A Study in Allegory and Iconography* (Princeton: Princeton Univ. Press, 1969), hereafter cited as Fleming.

11. "Solomon" is occasionally cited on sexual topics, but as just another philosopher, not as a voice of God. Reason's speeches occupy lines 2971–3098 in Guillaume's part and 4221–7230 in Jean's; her reference to Boethius as "Scripture" is 6291–99, citing *Cons.* IV, pr. 2, as noted by Ernest Langlois, ed., *Le Roman de la Rose*, SATF 71, (Paris: Firmin-Didot and Champion, 1914–24), 5 vols., from which all quotations are taken. The digression on mendicants, an ironic self-praise by the vice Faux Semblant, occupies 11006–12014, with Scriptural references passim (e.g., 11599 ff.). I am grateful to Professor Alice M. Colby of Cornell University for advice on the OF throughout.

12.   Ou se rent en aucun couvent,
        Qu'il ne set garder la franchise
        Que Nature avait en lui mise . . . .

He either repents his decision and leaves (Reason continues) or remains, held by Shame, and then:

        La vit a grant mesaise e pleure
        La franchise qu'il a perdue,
        Qui ne li peut estre rendue,
        Se n'est que Deus grace li face,
        Qui sa mesaise li efface
        E le tiegne en obedience
        Par la vertu de pacience. (4444–62)

Gerard Paré, *Les idées et les lettres au XIIIe siècle* (Montreal: Bibliothèque de la Philosophie, 1947), pp. 86, 187, reads all the lines quoted in the same way as I do and summarizes—in his earlier book *Le Roman de la Rose et la scolastique courtoise* (Ottawa: Institut d'Études Médiévales, and Paris: Librairie Philosophique J. Vrin, 1941), p. 202–"Certes, la morale de Jean de Meung ne respecte pas l'âme de la morale chrétienne; son roman n'est pas une recommandation de la fidélité conjugale, ni de la continence, et il n'a guère de sympathie pour les voeux de religion."

13. See C. F. Ward, ed., *The Epistles on the Romance of the Rose and Other Documents in the Debate* (Chicago: Univ. of Chicago Press, 1911). The only attacker of Jean's morality worth taking seriously is Jean Gerson, a century after the poem was written, and he fails to distinguish the speakers from the author and from each other in terms of credibility, and was so narrow-minded, as Paré points out (*Le Roman*, pp. 202–03), that he even condemned Aquinas.

14. "Narcissus, Pygmalion, and the Castration of Saturn . . . in the *Roman de la Rose*," *SP*, 71 (1974), 417 ff. This interpretation is adumbrated in Winthrop Wetherbee, *Platonism and Poetry in the Twelfth Century: The Literary Influence of the School of Chartres* (Princeton: Princeton Univ. Press, 1967), pp. 258–59. I am also indebted to Professors Hill and Wetherbee as well as to Professor Emerson Brown of Vanderbilt University for illuminating conversations on this and other problems in the *Roman*.

15. Wetherbee, *Platonism*, p. 258 and n. 34.

16. V. L. Dedeck-Héry, ed., "Boethius' *De Consolatione* by Jean de Meun," *Mediaeval Studies*, 14 (1952), 168–71, "experience" on p. 168.

17. Ronald Sutherland, *The Romaunt of the Rose and Le Roman de la Rose: A Parallel-Text Edition* (Oxford: Blackwell, 1967), pp. xxxiv–xxxv. The inauthentic Fragment B, which covers the unchristian sentiments of Reason cited above, does Christianize one of them, cf. *Romaunt*, 5030 with *RR*, 4547–48, and adds the line *Romaunt*, 5078 "Whanne in her love ther is no synne" between *RR*, 4589 and 4590, along with similar changes, passim. V. L. Dedeck-Héry does not mention any Christianizations of Boethius on the part of Chaucer, nor, for that matter, of Jean de Meun, "Jean de Meun et Chaucer, Traducteurs de la *Consolation* de Boèce," *PMLA*, 52 (1937) 967–91. At most, our authors perhaps add Christian nuances by translating words like *nefas* and *turpitudo* as "pechie/synne" and terms like *operante principio* as "de Dieu/by God."

18. E. Gilson, *Reason and Revelation in the Middle Ages* (New York: Charles Scribner's Sons, 1938), pp. 78–83. Aquinas, while usually a syncretist, adopted this perspective in the *Summa contra Gentiles* and also, according to Courcelle, in the strongly Boethi-

an *De aeternitate mundi contra murmurantes,* see *La Consolation,* p. 343. Other examples are given by Delany, Chapter 2.

19. "Lady Philosophy or Wisdom," pp. 126–27, 130–31. Since *"ventura* means 'fortune,'" she alludes to another Boethian and not particularly Christian theme. In the *Convivio,* the Boethian background of Dante's counselor, also called "Lady Philosophy," is explicit; see II, 12 and 15, ed. G. Busnelli and G. Vandelli, *Opere di Dante,* IV and V (Florence: Le Monnier, 1934–37), pp. 187–231; in some eds. the chapters are 13 and 16. Dante seems to have known that Boethius personally was a Christian, since he placed him in Paradise, *Par.* X, 124–29.

20. R. M. Lumiansky, "Chaucer's Philosophical Knight," *Tulane Studies in English,* 3 (1952), 47–68.

21. The speech occupies *KnT,* 2987–3072, though the direct echoes of Boethius end with 3015 (3030 possibly II, m. 1, a commonplace); principally *Cons.* II, m. 8 and IV, pr. 6 and m. 6, see also III, m. 9 and pr. 10. One stanza (XII, 6) of the speech attributed to Theseus in the source has been diverted to an earlier counsellor (Egeus) because, far from mentioning heaven or anything Christian, it lacks even the profounder of the Boethian consolations, 2837–52. On Chaucer's sympathy with and Boethian characterization of classical paganism, see T. P. Dunning, "God and Man in *Troilus and Criseyde,*" in *English and Medieval Studies Presented to J. R. R. Tolkien,* ed. Norman Davis and C. L. Wrenn (London: Allen & Unwin, 1962), pp. 164–82.

22. The *Monk's Tale* never mentions heaven in the sense of an afterlife. It is a significant anomaly—learned in the sense that its moral is derived from authority (see above) but falling short, as R. E. Kaske has shown, "The Knight's Interruption of the *Monk's Tale,*" *ELH,* 24 (1957), 249–68, of even the Knight's Boethian explanations for misfortune, let alone Christian explanations.

23. Edward Block, "Originality, Controlling Purpose, and Craftsmanship in Chaucer's *Man of Law's Tale,*" *PMLA,* 68 (1953), 572–616.

24. Article in progress.

25. The first question has long been recognized: R. E. Kaske has called attention to the second question, "Chaucer's Marriage Group," in Jerome Mitchell and William Provost, eds., *Chaucer the Love Poet* (Athens, Ga.: Univ. of Georgia Press, 1973), p. 47; the first formulation of it, however, is my own. The Franklin's relation to the Parson as I see it is similar to that which Donald Howard postulates, "The Conclusion of the Marriage Group: Chaucer and the Human Condition," *MP,* 57 (1960), 223–32, hereafter referred to as Howard.

26. Kathryn Hume, "Why Chaucer Calls the *Franklin's Tale* a Breton Lai," *PQ*, 51 (1972), 365–79.

27. Gertrude White, "The *Franklin's Tale:* Chaucer or the Critics," *PMLA*, 89 (1974), 456–7 et passim.

28. "Chaucer's Marriage Group," p. 54.

29. *Reason and Revelation*, pp. 58, 78.

30. A. J. Denomy, "The Two Moralities in *Troilus and Criseyde*," *Trans. Royal Soc. of Canada*, 3rd Ser., 44 (1950), 35–46. Andreas Capellanus, *The Art of Courtly Love*, trans. John Jay Parry (New York: Columbia Univ. Press, 1941). Delany goes further, declaring the latter as well as the former to be "the very model of fideism," pp. 26–27, 31–32, 116.

31. Carol V. Kaske, "Spenser's Pluralistic Universe: The View from the Mount of Contemplation (*FQ* I.x)," in R. Frushell and B. Vondersmith, eds., *Contemporary Thought on Spenser* (Carbondale, Ill.: Univ. of Southern Illinois Press, 1975), pp. 131–49 and 230–33.

32. I Tim. 1:4; 4:7; II Tim. 4:4; cf. 2:23. *Preface,* pp. 335–36 and n. 100. Two exegetes available to Chaucer and more popular than Robertson's *Glossa maior* are *Glossa ordinaria cum postilla . . . Nicolai de Lyra* (Venice: Paganinus de Paganinis, 1495) VI, f. 1277d; and Hugh of St. Cher, *Opera* (Lyon: Societas Bibliopolarum, 1645) VII, f. 203c. Both interpret I Tim. 1:4 of legends of the Jews; on I Tim. 4:7, each includes a literary interpretation similar to Robertson's: irrational fables without moral "fruit" should be avoided at least by the mature (*Glossa,* f. 1280d; Hugh f. 214d); on II Tim. 4:4 "fables" are again merely Mohammedan and Jewish apocrypha and superfluous doctrines (*Glossa,* f. 1386a; Hugh f. 229c).

33. Ralph Baldwin, *The Unity of the Canterbury Tales,* Anglistica, 5 (Copenhagen: Rosenkilde and Bagger, 1955), p. 99; E. Talbot Donaldson, ed., *Chaucer's Poetry: An Anthology for the Modern Reader* (New York: Ronald Press, 1958), pp. 949–50.

34. E. Talbot Donaldson, "Medieval Poetry and Medieval Sin," in *Speaking of Chaucer* (New York: W. W. Norton, 1970), pp. 168–69; Judson Allen, "The Old Way and the Parson's Way: An Ironic Reading of the *Parson's Tale,*" *Journal of Medieval and Renaissance Studies,* 3 (1973), 255–71. Besides my new evidence and disagreements of detail, my conclusions differ from those of Donaldson, Allen, and Dunning in seeing a pattern in the contradictions between the *Parson's Tale* and the secular tales.

35. Siegried Wenzel, "The Source of the 'Remedia' of the *Parson's Tale,*" *Traditio,* 17 (1971), 433 ff., esp. pp. 446 ff. Hereafter cited as Wenzel.

36. By a different route—namely, by tracing a Boethian limitation of perspective in works Chaucer seems to have read—I have come to a conclusion about the *Canterbury Tales* similar to that reached by Delany in the brief epilogue to her book on the *Hous of Fame,* which became available to me only when the present article was substantially completed. While I note a Christian voice almost from the beginning (that of the *MLT*), and hence cannot agree with her that religion is literally "not [Chaucer's] first idea but his last," my entire case is epitomized in her next words: religion "enters the structure of his work not as a credible solution to dialectic, but in fact as another term in dialectic" (p. 118).

9

The Historical Criticism
We Need

ROBERT O. PAYNE

A little more than ten years ago, sharing the excitement of that post-New-Criticism belief that we were beginning to come to terms with literary history in ways that did not require the abnegation of our aesthetic sensibilities, I wrote:

> We have sometimes been too easily trapped by the ease and specificity with which Chaucer's poetry suggests an interested, aware, and sensitive group of immediate respondents, and have concluded that Chaucer must have read it aloud before a select court circle, and dropped the matter at that. Yet *Troilus and Criseyde* not only expressed certain concerns about its own preservation and the durability of language in general, extending at least its ambitions for an audience far beyond any fourteenth-century court circle . . . All the members of the audience specified by the poem possess the same few characteristics, and these characteristics seem somehow to fit us all.[1]

When I wrote that, I was addressing some specific stylistic matters in one of Chaucer's poems, but I wish now to consider the broader theoretical implications.

179

The very phrase "Chaucer's audience" has been nearly pre-empted by an array of scholar-critics who would define it in a sense almost contradictory to my own. J. M. Manly (who had the virtue of never clouding these issues with any subtlety) said, in *Some New Light on Chaucer:*

> Chaucer was not writing for posterity or even for the whole contemporary population of England, but for a handful of courtiers, gentlemen, church-men, professional men, officials, and city merchants.[2]

A. C. Baugh, reviewing in 1951 a half-century of Chaucer criticism, confidently dismissed a considerable bundle of it with the apparently unexceptionable comment:

> I do not care to look too far below the surface of Chaucer's poetry to discern a meaning that few in the audience for which he wrote would have grasped.[3]

And to many of us the great surprise that closed the decade of the fifties was Bertrand Bronson's recantation of much of his own brilliant earlier criticism and his retreat, in *In Search of Chaucer,* to a near Manly historicism and the plea that, in the name of Chaucer's audience, we should severely inhibit our perverse modern concern with "meaning, structure, design, pattern, rhetoric, imagery, symbol, myth, and persona,"[4] and attend rather to "a poet who deliberately practised a style capable of being instantly followed by a moderately attentive ear, and who seems to have had a genuine liking for russet yeas and honest kersey noes."[5]

But for the past decade or so, the most obtrusive avatar of hard-nosed historicism has been the neo-exegetical dogma, with its insistence that literary theories call into being the art they define, and so can never be applied to any poetry that predates them. D. W. Robertson had made a laudably flat-footed statement of the position in his English Institute paper on "Historical Criticism" in 1950:

> [The historical critic] shares the respect of the literary critic for the artistic integrity of the works with which he has to deal, but he looks with some misapprehension on the tendency of the literary critic to regard older literature in the light of modern aesthetic systems, economic philosophies, or psychological theories. He feels that such systems, whatever their value may be, do not exist before they are formulated.[6]

Later, in *A Preface to Chaucer*, he hacked at the knot again with the same historical-deterministic axe:

> [Chaucer's artistry] depends for its effectiveness, like the artistry of any other period, on what the audience brings to it. . . . The fact that our minds are differently conditioned . . . makes the task of recovering Chaucer's art extremely difficult.[7]

Now, however oddly ironic it may seem to crowd Manly, Baugh, Bronson, and Robertson into the same bracket as literary critics, there is a single premise necessary to their several arguments (and to many others over the past century), namely, that the responses of Chaucer's immediate contemporaries are the only ones his poetry will properly allow. In the need to be brief, I must risk the appearance of rudeness to learned and perceptive men in order to argue bluntly that that is a fatally untenable premise, which produces both bad criticism and bad history.

First, we should make two or three distinctions, none of them new but all of them too frequently blurred by many of us when we entangle ourselves in this "historical criticism" question. To begin with, we must insist on a workable differentiation between linguistic and aesthetic analysis.

The documentation we can produce to throw light on Chaucer's times is related to his poems mainly as *linguistic* information; that is, if it is properly investigated and interpreted, it can tell us much about the correspondences between the evolving *common* forms of life and the evolving *common* forms of speech. Beyond that, historical-linguistic documentation can tell us almost nothing at all about what *new construct* a poet might willfully create out of languge in order to illuminate, resist, or alter the course of life—or perhaps even to express himself. With the exception of John Speirs and D. W. Robertson, I know of no critics (literary, historical or otherwise) who have ever argued that we need not attend as closely as we can to the language Chaucer wrote, as a pre-condition to the best understanding of his poetry. And even the neo-exegetes, despite the scorn they regularly avow in their prefaces for what the texts of medieval poetry actually say, have produced some useful glosses for several lines in medieval poetry.

Still, we *seem* too often to forget what we all had so carefully to learn about language study: that, in the historical/ statistical sense, all native speakers theoretically have a perfect knowledge of their own language; but how many of the native speakers you know would you trust to explicate a poem by Robert Lowell? This question is in no way frivolous. Surely, we will never begin to enjoy Chaucer's poetry until we know his language; equally surely, even a Ricardian courtier's perfect knowledge of Middle English would guarantee us next to nothing in the aesthetic comprehension of *Troilus and Criseyde*.

There is another distinction that is even more important—harder to make and harder to make clear: The history of taste is a fascinating and useful study, but it is not the same as literary history. What is most wrong with the negative historicism of the Manly-Baugh-Bronson-Robertson line is that it works only if we are willing to agree that what the people of a given era found good in a work of art is a necessary, sufficient, and limiting definition of what *is* good in it. The corollary—rarely if ever stated by such "historical critics"—would have to be that it is impossible for a poem to mean anything its contemporary audience did not perceive in it, or possess any values they did not appreciate. Since most of the poets I know, from before Chaucer to our youngest contemporaries, have complained at one time or another (many of them fairly constantly) that their audiences kept missing their best effects, it is hard to know what basis there is for confidence that, in literary criticism, the contemporary consumer is always right

It should also be mentioned that very few of those who urge us to restrict our responses to what Chaucer's contemporaries saw and felt in his poetry agree among themselves about what those fourteenth-century responses were—largely because, in simple fact, we have no way of knowing except through the most indirect and inferential kinds of evidence. No contemporary essays in criticism survive; not until Sidney (briefly), and still later Dryden, does anyone tell us even sketchily how he read Chaucer's poems. About nine times in ten, when someone tells us "this interpretation or evaluation of Chaucer's poem is wrong because Chaucer's audience could not have made it," he is really saying one of two things: "I know some other fourteenth-century book (maybe even a fifth- or eighth-century one) which I think says something different"; or, more likely, "I don't interpret the poem that way myself; I must therefore assume that no one else who really knows Chaucer sensitively and intimately—that is, his contemporary audience—could have read him that way either."

This embarrassment—the embarrassment of being committed to a critical method for which the materials necessary to exercise it just do not exist—is probably what generates the persistent negativism common to all the diverse "historical criticisms" I have mentioned. The one thing upon which they all agree, in the name of Chaucer's Ricardian readers, is that if a response to his poems is modern, it cannot be right. More than half a century before Robertson's pontifical longueurs and Bronson's graceful, elegant Alexander lectures, Manly made their point clearly in his famous essay on the Knight:

> It seems to me that this portrait—like all the others in this and other ancient galleries—has faded a little, that time has taken away the richness of coloring which was such a wonder and delight to the contemporaries of the artist and left us only line and hints of light and shade. I do not wish to retouch the portrait, to *spoil it with crude bright modern colors,* but, if possible, to apply to it a 're-viver' made of extracts from certain old documents. . . . [8]

The italics are mine, but the emphasis is authentically Manly's: modern colors could only spoil the portrait, are always crude and too bright.

This brings us to a third matter which it seems to me has become badly confused in much of our discussion of historical criticism. The negative, exclusivist version of historical criticism has constantly to try to live with two contradictory logics, one absolutist and one relativistic in the extreme. First we are told that there is one and only one "truth" about literature and that it is recoverable for us moderns if we use the one true method of repressing all our own responses and miming those of some prior era. At the same time, we are admonished that the 'truth" about literature changes with each period, is irretrievably locked in the souls of contemporaries, so that what subsequent readers think of it is nearly certain to be wrong. That paradoxical position is wrong on several counts, historical and literary as well as logical; probably most important is that it rules out *a priori* any diachronic theory of literature. In addition it is interesting to point out that the archeological view of literature, the urge to know exactly what a poem meant to its immediate contemporaries (and conversely, what it tells us about its surrounding culture), is itself a quite modern view.

Morton Bloomfield's indispensable essay on "Chaucer's Sense of History"[9] quite rightly reminds us that a new *Diesseitsstimmung* is dawning in Chaucer's own time, one which "is rather basically a new heightened attention toward past, present, and future . . . [and] may manifest itself in an emphasis on the pastness of the past or on the reality of the present. . . ." Although Bloomfield may be right that "Chaucer is historically minded as compared with his English contemporaries," the clearest expression I know in fourteenth-century poetry of a historical theory of literature comes in the opening of the anonymous *Gest Historiale of the Destruction of Troy*. In a passage that surely must have pleased Manly with its distrust of crude modern colors, the poet tells us he wants to save the old stories from being "swolowet into swym by swiftness of yeres" so that they

> May be solas to sum that it segh never,
> Be writyng of wees that wist it in dede,
> With sight for to serche, of hom that suet after,
> To ken all the crafte how the case felle,
> By loking of letturs that lefte were of olde.[10] (22–26)

But, especially in the context of the present argument, I believe a more common fourteenth-century sense of the matter is expressed by Gower in the preface to the *Confessio Amantis*:

> Of hem that writen ous tofore
> The bokes duelle, and we therfore
> Ben tawht of that was write tho;
> Forthi good is that we also
> In our tyme among ous hiere
> Do wryte of newe som matiere,
> Ensampled of these olde wyse

So that it myhte in such a wyse,
When we ben dede and elleswhere
Beleve to the worldes eere
In tyme comende after this.[11] (*CA*, Pro 1–11)

Gower's confidence that he can make his own aesthetic uses of the past, and that he writes for the future or for all time even more than for his own contemporaries, if given the rephrasing I have just given it, would certainly be stigmatized as "modernistic" and anti-historical by any of the four historical critics I cited earlier. Yet the passage from the *Destruction of Troy* is much the more "modern"; and if the neo-exegetes really mean it when they insist that we may not use in our exploration of fourteenth-century poetry any critical tools we cannot prove were available to fourteenth-century readers, then it is fortunate for them that the passage was not lost in the shuffle of manuscript transmission.

What is wrong, fundamentally, is that somehow we have allowed the phrase "historical criticism" to accrue almost wholly negative implications, to come to stand for a way of keeping ourselves from making wrong interpretations and evaluations. It is most saddening that this position stems ultimately from our distrust of our personal responses to great poems and our fear that they may be different from other's responses. Knowing, as all of us do, our critical fallibility, we seem almost irresistibly lured by the promise of the Rosetta stone, the key, the pony, the guaranteed response, and get rid of troublesomely different responses by "proving" that Richard's courtiers could not have made them. In that form, "historical criticism" is sheer self-deception. It only buries our personal fallibility another layer deeper. As far as literary criticism is concerned, we have to invent that Ricardian audience for ourselves; and the likelihood that in inventing it we will mirror ourselves is even greater than that we will project ourselves into the text of a poem which we did not invent. This, I feel sure, is a ma-

jor reason why those who are so certain Chaucer's audience can tell us what responses we can *not* make to his poems do not agree, any more than the rest of us, upon what
we *can* make of them.

The first thing we must do to provide a more positive historical criticism is to make it a search, however risky and
imperfect, for what can be discovered in the past, whether
or not we think it ought to be there. In an unpublished paper taking issue with Bronson's *In Search of Chaucer*, E. Talbot Donaldson put the matter nicely:

> We have excellent notions, grounded on firm pos-
> itive evidence, of how certain past eras character-
> istically thought, and we can safely generalize
> about them. But we may not legislate for every in-
> dividual in the lawless past; the one thing that
> people are capable of is imagining anything. We
> may not expect to find a certain idea in medieval
> literature, but we cannot ward it off with the Ber-
> keleian principle, "If I can't see you, you can't be
> you."[12]

Even that seems to me not to tell us enough about what
we *can* do as historical critics. For that, we may look at a
quote from the pre-lapsarian Bronson, from his 1940 essay
"Chaucer's Audience":

> If it be true that Chaucer kept in view while he
> wrote, the needs and predilections of those who
> were to hear him, *it is true also that, in a sense, his
> works are a judgment of his public.*[13]

That last clause can only mean that we must characterize
the Ricardian era by Chaucer's poems, and the only way to
do that is to make for ourselves the best independent judgments we can of the poems. It is a matter of great interest to
the literary historian which poems people preferred, what

things in them they responded to most, and what the preferences imply. He will never find out, if he is not prepared to make his own assessment of the poems—to know, or perhaps only to suspect, that some of the preferences were good and some less good or bad. To say of Chaucer's audience that it had a high or low level of literary taste is inescapably to say—at least in considerable part—that one's own critical judgment agrees or disagrees with theirs.

Rossell Hope Robbins was surely right in his tart reminder to John Speirs that "Literature, quite apart from its other qualities, is not an excrescence on life; it is something said, by a certain man, to a certain audience, at a certain time."[14] He would surely also agree that that is not all it is; for the rest of us, in far different times, do overhear and care. And all of us living through the Nixon years certainly know that the motives of the eavesdropper are seldom coincident with those of the parties he overhears.

There is no escape, finally, from the exercise of our own literary judgment. Just as George Kane, in his brilliant re-editing of the A-texts of *Piers Plowman*[15] concluded that the only solution was to exercise his best judgment as early, responsibly, and openly as possible, so I suspect that we historical critics have to come out of the closet and admit that we are not simply cultural historians.

Donald R. Howard made a similar point in his recent essay on the state of *Gawain* studies:

> . . . we must remember that the poem was not necessarily admired in its own time, not necessarily in tune with its contemporary background. Why did it fall into oblivion? Perhaps by mistake; or perhaps because its form and ideas seemed old-fashioned at the end of the fourteenth century; but perhaps also because its style and treatment did not suit the tastes of fourteenth- and fifteenth-century men, did not fulfill *their* literary and aesthetic expectations . . .
> . . . we can say that men of the nineteenth centu-

ry invented this poem: that is, they conceived the idea of what to look for among the shards of the Cottonian library. And we can say that we of the twentieth century invented it: that is, we conceived the idea of what to look for in the poem which gives it the status we honor.[16]

Still even that won't quite do it. It is not so much that we invent *Gawain* as that we create—we must create—the best whole literary past we can. We need not only a cultural history, but a *musée imaginaire*, a refined and informed sense of what we need most and love best in the past. We need to stock our literary *musée imaginaire* with things both this side and the other side of Chaucer. Once we have read Spenser, Yeats, and Stevens, there is no way that Chaucer can look the same to us as he looked to his contemporaries. If we are to have a literary past which doesn't end with Chaucer's death and which is still alive in our active sense of values, then it is aesthetic suicide to commit ourselves to the aesthetic charade we have been offered recently as "historical criticism."

There is one last point, though in the act of offering it I am uncomfortably reminded that the etymon of the word "critic" means "to weigh" more than it means "to conclude." However much the positivism of the nineteenth century and the relativism of the early twentieth may have discredited the notion, I am still not convinced that we may not, if we love poetry, be responding to the same or very similar things in the poetry of any age. If that is possibly true, it is a very important function of the historical critic to try to find out.

A very long time ago, long before the neo-exegetes had nearly reversed the import of his aesthetic perceptions, Augustine wrote:

Moreover, in the speeches and sayings of the eloquent, the precepts of eloquence are found to have been fulfilled, although the speakers did not think of them in order to be eloquent or while they were being eloquent; and they were eloquent whether they had learned the rules, or never came in contact with them.[17]

In this question, Augustine is a far safer guide than Robertson. Systems may indeed exist before they are formulated, and only a proper and open historical criticism will ever be able to find out. If modern readers value the complexity, the ambiguity, the formal ingenuity of Chaucer's poetry more than his Ricardian contemporaries did, that does not prove that those qualities are not in his poetry, although it may well indicate that all great poetry survives because no age ever exhausts it.

"Glose whoso wole, and seye bothe up and doun" that the only proper way to understand a medieval poem is to resist heroically the seductive delusions of what it says and how it makes us feel, "the experience woot wel it is noght so."

THE GRADUATE CENTER AND HERBERT H. LEHMAN COLLEGE
OF THE CITY UNIVERSITY OF NEW YORK

FOOTNOTES

1. Robert O. Payne, *The Key to Remembrance: A Study of Chaucer's Poetics* (New Haven: Yale Univ. Press, 1963), p. 228.

2. J. M. Manly, *Some New Light on Chaucer* (New York: Henry Holt, 1926), p. 76.

3. Albert C. Baugh, "Fifty Years of Chaucer Scholarship," *Speculum,* 26 (1951), 665.

4. Bertrand H. Bronson, *In Search of Chaucer* (Toronto: Univ. of Toronto Press, 1960), pp. 8–9.

5. Op. cit., p. 10.

6. D. W. Robertson, Jr, "Historical Criticism," in *English Institute Essays 1950,* ed. Alan S. Downer (New York: Columbia Univ. Press, 1951), p. 4

7. D. W. Robertson, Jr., *A Preface to Chaucer* (Princeton: Princeton Univ. Press, 1962), p. 502.

8. J. M. Manly, "A Knight Ther Was," *Trans. and Proc. of the American Philological Association*, 38 (1907), 89.

9. Morton W. Bloomfield, "Chaucer's Sense of History," *JEGP*, 51 (1952), 304, 305.

10. *Gest Historiale of the Destruction of Troy*, ed. G. A. Pantin and D. Donaldson, *EETS*, 39 (London, 1866), pp. 1–2.

11. *The Complete Works of John Gower*, ed. George C. Macaulay (Oxford: Clarendon Press, 1900), 2. 1–2. Also in *EETS*, es 81 (London, 1900), pp. 1–2.

12. E. Talbot Donaldson, a paper read at English Group 3, Modern Language Association of America, December 1972.

13. Bertrand H. Bronson, "Chaucer's Audience," in *Five Studies in Literature* (Berkeley: Univ. of California Press, 1940), p. 49.

14. Rossell Hope Robbins "Middle English Misunderstood: Mr. Speirs and the Goblins," *Anglia* 75 (1967), 275.

15. George Kane, *Piers Plowman The A Version: Will's Vision of Piers Plowman and Do-Well* (London: Athlone Press, 1960).

16. Donald R. Howard, "Sir Gawain and the Green Knight," in *Recent Middle English Scholarship*, ed. J. Burke Severs (Pittsburgh: Duquesne Univ. Press, 1971), pp. 44–45.

17. *De Doctrina Christiana*, Bk. IV, iii, trans. D. W. Robertson, Jr. (New York: Liberal Arts Press, 1958), p. 120.

10

Chaucer and Modernism: An Essay in Criticism

MARTIN STEVENS

One of the principal assumptions in D. W. Robertson's approach to Chaucer is that, to quote the Introduction to his *Preface to Chaucer,* "there are profound differences between the arts of the Middle Ages and those of modern times."[1] As a result, Robertson argues, we cannot rely on the canons of modern aesthetic theory to understand Chaucer and his times. What we need instead is a full acquaintance with the principles of medieval aesthetics, and our approach to Chaucer, once we have acquired such acquaintance, must become historically oriented. Robertson's application of medieval aesthetics to the study of Chaucer and to medieval literature at large has attracted sufficient attention elsewhere; hence I will not discuss that phase of his work here. What has not so far occupied the critics of Robertson's important book is his discussion of the modern temperament, a subject which occupies, directly or indirectly, the general introduction of the volume and which subsumes essentially all that follows. I believe that the gravest shortcoming of the Robertsonian approach lies squarely in its postulation of the "modern," not the "medieval aesthetic." Because the historical approach is finally justified by what Robertson considers the inadequacy of modern thought in coming to terms with the medieval aesthetic, it is important for us to take a second look at the Robertsonian conception of the "modern."

Perhaps the single most astonishing feature of Robertson's view of the modern is his pervasive identification of the romantic with all aesthetic movements that have taken place since 1800. Indeed, the year 1800 is, according to this formulation, the great watershed. We read:

> The extent to which the colorful harmonies and deliberate dissonances of romanticism still influence our historical and aesthetic ideals is not commonly realized. The various aesthetic systems that have arisen since art became an entity in itself have a valid application to post-romantic art and literature, but they have little relevance to the art and literature of the pre-romantic past. (p. 9)

Over and over in the pages of his introduction the words "romantic" and "modern" are used virtually interchangeably. We are told about the tenacity with which the romantic imagination dominates the modern mind (p. 18), about "our romantic expectations concerning what a good plot should be" (p. 46), about how "romantic art" has influenced the modern mind to a "non-discursive awareness of 'the mystery of things'" (p. 33). The so-called "modern" writers cited who demonstrate the romantic aesthetic in operation are the following: Goethe, Wordsworth, Blake, Coleridge, Byron, Shelley, Leigh Hunt, Jacob Grimm, A. W. Schlegel, John Stuart Mill, Rousseau, H. G. Wells, G. B. Shaw, T. S. Eliot, and W. B. Yeats. What is truly remarkable about this list of writers is the absence, once one gets past the name of Eliot, of any and all modern critics. One wonders, for example, what T. E. Hulme or F R. Leavis or Jose Ortega y Gasset would have to say to Robertson's facile identification of the modern with the romantic. Any work which addresses itself, even indirectly, to the modern temperament and relies on such a list of writers while disregarding names like Burke, Wilson, Richards, Beckett, Brecht, Artaud, Empson, Levi-Strauss, Robbe-Grillet, Langer and Barthes (to mention just a few) has to be hopelessly out of touch with the realities of contemporary criticism.

When one looks specifically into what Robertson deems the modern aesthetic, he discovers the following characteristics to dominate the critical outlook. (It should be added that these characteristics are nowhere clearly enumerated; they are extrapolated from a rather diffusive and digressive discussion in the Introduction.) First, modern thought, according to Robertson, is marked by a tendency to think in terms of polarities, "of opposites whose dynamic interaction leads to a synthesis" (p. 6). In contrast, the Middle Ages tended "to think in terms of symmetrical patterns" (p. 6). There is no systematic demonstration of the modern concept of opposites, but later in the chapter reference is made to the inapplicability of "dramatic contraries in the modern sense" to the discussion of such medieval topics as the Old Law and the New and of cupidity and charity (p. 24). Second, the modern (romantic?) temperament "envisages the artist as a man in dynamic opposition to the conventions of his society" (p. 10); in short, the romantic/modern is a rebel. In contrast, says Robertson, "rebelliousness in the Middle Ages was usually . . . within the limits of the hierarchical ideal" (p. 11). Third, the romantic/modern "is characteristically interested in tensions, in the pursuit of unsatisfied desires, in a dynamic quest which may be . . . a means of salvation" (p. 12). Such tension elevates to a primary position self-expression and "the unveiling of the sensitive heart" (p. 12). According to Robertson "the search for self expression of this kind in medieval literature almost always leads to disappointment" (p. 12). Fourth, the romantic/modern insists that "to be 'human' [is] a matter of the free development of the feelings rather than a matter of wisdom, a matter of 'nature' rather than a matter of 'grace'" (p. 44). As a corollary, romantic/modern art is emotional rather than intellectual in its appeal, "it 'moves' its audience, not to think necessarily, but to feel . . ." (p. 33). In sum, then, the "modern" way of perceiving, which includes making polarities, creating tensions, stirring oppositions, and surrendering to the feelings, blocks our capacity to understand the Middle Ages.

Quite apart from the crucial error of lumping all that is modern under the rubric of "romanticism," Robertson's analysis fails because it never demonstrates the validity of its thesis, particularly as it applies to the criticism of Chaucer. Who exactly are the misguided critics against whom he is tilting? The *Preface* was first published in 1962. By that time Charles Muscatine's influential book on *Chaucer and the French Tradition* had already been in print for five years. Was he speaking among others of Muscatine? Or about Ralph Baldwin's study of *The Unity of the Canterbury Tales,* published in 1955? Or perhaps about the work of Donaldson, Lumiansky, Malone, Patch, Root, Speirs, Tatlock, Manly, or even Kittredge and C. S. Lewis? Were these the Chaucer critics who created tensions, stirred oppositions, or made polarities? Robertson doesn't say. We get only the vaguest sort of generality about the criticism to which he objects: "it has become commonplace to think of the troubadors as rebels" (p. 10) or "we have shed many a misguided tear over the 'tragedy' of that sweet young thing the prioress" (p. 45). Nowhere in the introduction is there reference to a medieval scholar of the past fifty years to whose approach Mr. Robertson would take exception. (Indeed, the only two scholars of medieval literature whom he mentions by name, in footnotes, Vittore Branca and Dorothy Whitelock, he seems to admire greatly.) The nearest he ever comes to associating his general observations with a specific writer on the Middle Ages is his allusion to Walter Pater whose "elegant" description of *Aucassin e Nicolette* he praises. Is Robertson, then, in any way concerned with a serious reappraisal of twentieth-century attitudes toward

Chaucer or the Middle Ages? Manifestly not. At most, he seems to tell us that romantic critics and poets of the nineteenth century were not in consonance with the *Zeitgeist* of the Middle Ages, a message that will not come as a great surprise to anyone who has the least smattering of cultural history. All this is to say that the observations about the modern temperament in Robertson's *Preface* are either wrong or useless or both, and as justification for a new approach to Chaucer, they verge on the disingenuous.

On further consideration, Robertson appears to me to have trained his heavy artillery on the wrong target: he should have fired not on nineteenth-century romantic critics, who as readers of Chaucer remain reasonably blameless for the dominant mode of twentieth-century interpretations, but on the realists, who, until very recent times, have all but held sway over the critical study of Chaucer. A closer look at the so-called "modern" era of Chaucer criticism will make clear that, as in other areas of aesthetic concern, there is a vast difference between the canons that dominated the *fin de siecle* and those that dominate the contemporary scene. What was really objectionable in the outlook of most critics who preceded Robertson was not so much their general romantic proclivities but their realism. As is well known, it is especially the reaction to the latter which has shaped the contemporary view of the arts. Whether consciously or not, present-day criticism of Chaucer—as of all other major figures in English literary history—is guided, I believe, by a new realization that literature is not life and that art is governed by its own form and substance. I believe further that when one reexamines the dominant aesthetic of our times, one will readily perceive a very close resemblance between the modern and the medieval. In what follows I propose, therefore, to consider Chaucer and Chaucerian criticism in the light of what one of the foremost modern theorists, Jose Ortega y Gasset, has to say about modern art. My basic text will be Ortega's famous essay "The Dehumanization of Art,"[2] which is acknowledged by many as something of a manifesto for the contemporary consciousness.

I hope I shall not be belaboring the obvious by proposing first of all to review Ortega's principal conceptions of the role and nature of modern art as these are summarized in the aforementioned essay. Ortega begins his analysis by characterizing all that is modern in art as unpopular and anti-popular (pp. 4–5). For him, the romanticism of the last century "was the prototype of a popular style" (p. 5), making its appeal to the masses essentially by letting its works of art concentrate almost wholly on what he calls "a fiction of human realities" (p. 11). He envisages the last century and a half (speaking in 1925) as essentially an aberration in human taste, a surrender by the elite to the demands of the vulgar who have always dominated the arts in times of greatest excitement. Above all, Ortega y Gasset is disturbed by the preoccupation of the nineteenth century "with the human content" of artistic works, a content which, in his mind, is "incompatible with aesthetic enjoyment proper" (pp. 9–10). To illustrate the sort of human content that gives pleasure to the masses and hence that informs the art of the last century, he cites the following:

> A man likes a play when he has become interested in the human destinies presented to him, when the love and hatred, the joys and sorrows of the personages so move his heart that he participates in it all as though it were happening in real life. And he calls a work "good" if it succeeds in creating the illusion necessary to make the imaginary personages appear like living persons. In poetry he seeks the passions and pain of the man behind the poet. Paintings attract him if he finds on them figures of men or women whom it would be interesting to meet. A landscape is pronounced "pret-

ty" if the country it represents deserves for its
loveliness or its grandeur to be visited on a trip.
(pp. 8–9)

The modern consciousness, in contrast, puts all of its energy into the "dehumanization of art" (pp. 22–23). The artist
in our time, according to Ortega, does all in his power to
create an emotional distance between himself and reality;
indeed, for the modern artist "an object of art is artistic
only in so far as it is not real" (p. 10). The new style, then,
never confuses life with art, and it regards art as nothing
but an artifice. "Dehumanization" must, therefore, be interpreted to mean the removal of human concerns from the
artistic consciousness. The artist, as Ortega sees him, "is
brazenly set on deforming reality, shattering its human aspect" (p. 21) and constructing something that "possesses
any substance of its own" (p. 23). Such art is, as Ortega puts
it, "a thing of no consequence"; that is, it does not set out
to change human destinies or to create revolutions. Rather,
it is centrally concerned with its own perspective, with its
peculiar mode of seeing. It exists in the realm of play, and
because it conceives of the artist as the center of his own
creation, its vision is essentially ironic.

With this inadequate and necessarily partial summary of
Ortega, I would like to return to Chaucer and Chaucerians.
It seems to me that the course of Chaucer criticism over the
past hundred years or so has concentrated on its subject
much in the manner that Ortega y Gasset has characterized
as belonging to the nineteenth century. While we may wish
to moderate some of Ortega's more extravagant observations, I think it undeniably true that Chaucer criticism from
roughly 1850 to 1950 focused almost entirely on the
"fiction of human realities" and thus on a very partial and
often unenlightening aspect of its subject matter. To the extent that this criticism grew out of a confusion of art with
life, Robertson is no doubt right in characterizing it as ro-

mantic. But what Robertson does not seem to realize is, first of all, that the failure of that criticism lies centrally in its realistic assumptions (rather than its polarities or tensions), and, secondly, that it now has ceased to exist as a mode of interpretation to be reckoned with. Ironically, Robertson's own book is at the center of a newly-created school of interpretation which, for all its methodological differences in approaching Chaucer, yet puts the work of art and its aesthetic design at the center of its interest. If I am right in my characterization of the old "realist" school of criticism and the new "modernist" school (I am cognizant of the shudder that the term will bring forth), then we should be able to see in the Chaucer criticism of the past one hundred and twenty-five to fifty years an interesting reflection of the shifting consciousness in the arts generally. I think that shift in interpretation has already taken place, though not without its cultural lag, for applied criticism seems generally to follow its informing theory by one generation and the style that inspired it by at least two. In this sense the realist school of Chaucer criticism stands in the same relationship to nineteenth-century realism as, in the eyes of O. B. Hardison, the organic structure theory in drama stands to the social-Darwinians. Indeed, as Hardison has so brilliantly shown, even the essential scholarship can be deeply influenced by a prevailing *Weltanschauung*.[3] It is my firm belief that both the realist and the modernist schools of Chaucer criticism are the expression of their times. Let us take a closer look at a specific problem.

One of the most enduring conceptions in Chaucer scholarship and criticism over the past hundred or so years has been that which regards the *Canterbury Tales* as a form of "roadside drama." According to this interpretation, the real structure of the work, despite the absence of the usual conventions, is dramatic, and the tales themselves—or at least those worth bothering with—are of interest in direct proportion to how much they reveal of their tellers. Roadside drama critics focus on the believability and consistency of

the pilgrims as characters; the tales become the vehicle by
means of which Chaucer gives life to his personages. And
all is done in the service of realism: the storytelling contest
is seen against the backdrop of the Tabard Inn and the road
to Canterbury, and the whole is carefully measured to fit
the time span of an actual pilgrimage. Art is thus seen as an
extension of medieval life in which characters are admired
most for being lifelike.

More than a hundred years ago, roadside realism was
first invoked by Henry Bradshaw to adduce an order rival-
ing the Ellesmere order for the *Canterbury Tales*. Basically,
Bradshaw and his adherents argue that Chaucer was so attentive to place and time in constructing his framework that
he would never have alluded, out of sequence, to Sittingbourne before Rochester on the way from London to Canterbury. The guiding notion behind one of the major order-
ings of *The Canterbury Tales* is, therefore, strictly a matter
of realism: the representation of place and time is taken as
the very mortar of Chaucer's fiction; it takes precedence
even over the evidence accrued from the best surviving
manuscript. When Robert A. Pratt revived the Bradshaw
shift in 1951, he opened his now famous article as follows:

> Chaucer envisaged the *Canterbury Tales* as pre-
> sented on the actual London-Canterbury road at
> various times during successive days, for he offers
> about seven allusions to place and at least five to
> time, scattered throughout eight of the nine Frag-
> ments which make up the work.[4]

The crucial word in this sentence is "actual," for it is solely
actuality that ultimately determines Pratt's preference. (It is
well to remind ourselves that the *Canterbury Tales* took
place on a fictional, not an actual, road from London to
Canterbury.) And perhaps even more revealing, Pratt discards the Ellesmere order entirely on the basis of geograph-
ical distortion. So strongly, then, was realism entrenched in

the critical outlook of Chaucerians over the nearly one hundred years between Bradshaw and Pratt that a whole new ordering of the *Tales* was accomplished in its service. As a criterion for editing, the "reality–principle" offered opportunity for one and all textual architects to build their structures. Upon discovering the "Bradshaw shift," F. J. Furnivall exclaimed, "A happy hit! and it sets us free to alter the arrangement of any or all of the MSS, to move up or down any *Groups* of Tales, whenever internal evidence, probability, or presumption, requires it." He then proceeds to move Fragment VI after Fragment VII because the Pardoner "wole bothe drynke and eten of a cake" (322), clearly, in Furnivall's view, referring to breakfast and thus an indication that a new day's tale-telling is about to begin.[5] Such is the house of fiction that realists build!

What the realists fail to take into account is that Chaucer was not one of them. Anyone who can make Troy into a medieval city is not likely to be deeply concerned over or even cognizant of the fact that Sittingbourne should come after Rochester on the way from London to Canterbury. And especially is such the case when literally quires of pages intervene between the two references (Sittingbourne is mentioned in Fragment III; Rochester in Fragment VII). Chaucer simply was not obsessed by an urge to create a faithful illusion of reality. He needed occasional milestones to highlight the general setting of his fictional pilgrimage, but he was not over-concerned in rendering a unified photographic account of the journey. Nor was he otherwise bound by the broadly representational design of his fiction. It was perfectly possible for him to have the Miller and the Reeve engage in a lingering roadside argument, even though one was at the head of the file and the other at the end. It was likewise possible for him to break the storytelling frame almost at will. Take, for example, such a simple lapse as line 1201 of the *Knight's Tale,* when the narrator says "But of that storie list me nat to write."[6] Here, with one stroke of the pen, Chaucer has suddenly removed fictive narrator and audience altogether, and what remains is a straightforward telling of the story of Palamon and Arcite by the poet to the reader. All this is to say that Chaucer used his design when he needed it, but he was also entirely free to discard it when it did not serve his purposes.[7]

Before we continue with our consideration of the "roadside drama" theory, let us pause just long enough to make some general observations about the rise of realism in the literature of Western civilization. While it is true that, as Ortega y Gasset has shown, realism is a dominant force of the nineteenth century, especially in its dictation of the canons of criticism, it gained its rise with the advent of the Enlightenment. Ian Watt observes in *The Rise of the Novel* that "modern realism . . . begins from the position that truth can be discovered by the individual through his senses: it has its origins in Descartes and Locke, and received its first full formulation by Thomas Reid in the middle of the eighteenth-century."[8] Watt, in fact, sees the novel as the formal narrative structure of realism; it was not possible, in his view, for any fiction to contain "a full and authentic report of human experience," until literary artists concerned themselves with the faithful representation of particularized time and space, and that first happened systematically in the fiction of Daniel Defoe.[9] It follows, therefore, that Chaucer was neither a realist nor a novelist. Like Shakespeare, he is concerned with temporal flux only as it contrasts with the eternal designs of the universe and never as an end in itself. Ian Watt ascribes to Shakespeare and his predecessors an "a-historical outlook" which is "associated with a striking lack of interest in the minute-by-minute and day-to-day temporal setting" and which causes all kinds of dislocations in the time schemes of their narratives.[10] Indeed, the word "anachronism" did not appear in our language until the middle of the seventeenth century (and in the critical sense of "something existing out of date" not until the nineteenth century; see *O.E.D.*, s.v. "Anachronism"). For Chaucer, as for Shakespeare, the historical past

was an extension of the present, and both were manifesta-
tions of an eternal scheme of events. The progress of the
pilgrimage was not meant to be measured by the minute
hand and the milestone; indeed, as Ricardo Quinones observes in a recent study, life in the Middle Ages was governed much more centrally by the church bell tolling the
canonical hours than the mechanical clock, which, in Chaucer's time, was still a novelty as a functional timepiece.[11]
Chaucer was, of course, aware of clock time, but his calculations are characteristically made on the basis of the sun
or moon, as witness the following passage from the Headlink to *The Man of Law's Tale:*

> Our Hooste saugh wel that the brighte sonne
> The ark of his artificial day hath ronne
> The ferthe part, and half an houre and moore,
> And though he were nat depe ystert in loore,
> He wiste it was the eightetethe day
> Of Aprill, that is messager to May;
> And saugh wel that the shadwe of every tree
> Was as in lengthe the same quantitee
> That was the body erect that caused it.
> And therfore by the shadwe he took his wit
> That Phebus, which that shoon so clere and brighte,
> Degrees was fyve and fourty clombe on highte;
> And for that day, as in that latitude,
> It was ten of the clokke, he gan conclude . . .
>   (II, 1–14)

This is not a simple, matter-of-fact allusion to clock time, as
the roadside realists would have us believe; rather it is a
playfully elaborate calculation of solar time, the purpose of
which is much less to record the hour than to allow Harry
Bailly to make a speech, ironically, about how the "los of
tyme shendeth us" (II, 28). We must be aware, then, that
Chaucer's references to time and place are far removed in
function and in type from those that characterize the realis-

tic novel. For Chaucer, finally, the *Canterbury Tales* was not a travel story, and the references to time and place, though authentic enough, serve only to link this particular fictional journey with the universal pilgrimage, as Egeus reminds us in the *Knight's Tale,* in which we all "been pilgrymes, passynge to and fro." (I, 2847–2848)

The criticism of Chaucer's *Canterbury Tales,* much like the textual scholarship, has for the larger part of the past century been significantly influenced by the roadside drama theory. It was George Lyman Kittredge who first gave currency to the notion that the several stories of *The Canterbury Tales* must be regarded from "the dramatic point of view."[12] He tells us that the Canterbury pilgrimage is "a human comedy" of which

> the Knight and the Miller and the Pardoner and the Wife of Bath and the rest are the *dramatis personae.* The Prologue itself is not merely a prologue: it is the first act, which sets the personages in motion. Thereafter, they move by virtue of their inherent vitality, not as tale-telling puppets, but as men and women. From this point of view, which surely accords with Chaucer's intention, the Pilgrims do not exist for the sake of the stories, but *vice versa.* Structurally regarded, the stories are merely long speeches expressing, directly or indirectly, the characters of several persons.[13]

Others before me, notably Robert Jordan, have pointed out the limitations of this dramatic conception of the *Canterbury Tales.* For one thing, it leaves out of consideration the voices of the poet and the narrator altogether, and it disregards wholly the subtle imaginative interplay between Chaucer and his reader.

What is more germane to my central point is that the roadside drama theory embodies all the most fundamental characteristics ascribed by Ortega y Gasset to the realistic art of the last century. It is well for us to remember that Kittredge first published his book in 1915, at a time when the "fiction of human realities" dominated artistic expression. In effect, Kittredge reduced the complex, refractive art of the *Canterbury Tales* to a slice of medieval life. As Robert Jordan has put it, in his excellent general chapter on the *Canterbury Tales,* the roadside drama theory promulgated by Kittredge creates the misconception "that the fictional characters are real persons consorting with the poet Chaucer."[14] The ultimate end of such an interpretation is to put reality above art and to make literary expression nothing more than historical reportage. The marriage controversy, after all, finally serves to reduce four major tales into simple monologues designed to characterize their tellers. The effect of all this is to create "real people," like Alice of Bath, whom we finally perceive and admire not for their literary dimensions but for themselves, as if they were historical personages living outside the pages which gave them birth. It is only a short step from Kittredge's vision of "The Wife of Bath [as] an individual expressing herself in character" (p. 200) to John M. Manly's search for the real historical prototypes of the Canterbury pilgrims and to Eileen Power's ingenious creation in the book *Medieval People* of a whole new order of reality based, to begin with, on Chaucer's characters (her chapter on Madame Eglentyne is subtitled "Chaucer's Prioress in Real Life.").[15] Roadside drama from Kittredge's time until very recently has dominated the critical discussion of the *Canterbury Tales* as critic after critic added yet another perspective by which tale could be fitted to teller or teller to tale. The culminating effort in the delineation of roadside realism is Robert Lumiansky's book, *Of Sondry Folk,* published in 1955.[16] Lumiansky characterizes Chaucer primarily as a keen observer of mankind who "regularly conceived and developed his narratives as vehicles for character portrayal" (p. 3). The individual tales thus become, as labelled in the Table of Contents, "twenty-three performances" which take place on "the movable stage" of the General Prologue and the Links. Significantly, Lumiansky sees the *Canterbury Tales* as a composite of "artifice and realism." Artifice refers to all those conventions of late medieval storytelling which break the illusion of reality (e.g., "that thirty-odd people can all hear the storyteller despite the narrow, muddy road," p. 12). Literary realism, in turn, is "a collective term for the devices that give the effect of reality" (p. 12). Lumiansky concludes that Chaucer

> by his minute observations of dress and manners, by his frequent recordings of personal likes and dislikes, and by numerous other devices . . . treats his company as a group of *real* people on a *real* pilgrimage, and it is as such that we shall examine them. Actually, the *Canterbury Tales* presents the effect of dramatic realism within a framework leading to the easy acceptance of certain artificialities. (p. 12; italics mine)

In consonance with this viewpoint, Lumiansky accepts the order proposed by Bradshaw and Pratt, which, as we have seen, similarly focuses on realism as the cardinal fact in the artistic design of the *Canterbury Tales*.

So much for roadside realism as an approach to the *Canterbury Tales* in twentieth-century Chaucer criticism. In my sometimes harsh review of its premises, I did not mean to suggest that this approach lacked value for its insights. On the contrary, much that the realist critics wrote about was deeply perceptive and helped appreciably to elevate the general understanding of Chaucer's narrative art. Nor am I saying that any dramatic reading of Chaucer is necessarily a distortion, as, in fact, Robertson argues in his *Preface*.[17] Much of Chaucer is indeed dramatic, not only in situation but also in conception. What I am saying about roadside realism is that it limits our total understanding and appreciation of Chaucer's art. The roadside realists, as I call them for lack of a better name, concentrated on the humanization of Chaucerian fiction. In this enterprise, they shared the outlook of nineteenth-century realism at large and thus also what Ortega calls the artistic sensibility which must be "put down as a freak in aesthetic evolution" (p. 25). For it was, according to his analysis, only in the nineteenth century that art "revolved about human contents," became "reflected life," and abandoned style altogether. This view so infused the reading of Chaucer that for much of the modern period, until very recently, critics were blind to the genuine artistic substance of his works. But since World War II, there has been a noticeable shift to the dehumanization of Chaucerian art.

One illustration of this trend may well be seen in the latest important critical work concerned with the roadside drama theory. I have in mind the book by Robert Jordan, *Chaucer and the Shape of Creation.* I quarrel with Jordan, almost as much as with Robertson, in his characterization of the modern; however, his criticism is nevertheless a sound antidote to the realists. Jordan begins his book by stating that "it is no longer satisfactory to celebrate the poet for his 'modernity'" (p. 1). This modernity, in Jordan's eyes, is the antithesis of medievalism, and it consists essentially in the quest for organic unity. Relying on M. H. Abrams' distinction between "mechanism" and "organism" as basic metaphors describing the function of the mind, Jordan sees the latter as the earmark of modern fiction, as inherently "the criterion of verisimilitude" whose primary requisite is "consistency of illusion" (p. 6). This is to say, in so many words, that all modern fiction (Jordan focuses on the post-Jamesian novel) is illusionist. The novelist, we are told, excludes himself from his fiction, gives no evidence of his shaping hand, is an omniscient external force. As a result art becomes alive, organic, "rather than inert and submissive to externally imposed limitations" (p. 5). All this is, of course, a characterization of realism. For Jordan, therefore, modernism is equatable with "realism" as for Robertson it was with "romanticism."

As I have already indicated, I find Jordan's approach to the *Canterbury Tales* much more useful than Robertson's. For one thing, it squarely confronts the roadside realists, while Robertson, his professions aside, confronts no one. For another, it offers deeply discerning interpretations of Chaucer which, ironically, are very modern indeed (as they are also medieval). In fact, there, for me, lies the central flaw of Jordan's book: its failure to recognize the substantial similarities in the aesthetics of medievalism and modernism. Take, for example, Jordan's treatment of the *Merchant's Tale*. Arguing against the dramatic interpretation of the realist critics (like Kittredge, Tatlock, and Bronson), Jordan discards the view that the tale derives unity from "a supposedly full and rich psychological characterization of the Merchant-Teller" (p. 133). Indeed, he discovers in the tale a studied inconsistency of illusion which serves "to distance us from the characters" and allows us to perceive them as personifications rather than as persons. Once we read the story as a narrative (instead of a drama) told by a removed narrator rather than an aggrieved Merchant-Teller, we become aware of "an astonishing diversity in attitude and tone" (p. 143), ranging from academic debate to epic apostrophe. The effect of the whole is, therefore, as stated in the subheading of the Chapter title, "dramatic disunity and inorganic unity." I find myself in full agreement with this view of the tale, having argued elsewhere for a disassociation of the Merchant and January.[18] However, we should recognize that such a reading is not inconsonant with the mode of modern fiction. The terms "inorganic" and "disunity" are, indeed, fully in keeping with the modern aesthetic, so much so that a recent splendid collection of writings on the "contemporary consciousness," by Sallie Sears and Georgiana W. Lord, is entitled *The Discontinuous Universe*.[19] We have, in our time, advanced far beyond the tenets of romanticism and of realism, and I think we are perfectly capable, as a matter of general disposition, to shun organicist interpretations where they were not intended in the first place. I would not wish to argue that the

medieval and modern world views are identical—far from
it, since the sources of disunity differ vastly in the two
epochs. But they do share some fundamental attitudes
about the nature of art, not the least among which is the
artist's own image of his centrality within his created universe.

Let me demonstrate this point very briefly as it relates to
Chaucer. It has become fashionable, ever since the publication of Talbot Donaldson's famous essay on "Chaucer
the Pilgrim" in 1954, to speak of two Chaucers: one being
the poet, the other his literary persona (in the *Canterbury
Tales,* Chaucer the Pilgrim.)[20] When Donaldson first
proposed this division, he offered it as a much needed
corrective against the autobiographical interpretations of
Chaucer's poetry by the realists. At the outset of his essay,
Donaldson writes: "I am under the impression that many
readers, too much influenced by Chaucer's brilliant verisimilitude, tend to regard his famous pilgrimage to Canterbury as significant not because it is a great fiction, but because it seems to be a remarkable record of fourteenth-
century pilgrimage."[21] Donaldson then proceeds to demonstrate just how important the persona is for our reading
of the *Canterbury Tales* as a "great fiction." While I have
been personally very much indebted to Donaldson's brilliant essay, I have also in a recent reconsideration of its
premises become somewhat skeptical of the approach that
it implicitly proposes for the reading of the *Canterbury
Tales.* It seems to me that the rather arbitrary separation of
poet and pilgrim can lead us to read Chaucer's fiction on
simply a different level of realism from the old biographical
interpretation. If we insist that Chaucer the Pilgrim is, indeed, a dramatic character with his own motivations and his
own internal consistencies—in other words, a personality
separated by the laws of fiction from his creator—we make
for a new kind of organic unity in the *Canterbury Tales.*
Admittedly, Donaldson himself is aware of the limitation of
the persona and never argues his proposition to the break-

ing point; he even warns that the fictional first person is, on the deepest level, "no fiction at all."[22] Yet the emphasis Donaldson provides does finally make something of a realistic fiction out of the *Canterbury Tales* with its varieties in point of view. I find myself attracted, therefore, to the caveat entered by Donald Howard in his essay on "Chaucer the Man":

> My theme is that this man, whom we feel that we know, is a real and living presence in his works, and that his presence in them is what makes them interesting and good. I present this not as a corollary of any humanistic or existential principles, but as a fact. I say that we are interested in the fictional narrator, the rhetorical workings of irony, the method of creating illusion and reality . . . not because they are devices, but because everywhere *in* and *behind* them lies Chaucer the man. I will even go a step further: I say that this is the point which various analyses of "narrator" and "persona" have really proved.[23]

The phenomenon of the artist obtruding in his own works is very much a symptom of both the medieval and the modern scenes. For the poet or even the painter in our own time the device is a useful anti-illusionist one designed to break a too steadily-held fictional perspective. In essence, this emergence of the artist as a part of his own creation is what Brecht means by the "alienation effect." I doubt that it worked in quite the same way or for quite the same reason in the Middle Ages, and yet the striking appearances of Chaucer in his fictional world cannot but jolt the reader into a recognition of the writer's presence. The illusion is not necessarily broken, but it is brought into question, and it reminds us that the *auctour*, "one who augments" (as Ortega reminds us, p. 31), is there at all times to realign the worlds of "auctoritee" and experience. I believe that the

emergence of the self-consious artist who delights in nam-
ing himself may well be the real and most revolutionary literary development promulgated by the Twelfth-Century
Renaissance (note Gottfried and Wolfram, and eventually
Dante, Chaucer, and Langland). In our own time, we are
flooded with images of the "Performing Self," which is but
an extension of the tradition of which I speak. As Roland
Barthes tells us, " . . . the modern writer (*scriptor*) is born
simultaneously with his text; he is in no way supplied with a
being which precedes or transcends his writing; he is in no
way the subject of which his book is the predicate."[24] That,
I believe, applies also to the medieval writer, and too much
concentration on literary personae can make us forget this
point.

In concluding this paper, I want briefly to return to Jordan's approach. Giving us "the aesthetic possibilities of
inorganic structure," he urges that we look at Platonic ex-
emplarism as a philosophic base and the high Gothic cathedral as a paradigm for Chaucer's art. He does so because he
believes that the modern ages otherwise have no key by
which to open the door to Chaucer's realm. I believe, as I
hope I have shown, that this view is wrong. We have tried
for too long now to approach Chaucer's artistry over the
highways, and even more often the byways, of the past.
True, the *De Doctrina Christiana*, the Gothic cathedral, the
cumulative French tradition, the icons and allusions of
Christianity, the topoi and structures of medieval rhetoric,
the study of the Bible and the Saints, the intimate acquaintance of Ricardian life and times—all these and more subjects are of vital concern to students who seek to know fully
Chaucer the man, his times, and his works. But they will
suffice only to bring knowledge, not understanding at the
deepest level of all those qualities that we finally recognize
as the artistry of Chaucer. I propose, therefore, that
Chaucerians abandon the common practice of deploring
and eschewing the modern, that instead they make every
effort to know its impulses and substance, for I believe that,

properly defined and understood, it will help us to reenter the realm of Chaucer's art more meaningfully and profoundly than we can expect from any other avenue of approach. Chaucer began one of his poems with the echo of a famous aphorism "the lyf so short, the craft so long to lerne." I interpret *craft* here to mean principally the art of poetry, his great subject in all that he wrote, and only secondarily and ironically the art of love. It is this craft of poetry which is peculiarly in the domain of literary critics and it must be the first and foremost concern of Chaucerians.

To demonstrate that the literary questions posed by Chaucer are fundamentally still with us, one need only examine what present-day writers have to say about their own craft. One such, Jorge Louis Borges, in a vignette entitled "Borges and I," provides a fitting conclusion for this paper in what is the modern writer's reflection about his literary identity. I think Chaucer might well have written likewise about himself:

> It's the other one, it's Borges, that things happen to. I stroll about Buenos Aires and stop, perhaps mechanically now, to look at the arch of an entrance or an iron gate. News of Borges reaches me through the mail and I see his name on an academic ballot or in a biographical dictionary. I like hourglasses, maps, eighteenth-century typography, the taste of coffee, and Stevenson's prose. The other one shares these preferences with me, but in a vain way that converts them into the attributes of an actor. It would be too much to say that our relations are hostile; I live, I allow myself to live, so that Borges may contrive his literature and that literature justifies my existence. I do not mind confessing that he has managed to write some worthwhile pages, but those pages cannot save me, perhaps because the good part no longer belongs to anyone, not even to the other one, but

rather to the Spanish language or to tradition. Otherwise, I am destined to be lost, definitively, and only a few instants of me will be able to survive in the other one. Little by little I am yielding him everything, although I am well aware of his perverse habit of falsifying and exaggerating. Spinoza held that all things long to preserve their own nature: the rock wants to be rock forever and the tiger, a tiger. But I must live on in Borges, not in myself—if indeed I am anyone—though I recognize myself less in his books than in many others, or than in the laborious strumming of a guitar. Years ago I tried to free myself from him and I passed from lower-middle-class myths to playing games with time and infinity, but those games are Borges' now, and I will have to conceive something else. Thus my life is running away, and I lose everything and everything belongs to oblivion, or to the other one.

I do not know which of us two is writing this page.[25]

STATE UNIVERSITY OF NEW YORK AT STONY BROOK

FOOTNOTES

1. D. W. Robertson, Jr., *A Preface to Chaucer: Studies in Medieval Perspectives* (Princeton: Princeton Univ. Press, 1962), p. 3. Henceforth cited within the text.

2. Jose Ortega y Gasset, *The Dehumanization of Art and Other Essays on Art, Culture, and Literature* (Princeton: Princeton Univ. Press, 1968), esp. pp. 3–54. Henceforth cited within the text.

3. See especially the essay on "Darwin, Mutations, and the Origin of Medieval Drama," in O. B. Hardison, *Christian Rite and Christian Drama in the Middle Ages: Essays in the Origin and Early History of Modern Drama* (Baltimore; The Johns Hopkins Press, 1965), pp. 1–34.

4. Robert A. Pratt, "The Order of the Canterbury Tales," *PMLA,* 66 (1951), 1141.

5. F. J. Furnivall, *Temporary Preface,* Chaucer Soc. Publ., 2nd Ser., No. 3 (London, 1868), pp. 22 and 24–26.

6. All Chaucer quotations and references are from *The Works of Geoffrey Chaucer,* ed. F. N. Robinson, 2nd ed. (Boston: Houghton-Mifflin, 1957).

7. I would not wish to suggest that Chaucer was incapable of writing realistic scenes. On the contrary, there is much that is true to life in Chaucer's fiction throughout; but his realism is essentially scenic or episodic rather than thematic or unified. In this respect, the *Canterbury Tales* resemble the medieval mystery cycles, which, in the largest terms, by the very nature of their subject, were forced to eschew realism (how do you stage Noah's Flood or, for that matter, the Creation of the World?), but which nevertheless contained some graphically realistic scenes like the building of the ark or the torture of Christ. The point is that Chaucer's realistic scenes—like the dramatic linkage of the *Wife of Bath's Prologue* and *Tale*—never fuse into an organically unified panorama. For further discussion of scenic realism in the drama, see my article, "Illusion and Reality in the Medieval Drama," *College English,* 32 (January, 1971), esp. pp. 457–58.

8. Ian Watt, *The Rise of the Novel* (Berkeley: Univ. of California Press, 1957), p. 12.

9. Ibid., p. 32.

10. Ibid., p. 23.

11. Ricardo Quinones, *The Renaissance Discovery of Time* (Cambridge, Mass: Harvard Univ. Press, 1972), pp. 4–6.

12. George Lyman Kittredge, *Chaucer and His Poetry* (Cambridge, Mass: Harvard Univ. Press, 1915), p. 151.

13. Ibid., p. 155.

14. Robert M. Jordan, *Chaucer and the Shape of Creation* (Cambridge, Mass: Harvard Univ. Press, 1967), p. 122. Henceforth cited within the text.

15. Eileen Power, *Medieval People* (London: Methuen, 1924), Chapter 4.

16. Robert M. Lumiansky, *Of Sondry Folk: The Dramatic Principle in the Canterbury Tales* (Austin: Univ. of Texas Press, 1955). Henceforth cited within the text.

17. For Robertson, drama seems to be synonymous with heightened states of emotional feelings, and he resorts almost exclusively to a work by Gustav Freytag entitled *Die Technik des Dramas,* first published in 1863, to demonstrate that the well-made plot—which Robertson regards as a classic modern con-

figuration— is out of touch with the medieval temperament. But Freytag has about as much to do with true modern drama as Walt Disney has with *cinema verité*. For Robertson's discussion of dramatic theory, see *A Preface to Chaucer,* pp. 33 ff.

18. Martin Stevens, " 'And Venus Laugheth': An Interpretation of the *Merchant's Tale,"* *Chaucer Review,* 7 (1972), 118–31.

19. *The Discontinuous Universe: Selected Writings in Contemporary Consciousness,* ed. Sallie Sears and Georgiana W. Lord (London: Athlone Press, 1972).

20. E. Talbot Donaldson, "Chaucer the Pilgrim," *PMLA,* 69 (1954), 928–36; rpt. in E. Talbot Donaldson, *Speaking of Chaucer* (London: Athlone Press, 1970), pp. 1–12. Citations in this paper are from the latter edition.

21. Ibid., p. 1.

22. Ibid., p. 10.

23. Donald R. Howard, "Chaucer the Man," *PMLA,* 80 (1965), 337; rpt. in *Chaucer's Mind and Art,* ed. A. C. Cawley (Edinburgh: Oliver and Boyd, 1969), pp. 31–32.

24. See Sears and Lord, *The Discontinuous Universe,* p. 10.

25. See Jorge Luis Borges, *Dreamtigers* (New York: Dutton, 1970), p. 51. I am indebted to my student Tim Lally for bringing the Borges' vignette to my attention.

A Note on the Contributors

JAMES WIMSATT, who took his doctorate at Duke, is Professor of English at the Universty of North Carolina at Greensboro. He is the leading authority on the French influences on Chaucer. His publications include *Chaucer and The French Love Poets*, *The Marguerite Poems of Guillaume de Machaut*, and *Allegory and Mirror: Tradition and Structure in Middle English Literature*.

DONALD K. FRY has been Professor of English since 1968 at the State University of New York at Stony Brook. His doctorate is from Berkeley. To date most of his research has been in Old English: *The Beowulf Poet: A Collection of Critical Essays; Finnsburh Fragment and Episode; Beowulf and the Fight at Finnsburh, A Bibliography*.

BERYL ROWLAND, one of North America's senior medievalists, has published extensively on Chaucer and Middle English, and in addition on nineteenth-century American literature. Her publications reflect some of her interests, like *Blind Beasts: Chaucer's Animal World* and *Animals with Human Faces*. She edited the *Companion to Chaucer Studies* and, most recently, *Chaucer and Middle English Studies in Honour of Rossell Hope Robbins*.

ROBERT WORTH FRANK, JR., has been a Professor of English, and for some years Chairman of the Department, at the State University of Pennsylvania since 1958. He helped found the *Chaucer Review*, of which he is now the Editor. His two major books are *Piers Plowman and the Scheme of Salvation* and *Chaucer and the Legend of Good Women*, the subject of his paper included here.

217

Robert M. Jordan, with his Ph. D. from Berkeley, is Professor of English and Head of the Department at the University of British Columbia. Along with numerous articles, his main Chaucerian criticism is his *Chaucer and the Shape of Creation.*

Ann S. Haskell, Professor of English at the State University of New York at Buffalo, is a frequent speaker at academic gatherings. She has edited *A Middle English Anthology,* and the topic of her paper included here is an extension of her *Essays on Chaucer's Saints.*

Charles A. Owen, Jr., with a B. Litt. from Oxford, is Professor of English at the University of Connecticut, which he joined in 1946. Most of his publications deal with the development of the concept of the *Canterbury Tales,* and his present essay is his most developed presentation of his theories. His early collection, *Discussions of the Canterbury Tales,* is still valued in graduate courses.

Carol V. Kaske, with her doctorate from Johns Hopkins, teaches at Cornell. She is a younger scholar whose main publications to date have been in Renaissance literature, especially Dante.

Robert O. Payne, whose Ph. D. is also from Johns Hopkins, was formerly at the University of Washington, but has now moved to the Graduate Center of the City University of New York. He is well known for his *Key to Remembrance: A Study of Chaucer's Poetics.*

Martin Stevens is Professor of English and Chairman of the Department at the State University of New York at Stony Brook. He is especially interested in medieval drama; his publications include *Masterpieces of English Prose* and *Old English Literature: Twenty-two Analytical Essays.*

A Note on the Conference

The Chaucer Conference of 1973 (probably the only all-Chaucer meeting ever held) proved one of the major happenings at Albany during its relatively short existence as a university center and prompted these papers. Before its memory has faded, it should be memorialized in a brief note.

The Conference grew out of the Faculty Seminar in Medieval Studies, an unstructured scholarly handful of medievalists, first gathered together at Albany in 1971. As well as introducing medievalists in Albany to each other, the Seminar sought out isolated medievalists on campuses within a range of a hundred miles or so, in order to acquaint them with recent research in their own and allied disciplines. The profit to those attending was not only the acquisition of new learning but (in my view more important) the sustenance of scholarly morale.

The goals of the Conference were limited and specific: to encourage a continuing friendship among medievalists in the capital area for the easier interchange of ideas; to minimize the feeling of isolation and wanhope which thwarts scholarly growth; to afford professors at smaller colleges an opportunity to meet and confer with others more active in medieval studies; and to strengthen the fledgling Faculty Seminar. I had in mind another purpose: to explore the chances for short refresher courses for teachers at weaker institutions, for teachers restricted to elementary courses, for teachers lacking library facilities, and in fact for all who are deprived of intellectual stimulation. This Conference showed how profitable extended teaching sessions could be, and how necessary and popular. So far, however, no administrator has pursued this idea.

The Conference itself was an outstanding success, but

its purposes failed, and (for several reasons, including lack of institutional encouragement) for the time being I have disbanded the Faculty Seminar. But for three years, for a couple of dozen scholars, the monthly dinner meetings of the Seminar provided a reprieve from apathy, informative talks, and indeed the *raison d'etre* for a Chaucer Conference. And without the Seminar and the Conference, it is probable that these papers would have been delayed or never written at all.

Over one hundred and twenty scholars participated during the three days of November 2, 3, and 4. What had been conceived originally as a small "conversation in the disciplines" rapidly swelled into an important regional meet. Speakers and registrants came from England and Canada—a sizable group from seven universities: British Columbia, Simon Fraser, York, Ottawa, Windsor, Western Ontario, and Montreal. Other guests came from distant universities like Texas, Stanford, Tulane, Maine, and North Carolina; more from universities nearer Albany such as Boston, Cornell, Rochester, Massachusetts, Vermont, Pennsylvania, Haverford, Connecticut, New Hampshire, as well as from the colleges and universities in the greater New York City area. Twelve campuses of the State system were represented.

Everyone will remember this gathering with warmth and affection. From the outset the registrants generated an intellectual and social camaraderie, heightened (on our part, as hosts) by the social hours before lunch and dinner and again after the late evening sessions, by the magnificent banquet (arranged by Mr. Les Hynes), dinner in our own Patroon Room, and the lavish lunch at the College of St. Rose, by the coffee breaks and the afternoon and evening entertainment (including a demonstration of late medieval court dances directed by Professor Paula Jeanne Schomberg of Russell Sage College). Most notable in this crowded long weekend was the celebration of a Sarum mass on Sunday morning, November 4. Liturgically it was a rare event; the celebrants, in precise vestments secured from many outlying religious houses, with full ceremonial and full choir, followed faithfully the order and music of the end of the fourteenth century, the kind of mass Chaucer himself might have attended. Ecclesiastically it was also unusual, inasmuch as two Roman Catholic priests and one Anglican participated ecumenically in a full Latin mass, both communions taking advantage of the age-old custom that universities conduct their services in the universal language of learning. The mass was videotaped, and copies are available. For the planning and coordination of the Sarum mass I am deeply indebted to Professor K. Drew Hartzell, Jr. For several months he worked round the clock, finding suitable celebrants, researching text and music, and rehearsing several times a week. My thanks too are due Professor Ernest Kaulbach, who chaired one of the sessions, for preparing a small brochure on the rite. To Professor Townsend Rich, who selected from his extensive collection of brass rubbings an exhibition of those with Chaucerian connections and wrote an annotated catalogue, also go my thanks.

The Chaucer Conference was financed by a grant from the Chancellor's Fund for a "Conversation in the Disciplines"; by state funds for Fellows of the statewide Medieval Seminar in attendance, by transfer of limited funds from my Faculty Seminar at Albany, by a generous gift from George Allen & Unwin, London (the publishers of my festschrift), by the very kind help from the College of St. Rose, by a number of small donations from registrants at the Conference, and by my own assumption of a deficit of nearly one thousand dollars. To the organizations and individuals I am grateful.

Two final acknowledgments of appreciation should also be recorded. First to four loyal students, the entire "staff" who assisted me—I had no institutional help: Brother (now Dr.) Patrick Horner, my research assistant for some three years, an indispensable factotum before, during, and after the Conference; and three young graduates, who during the Conference womanned the registration tables, chauffeused guests to and from various terminals, and cheerfully performed the chores: Mary Stutzman, Helene Grossman, and Susan Margaret Brown. Second to my wife, for her devoted encouragement and uncomplaining tolerance of my own reactions to pressure (a devotion she has bestowed on me for some thirty-six wonderful years), for her performing many clerical and administrative duties, and for her gracious presence throughout the whole Conference.

R. H. R.